D1471791

Michael Marra
Arrest This Moment

First published in 2017 by
Big Sky Press
www.bigsky.scot

Big Sky Press is an imprint of
Creative Services (Scotland) Ltd,
Drumderfit, North Kessock, IV1 3ZF

A catalogue record for this book is available from
the British Library.

Paperback: ISBN 978-0-956957-86-3
Hardback: ISBN 978-0-9569578-1-8

Typeset in Caslon.
Printed by Bell and Bain, Glasgow
Designed and Typeset by Andrew Forteath
www.andrewforteath.co.uk

This publication was supported by
Creative Scotland

Michael Marra

Arrest This Moment

James Robertson

Acknowledgements

This book is neither a definitive biography of Michael Marra nor a comprehensive study of his music. It is not meant to be. If, as Sheena Wellington told me, Michael's life and work are a rich field, then this is just a first furrow. In any case, it would be impossible for a single book to contain Michael in his entirety.

The people I interviewed while researching and writing the book are far outnumbered by those to whom I did not speak. As a result many facts, stories and opinions that might have been included here are absent. Nevertheless, I hope the Michael Marra portrayed in these pages looks and sounds familiar to those who knew him better than I did. If any of the information contained in these pages is wrong, I apologise and would be grateful for corrections to be forwarded to the publisher for inclusion in any future edition.

My sincere thanks go to the following for their help of various kinds:

For entrusting me with Michael's story and supplying me with countless anecdotes, artefacts, contacts and clues: Peggy, Alice and Matthew Marra.

For allowing me to interview them, quote their own words and the words that Michael wrote to or for them, or for giving me their reminiscences and views: Nicky, Mary and Chris Marra; Michael Craig (especially for his 'Marra Musings' material); Barbara Dickson; Alan Gorrie; Andy Hall; James Kirkpatrick; Ray Laidlaw; Ian Lamb; Liz Lochhead; Frank McConnell; Allan McGlone; Eilidh Mackenzie; Iain McKie; Gordon Maclean; Joan Michael; Andrew Mitchell; Marianne Mitchelson; Hamish Moore; Rab Noakes; Rod Paterson; Andy Pelc; Karine Polwart; Ricky Ross; Sheena Wellington; Gary West.

For permission to reproduce images of paintings, photographs, cartoons, drawings, tattoos and tapestries: Peter Baillie; Doreen Cullen; the family of Mrs Gorrie; Gabriel Gudaityte; Andy Hall; Eileen Hughes; John Johnstone; Peggy Marra; the family of Vincent Rattray; Alan Richardson; Ken Sharp; BJ Stewart; Gavin Wilson, Lorenz Zatecky.

For permission to reproduce the portrait of Michael Marra on the cover of this book, and the line drawing on the page following the title page: Calum Colvin.

For general assistance, encouragement and enthusiasm along the way: Ange Cran; John Douglas; Kenny Farquharson; David Francis; the late Rod Mackenzie; Jan Miller; Catriona Rioch; Susie Clark; Carolyn Scott.

For invaluable information and interview material in his 2004 Odyssey Productions feature for BBC Radio Scotland, *Hermless: A Portrait of Michael Marra*: Billy Kay.

For similarly useful material in the 2012 *Travelling Folk* tribute programme and the 2013 *Michael Marra Family Album* programme: BBC Radio Scotland.

For compiling the equally useful programme for *Resolis Remembers Michael Marra: A Highland Tribute* (2014): Diana Gilbert.

For background material on the history of rock, pop and folk music in Dundee: Jim Wilkie in his book *Blue Suede Brogans* (1991); Lorraine Wilson in her book *Take it to the Bridge: Dundee's Rock and Pop History* (2011).

For designing this book: Andrew Forteath.

For allowing us to reproduce his Michael Marra discography: Alastair 'Breeks' Brodie.

Thanks also to Bryan Beattie and Anna Day at Big Sky.

Special thanks for her support and attention to detail to Marianne Mitchelson, who knew Michael long before I did.

The illustrations at the start of chapters are all from original work by Michael Marra, with the exception of the painting by Vincent Rattray on p.214.

James Robertson
(Newtyle, August 2017)

I wanted to be a songwriter of the old school. I didn't want my name in lights, I wanted it in brackets.

Michael with self-portrait,
early 1980s.

Preface
Michael Marra (1952-2012)
– The Nicest Man I Never Met

by Craig Coulthard[1]
(31st October 2012)

Yesterday saw the funeral of Michael Marra take place in Dundee.

Ten years ago, I stepped into the Virgin Megastore on Princes Street to look for a Christmas present for my Mum. I walked up to one of the listening posts, and looking at the CD covers, I was struck by a black and white photo of a slightly bedraggled-looking man in a tweed jacket. *Posted Sober* – Michael Marra. I had never heard of Marra, but was intrigued by some of the song titles – 'Frida Kahlo's Visit to the Taybridge Bar' and 'Bob Dylan's Visit to Embra'. Once I reached the second song, 'Letter from Perth' and heard the line, 'I would rock in your sweet and tender arms, if I wasn't doing time', I realised it was a love song from Perth prison. I decided to buy the CD for myself (I can't remember if I bought my Mum a copy too).

A couple of years later, I finished recording my first 'album'. I decided to send Michael Marra a copy, to let him know that I thought he was an incredible songwriter, and that *Posted Sober* had affected the way I wanted to write songs. Just before my first gig at the Wee Red Bar,

I received a written letter in reply to my email. Michael wished me luck, congratulated me, and gave me some advice: 'If you're anything like me, you're probably a bit neurotic – leave your real self off stage before you play.'

That was the first of a number of letters he wrote me, usually after I had sent him a copy of my own new music. Always engaging, supportive, funny and humble, he often sent me a CD and more recently a DVD of his most recent work (including work with 'Saint Andrew'). I probably saw Michael play around ten times between 2002 and 2012, and after each gig I wanted to go and speak to him, introduce myself and thank him in person, but I always chickened out. Part of me also liked the idea of only communicating by letter.

Anyway, this summer, just a week before I was due to do *Forest Pitch* (before it was postponed) I received a voicemail message. It was Michael Marra asking me to phone him. I did so, and what followed was one of the most encouraging conversations I've ever had. He wanted to tell me that he liked my idea for *Forest Pitch*, but wouldn't be able to come as he was very unwell. Then he told me, in response to my idea, he was going to plant a football pitch of bluebells in his back garden. When I told him that there was a possibility the match would be postponed due to bad weather, he told me, 'It doesn't matter, it's the idea that matters – you almost don't have to do it.'

I was glad to be given the opportunity to tell Michael how much I admired his work, and we hoped to meet up at some point after *Forest Pitch* – obviously that never happened. But while I attended the very busy service yesterday, I was struck by the genuine emotion felt by everyone (fans, friends, family) who praised Michael's warmth, humanity and generosity. I realised how generous he had been to me; and how grateful I was to have been able to have even the smallest kind of communication with him.

I was asked by Creative Scotland a couple of months ago (about a week before the phone call) to do a little Q&A interview for their website. One of the questions was, 'Who is your "one to watch" for the future, or someone overlooked from the past that you feel should be better known?' And I answered 'Michael Marra'. I really do think he is one of the best songwriters Scotland has ever produced, and he is far from being the household name he should be.

Michael wrote songs with humanity, sympathy, humour and an attention for detail that is sadly lacking nowadays. His songs plead for fairness and justice, most of all a desire for understanding and honesty. He had a great ability to be able to use his locality, his friendships, his loves, to provide the listener with a chance to think a little deeper about things. He could join the macro and the micro with great skill in a single line, let alone in a song. One of his trademarks was to present a major character from the wider world in settings familiar to Scots (particularly Dundonians): for example, 'King Kong's Visit to Glasgow' ('why don't you take him to Ibrox / there we think he might blend in)'; 'General Grant's Visit To Dundee' ('what a mighty long bridge for such a mighty little old town'); 'Frida Kahlo's Visit to the Taybridge Bar' (Buenos dias boys this looks like the place /To make my re-entry to the human race'); 'Bob Dylan's Visit to Embra' ('From a Buick Six in Cockburn Street / Come Boots of Spanish Leather'); and 'Mac Rebennack's Visit to Blairgowrie' ('There's a poster on the launderette wall / Stating clearly in a bold typeface it says / Dr. John is playing Blairgowrie tonight / And I know that every little thing in Blairgowrie's / Going to be all right').

So many of his songs are filled with beautiful, imaginative, loving lines like these. His dedication to his surroundings is admirable and inspiring. As Jonathan Meades says, 'There is no such thing as a boring place.' This dedication undoubtedly helped Marra achieve a close and loyal relationship with his fans. Every gig I went to was a like a family get-together, where no one is fed up with each other yet. His songs were often introduced with witty and revealing stories, and though these rarely changed from gig to gig, they became as important as the songs during the performance. In a recent live album recorded with Mr. McFall's Chamber, these intros are retained and given their own track numbers.

Musically, Marra is described as a 'folk' musician – which for me is too narrow (as wide a field as it is) a description. His songwriting has much to recall Randy Newman, Tom Waits and Dr John – and his piano-playing is also reminiscent of Dr John, along with Professor Longhair and Fats Domino. His phrasing, both on the piano and in his vocals, is so subtle yet effective – and I haven't even mentioned the deep and warm yet smoky, crumbly voice. He also incorporated reggae, jazz, operatic music, ballads and more. In his music with 'Saint Andrew' Marra provided very Dundonian lyrics and midi keyboard production as well as lo-fi cut-and-paste collage videos. On top of this he wrote music for and acted in the theatre (*The Mill Lavvies* and *A Wee Home from Home*). He was an artist keen to soak up inspiration of all sorts, and to write songs about whatever he liked. His songs about football helped me to realise that there was no reason I couldn't attempt to make art and songs about whatever I wanted to.

In the last week, I have felt so sad and yet delighted that a man such as Michael was able to live his life in a creative and rewarding way. At the funeral, his brother said, 'Listen to Michael's music. Play it to your friends.' And so, I ask you to do exactly that. There will be no more music from Michael Marra, so make the most of what he did produce.

He was a very special talent, a man who revealed beauty in unexpected places, but was also capable of providing a non-sentimental, barbed analysis of Scotland and its history. His music is exactly the kind of thing Scotland needs, and something we should share with the rest of the world.

Thank you Michael Marra, love Craig.

Don't wipe your nose with the back of your hand, Use your sleeve like a civilised man.

Notes

1   Craig Coulthard is a Scottish artist working in a wide range of media. His project *Forest Pitch* was created as part of the Cultural Olympiad of 2012. On 25th August, two amateur football matches were played in the middle of a forest near Selkirk, by teams made up of people who had recently been granted UK residency status or British citizenship. The spruce trees that were felled to create the pitch were used to build the goal posts and the changing rooms for the teams. After match day, the lines of the football pitch were planted with native trees to create a living, evolving sculpture, a 3D representation of the pitch that also questions the changing nature of environment and of national and individual identities.

Introduction

Behind the Door, Beneath the Underdog

Eh'm no as bad as Muggie Sha'

'Muggie Sha''

In the pantry next to our kitchen hangs a large photograph of Michael Marra. It is one of a series taken by participants in a masterclass run by Calum Colvin, whose portrait of Michael, now in the McManus Art Gallery in Dundee, is reproduced on the cover of this book. In fact, the photograph was part of a number of studies for Calum's portrait. Michael is sitting on a stool, hands resting on thighs, with his beret pushed back from his brow and his head turned towards something or somebody off-camera, to his right. It's a fine picture, capturing as it does the resignation of a man who doesn't like to pose.

With the pantry door closed, a stranger to the house wouldn't know that Michael is behind it. Often, though, the door lies open, and then it seems, looking at him, as if he is listening to whatever conversation is going on in the kitchen. But whether the door is open or closed really makes no difference: he is still there. It is amazing how much he is still there.

Michael and I spent a lot of hours sitting on either side of the kitchen table, talking. He could make a cup of black coffee last a very long time. I wish now I could remember all the things he told me across that table. I can't, but I do remember a lot.

During the summer of 2016, I worked my way through a box of photographs, theatre programmes, scrapbooks and other miscellanea amassed by his wife Peggy, as I tried to find a way into telling Michael's story. I had been trying for a while. To begin at the beginning and follow a chronological line from there might have been the obvious route but it didn't seem to fit with the kind of man he was. 'Obvious' isn't the first word that comes to mind to describe Michael. Clear, coherent, audible, unmistakable, distinctive – all of those, yes. But Michael Marra, *obvious*? I don't think so.

So I began to wonder how *he* would do it. Where would he start, if it was down to him to make sense of that accumulation of memories? Possibly by saying it was not a project that interested him or one in which he wanted to invest any of his energy. After he died his family were united in their opinions of how he would have felt about the outpouring of tributes and appreciations of him as a songwriter, performer and person. 'Horrified', his wife Peggy said. 'Mortified', 'highly embarrassed', his daughter Alice and son Matthew were sure. 'He would have winced,' his older brother Nicky said. 'Double-winced,' his sister Mary added. Or, as his younger brother Chris put it, it would have been 'a pure minter'. So maybe he would tell me he had better, more important things to do with his time than tell his own story. Then I might reply, 'But it's not your time, Michael, it's mine.' And he would stop and consider that. Thinking of it as somebody

else's project, he would want to make some observations, even offer some help. Because he was *that* kind of man: considering, considerate, thoughtful, observant, helpful. He would want the thing to work, for the other person.

I was also, for reasons largely beyond my control, way behind schedule. Michael would have understood. Running late? He could easily have advised slowing down, or even stopping and going back a few stages. He had a good appreciation of effort and attention to detail. He understood that some jobs take more time than you thought was available. 'The apple will fall when the tree is ready,' he said once, when asked when the next album was coming out. He always wanted to get things right. More than once he told me, 'If it's easy, it's probably not worth doing.' Which is a sentence containing reassurance and discouragement in equal measure: the sort of formula Dundonians pride themselves on. And Michael, to the marrow, was a Dundonian.

The writer and journalist Neal Ascherson likes to quote the following dark joke: 'I hit bottom. But then I heard somebody tapping underneath.' Ascherson declares this to be a Polish saying, but I can't help thinking how Dundee it is. Maybe it was exported a few centuries ago, when the Scots were migrating to Poland in great numbers, as soldiers, merchants and craftsmen; when Cochrane, MacLean and Weir became Czochranek, Makalienski and Wajer. [1] And maybe, like a homing pigeon, the joke found its way back again.

Michael said in an interview, 'For any artist, Dundee is just the perfect place to look at the rest of the world. Charles Mingus had a book called *Beneath the Underdog*. I always thought they should put that under Dundee on the sign outside the city.'[2]

I remembered how he came to write the song 'Muggie Sha''. It was inspired by photographs from a book circulated by the Dundee police round the city's pubs in Edwardian times. Michael had got hold of copies of some of the pages of this book. On each page were two photographs, one facing the camera, one in profile, of an individual barred from all of Dundee's pubs. These were folk who were down on their luck. They were troubled and troublesome people, and in terms of social strata they were some distance below the meanest underdog.

And Michael admired them, especially the women, and he admired their achievement in earning themselves a citywide drinking ban. I could hear his voice, 'I wanted to celebrate these magnificent women.' Which he did. From their point of view. And what did he have them say? 'Eh'm no as bad as Muggie Sha'.' Who but you, Michael, could have homed in on that place of intense, black-humoured empathy?[3]

So already I found I was talking to him and he was talking to me, and not for the first time since he left us. When he was alive, the prelude to such a conversation would be a phone-call. 'Hello. James?' The unmistakable gravel of his voice. 'It's Michael.' As if it could be anybody else. 'Are you working?' (He expected you to be.) 'Do you have time for a chat? Good. I'll come round.' By the time I'd made the

coffee, round he would have come. And we would go from there.

Notes

1   As described by another Dundonian, Matthew Fitt, in his poem, 'Schotten'. The poem appears in *Kate o Shanter's Tale and other poems* (2003).

2   *Sunday Times*, 11th January 2004.

3   For Michael's own version of this story, see p.192.

Dundee

Dundee, home of the Beano,
You are the saving grace,
A volcano full of soldiers
With Winston Churchill's curse upon
   the place.
Dundee, home of Mary Slessor,
All the boys know she's game,
Stuck out in the jungle, it's pleasant
   but it's not the same.

'I Don't Like Methil'

People don't need your biography, was Michael's opinion, they need your songs. His own attitude to biography was, shall we say, creative. In 1979, when he signed a two-record deal with Polydor, the company wanted him to have a back story. So Michael constructed one. In fact he made several. Such as this one, from early 1981:

> **MICHAEL MARRA (1952 – ?)**
> Since joining Polydor at the close of '79 this burly Scot has repeated the success of his previous groups the folk-rock band Hen's Teeth, the rock and roll show Mort Wriggle & the Panthers and the snappy pop combo Skeets Boliver, unfortunately. These results have his record company confused, his manager embarrassed, the former Catholic priest and his family penniless, and all the major stars in the world without hits written by this fine amateur footballer. One of Marra's singles 'The Midas Touch' from the album of the same name could be scientifically proven to be a better song than 'Bright Eyes' or 'Bridge Over

Troubled Water'. Unfortunately none of his songs were ever recorded by the late ELVIS PRESLEY, and STEELY DAN have no immediate plans to make him wealthy. This entertaining graveside orator has been doing gigs for eleven years and recently appeared at R. Scott's and the Royal Albert Hall in London. After none of these shows has he ever been brutally murdered but he was once struck on the face by a tumbler full of Fuller's beer in a pub called the Nashville in W. Ken. while doing a highly invigorating support act for Howard De Voto's Magazine. Undaunted, the optimistic Celt has stylishly confronted each dashing failure with a real sense of occasion displaying a heart-warming unawareness and naiveté and belying the fact that praise and glory are no stranger to this unaffected prize-winning gardener. Inspired by Francois Mitterand's recent success in the French elections Marra's current single, 'Like a Frenchman I said Oui', is the soul of illogical optimism itself and should place this athletic scholar firmly in the charts and give him a real chance to become thirty years old next February. [1]

Burly Scot? Graveside orator? Prize-winning gardener? I don't know if the marketing men at Polydor ever saw this concoction of misinformation, but it would not have been what they were looking for. How do you sell somebody who deliberately undersells himself in every sentence? And why would anyone *do* that?

Meanwhile, Michael redrafts. In a second attempt, he anticipates living until June 1981 at least. It is already May of that year, so this is not the most optimistic outlook. He notes that his album released the previous year, *The Midas Touch*, is being 'enjoyed by everyone but the public' and that 'the single of the same name was a highly educational "turntable hit" teaching the composer that you can't eat turntables.' He ends by explaining that he is 'busy writing and recording and contemplating the dreary inevitability of success.'

Again, you can see why the record company might have thought this was not striking the right tone. They might have suspected Michael of having an attitude problem. He did: he had a problem with *their* attitude, and indeed his ironic approach is an indication that the relationship was somewhat strained.

Michael was torn between the promise of success if he allowed himself to be moulded by the London music industry – a promise which he regarded with the utmost suspicion – and the familiar attractions of home, where he could shrug off all pretensions, breathe more easily and be true to himself.

Home, by then, was the village of Newtyle, ten miles northwest of Dundee. He and Peggy had settled there in 1975. At the end of 1979 their daughter Alice was born. Their son Matthew arrived two years later. But really, everything starts three decades before that, in Dundee.

*

Michael, aged about seven.

Michael William Marra was born in Dundee on 17th February 1952, the fourth of five children: Edward, Mary, Nicholas and Michael were all born within four years of one another; there was nearly a five-year gap between Michael and Christopher. Their father, Edward Marra, was a printer. Michael recalled, 'He worked a Heidelberg cylinder, the proper old letterpress printing', which puts a slightly romantic gloss on what was often mind-numbingly tedious work. Their mother, Margaret (née Reilly), was a primary school teacher, although she stopped teaching for several years in order to look after a house full of young children. Margaret was one of six children herself, and her family had struggled to find the means to enable her to go to teacher-training college at Craiglockhart in Edinburgh. Her mother, the only grandparent still alive when the Marra children were growing up, felt the loss of a wage keenly, but her father believed that only through education could you change your life: in a sense, Margaret became a teacher on behalf of the whole family, and that weight of responsibility remained with her all her life. Michael would celebrate her achievement on *On Stolen Stationery* with the track 'Margaret Reilly's Arrival at Craiglockhart'.

The name Marra has been present in Scotland for centuries, with early concentrations in Ayrshire and Galloway and, on the east coast, in and around Montrose. There is some mystery as to how it arrived.

It is a common Italian name, particularly in southern Italy and Sicily, and one theory is that when part of the Spanish Armada was wrecked off the Irish coast in 1588 there were Italian mercenaries aboard who survived, and that either they or their descendants later made their way to Scotland. Whatever the truth of this, there were other, more direct links with Ireland.

Michael's paternal grandmother was a Clarke: her family origins were in Bailieborough in County Cavan: her uncle Francis would be the subject of one of Michael's best-known songs. [2] But many of Edward Marra's friends' parents or grandparents also hailed from Bailieborough, so the ties with that part of Ireland were communal as well as familial. The Reilly side of the family's Irish connections were mainly with Dublin.

There was a legacy of political activism on both sides of the family, although of very different kinds. Margaret Reilly's father James was involved in Dundee street protests against the hunger and unemployment of the 1930s, while the politics of Michael's paternal grandfather Nicholas Marra followed more institutional lines via the trade union movement and the Labour Party. As a Justice of the Peace, local councillor and chairman of the Dundee Labour Party, his was a well-known face in Dundee civic life.

He worked a Heidelberg cylinder, the proper old letterpress printing.

Quick! Get out of bed! Today's the day we shed our skin!

Lochee, where the family lived, was and is a working-class district, with a long history of immigration, especially from Ireland but with significant numbers also coming from Italy and Poland. This helped to create a diverse and vibrant culture. The singer Sheena Wellington, eight years older than Michael, was raised in the same area of Lochee as the Marras, Clement Park, and remembers it as a good and safe place to grow up: the houses had their own bathrooms, and coal fires with back-boilers to heat the water; children played in the middle of the street because nobody owned a car; everybody used the bus.

It was a close community where everybody knew their neighbours and where many were connected through marriage and kinship. 'There were a lot of big families because Lochee was at least fifty per cent Catholic, with a big Irish contingent, but I never remember any trouble, any fallings-out or arguments. There were no Orange marches or anything like that.' Sheena and her wee pals used to chap the Marra door and ask if they could 'take the bairn oot'. 'Mind you, we very rarely got to take him oot, because we were very rarely clean enough. Mrs Marra being a teacher, if you had the slightest hint o' a cold or if your nails werenae perfectly clipped, you didnae get!'[3] 'The family itself had a faith, an ethic, and a working-class decency which Michael grew up with…. He knew what was right, what was wrong, and in the middle was compassion and I think that very much came from his background.'[4]

(Preceding pages) Lochee High Street in the late 1950s.

(Opposite, top) The Marra bairns: left to right, Mary, Eddie, Michael, Nicky and (in pushchair) Chris.

(Opposite, bottom) A few years on, Margaret Marra with, left to right, Michael, Mary, Nicky, Chris and Eddie.

There was always a lot of conversation in the Marra house. Discussion on almost any subject, apart from sex, was encouraged. Religion tended not to be discussed much either, unless the priest called: although Margaret had a very strong personal faith, Edward's was more passive and he was not a church attender. Among the four oldest children there was a high level of competition for attention, and a delight in scoring points off one another. Nicky: 'The four of us were so close together in age that we tended to be dealt with as a unit. How else were we to achieve individuality? The point-scoring was without malice, but there was no let-up, and of all of us Michael was the expert.'[5]

Mary: 'He had no conscience. He didn't hold back where I probably would have.'[6] The biggest battlefield was at family meal-times, when he was adept at lobbing in apparently innocent questions or comments that were in fact small bombs with delayed detonators. Nicky: 'Michael was like a tea-table guerrilla. He would get the teapot and pour it, he would pour right up to the lip of your cup so you couldn't get any milk in, and then he would just look at you from under his brow: deal with that. The winner was the one that got Dad to say something to one of the others: "Would you cut that out?"'[7]

Chris was treated somewhat differently, the butt of some fairly intense teasing as well as being protected by his older siblings. On one occasion, having absorbed the necessary information from a radio documentary on the life-cycle of snakes, Michael excitedly shook his infant brother awake: 'Quick! Get out of bed! Today's the day we shed our skin!' Shortly afterwards Chris, confused and fearful, was being consoled by his mother while Michael chuckled wickedly in the wings.

He was constantly playing with words, and would regularly try out new names on Chris: 'Wallpaper, that's a good name for you. We'll call you Wallpaper. Or what about Linoleum?' The name he eventually settled on for Chris, and used almost always when addressing him, was 'M'Lach'. (When interviewed for this book about the origin and meaning of this name, Chris Marra replied, 'Haven't a clue.'). He was always looking for alternative versions of what was normal or accepted. Inventing noms de guerre became a lifelong habit: a small selection from his album covers and show programmes down the years includes Pip Locherty, Rock Newtyle, Colm Calvin, Clement Park, Beauregard Low, Harold Walls, Al Martini, Lochee Luciano, Pacquet Bonheure, Peem Porteus, Blair Gowrie, Sandy Limestone, Liam Reilly, Alec Gorrie, Memus Slim, Hamish Watt, Phillipe DuBiety, Fabio Lino and Chick Singer.

*

Both Michael's parents had a great appetite for music, which was part of daily family life: Margaret played piano and sang in both the Cecilian and Diocesan choirs; Edward did not play an instrument but loved jazz and classical music. Duke Ellington and Ludwig van Beethoven were Edward Marra's great heroes: the only time Michael ever saw his father combing his hair was the night he went to see Ellington and his band play the Caird Hall in 1967.

One feature of the household, an item which in time Michael would inherit, was a very fine Blüthner piano. Edward had bought it for Margaret when a family friend, Charles McHardy (who himself played piano in a jazz band), spotted it for sale, couldn't afford it himself, but alerted Edward to the fact that it was going for a reasonable price. Michael's oldest brother Eddie learned to play on this instrument and passed on a few tricks to Michael. Michael learned mostly by ear and by accident, discovering 'the good stuff' through perseverance: 'I love the shape of written music, but it looks like an adventure with Neptune rather than what [the notes are] supposed to convey. To me, the piano is all lying in front of you. It's difficult to make a mistake as everything leads to something else.'[8]

All the Marra children were encouraged to learn to play an instrument but, as Nicky explained it, while Eddie, Michael and Chris took their mother's genes, Mary and he followed their father's path, not playing but nevertheless developing a deep love of music.[9] There were opportunities to learn to play at school and, although money was tight, Edward Marra believed that music lessons were worth paying for. His understanding was that you learned music by a formal process of working your way up through the grades: Chris followed this path but Eddie and Michael took a more recreational route towards proficiency. When Michael was in his teens, Eddie brought home a guitar for him and Chris. Both of them were interested in learning how to play it, taking their cues from the likes of James Taylor and Joni Mitchell.

But while Chris would become a professional musician, for Michael instruments were always only a means to an end; and the end was to write songs.

If Edward was willing to pay for music tuition, Margaret paid – on the 'never-never', which Edward did not approve of – for some of the instruments the boys wanted out of Larg's Music Shop in Whitehall Street. (However, as Chris Marra remembered, 'It was my Dad who filled in the H.P. forms for my guitar and amp, the only debt he ever took on. Even at a young age I could understand how it must have pained him to go against his principles for my benefit.') On one occasion, when Margaret was in Larg's with a friend, a demonstration was being given on a baby grand piano. As they listened, a salesman spotted them and asked if they were interested in the piano. Margaret explained that she already had a piano at home.

The salesman said it could be traded in and asked what make and model she had. Margaret described the Blüthner and asked if that would be good enough. 'Madam,' he replied, 'I think *we* would be giving *you* money on such a trade-in.' When she got home, the stacks of *National Geographics* and other items were cleared from the top of the piano and it was given a good polish.

There was always singing in the Marra household. The range of music to which the children were exposed at home was wide and inclusive, from Uncle Mac's *Children's Favourites* on Saturday morning radio to opera and much in between. To some extent this reflected the variety of music that could be experienced more generally in Dundee in the post-war period. The

big bands of the dancehall era gave way to smaller jazz outfits in the 1950s; and there was an undercurrent of traditional Scottish music (which rose to the surface during the folk revival: the Dundee Folksong Club – later the Dundee Folk Club – first convened at the Royal British Hotel in Castle Street in 1963). However, into the mix came American-influenced skiffle and rock'n'roll, which laid the foundations for the pop and rock explosion of the Sixties. Amongst many other bands, The Beatles played the Caird Hall in October 1963, The Rolling Stones were there in January 1964.

Eddie, being the oldest child, was the first to get into this new wave of music, which did not however meet with the approval of Edward Marra. As in so many other families, when a television was acquired (in 1964) and the children became caught up in the excitement offered by *Top of the Pops* and *Juke Box Jury*, their father would keep up a running commentary on why what they were listening to was so awful. Kathy Kirby's lipstick, the Walker Brothers' hair and Gene Pitney ('greetin' all the way to the bank') were all the objects of his derision. In time, Michael would inherit his father's habits in this regard, inventing new names for panel show contestants or soap characters ('Total Eclipse of the Pavement' or 'Rotunda', for example, for somebody overweight), and mercilessly criticising their behaviour. 'One of the short stories in Michael's collection *Karma Mechanics* is called "Tacit",' said his son Matthew. 'It starts with the main character Gourlay barking at the stuff on daytime TV. That, to me, comes straight from Dad's own behaviour.'[10]

Michael absorbed everything, from hymns sung at church (the melody of 'Soul of My Saviour' would find its way into the opening bars of Michael's 'Mother Glasgow') to Elvis Presley – 'Jailhouse Rock' was his earliest, indelible musical memory. The Beatles impressed not just because of their energy and enthusiasm but because they wrote their own songs. In fact, Michael said, it was John Lennon who 'forced' him to be a songwriter: 'his voice was more than language.'[11]

The Beatles seemed almost American, coming in on a big wave that also contained early Motown – the Four Tops, Stevie Wonder, the Temptations and others. Dundee responded at some deep-seated emotional level to soul music – 'the Dundee disease', Michael called it. Maybe this was explained partly by the city's long history of being sneered at, denigrated or just ignored by people elsewhere who thought themselves culturally superior: 'I think of Dundee being like a sort of black ghetto of Scotland. I read the columns in the Scottish papers, the *Herald* and the *Scotsman* and so on, and the journalists are always ready with a snide remark for Dundee.'[12]

The pre-eminent expression of the city's infatuation with soul was the Average White Band, hugely successful in the 1970s and continuing to perform and record today; one of Michael's greatest delights in his last year was to play with them at Celtic Connections in Glasgow. 'By the way, he's right when he says Dundee's "disease" was soul music,' Alan Gorrie confirmed. 'Average White Band took many cues from

Dougie Martin and the Poor Souls, the city's "Big Boys" of soul music long before we cut our wisdom teeth.'[13]

Bob Dylan also made a huge impression on Michael. He wrote lyrics full of literary allusions and packed words and rhymes into melodies in a way that was totally ground-breaking. When Michael first heard Dylan's voice, he assumed it belonged to an old man. That such songs were being made by a man in his twenties was both a revelation and an inspiration. Years later, in the notes to his song 'Bob Dylan's Visit to Embra' on *Posted Sober*, Michael wrote:

> This is my wee tribute to the great man and was written so that I could use a mouth organ and harness which was given to me by my son Matthew. Bob's sixtieth birthday is approaching and I'd like to celebrate, maybe a gig with Bob's songs for the whole night would be good.[14] When I first heard him I thought he was an old man. I would have been about ten or eleven. I was pleased when I saw his photograph (with Suzy Rotolo) because he looked young and he was wearing jeans, then I thought he must be the coolest and most wise young man on the planet. AND he had a girlfriend. I loved the way people put their faith in his vision and took him seriously while enjoying the landscape of his imagination.[†] Dylan sang directly to me, that songwriting was huge, that nothing should be discounted, big songs, 'Masters of War' and 'Hard Rain', 'Ramona'. Personal and political.

[†] This was tempered by my brother Eddie telling me that what 'Hard Rain' REALLY meant was that I should clean his boots.

Michael first publicly articulated his long-term ambition while still at St Mary's Primary School in Lochee. A group of boys in his class were discussing what they wanted to be when they grew up, and he said he wanted to be a songwriter. As the others mostly intended to have glittering football careers, this was not a popular option, in fact he expected derision, but then another boy, John Duncan, chipped in, 'My uncle's a songwriter.' This assertion too was met with a degree of scepticism. 'Oh aye. And who is he?' 'Stephen Sondheim.' None of them had heard of Sondheim or *West Side Story* (the show opened on Broadway in 1957), but it turned out that John Duncan was telling the truth. 'The mere fact that somebody had a relation who wrote songs as a job was impressive: it was a big thing for me.'[15]

*

Out of school, the Marra boys played together a lot. 'Most of our play was just typical boys' stuff of that time,' Nicky recalls. 'Going up the backies, digging holes, covering them, making traps, building dens in trees, stuff like that. On a rainy day when you couldn't go out, we would collect all the pillows in the house and go up to our bedroom and play at stacking jute-bags. All the pillows would be on the floor and Michael would stand on the bed, and I would pick up a pillow and go "Hup, jeeb!" To us, that was what the guys down at Camperdown Mills said when they were stacking jute-bags, so that was the sound we made. And once the pillows were all up on the bed the next job was to get them down again. It was just reflecting what we saw going on.' [16]

Playing football mattered hugely to the brothers, as Nicky recalled:

> The Marras were not greatly into football, but the Reillys were. There was a real talent in the Reillys. We had cousins who were really good players, so it was a big thing for us. Just underneath the line of plane trees on Harefield Road there was a flat area which we developed into a football pitch, in other words eventually there was no grass left on it. There were always other boys looking for a game. That could be a bit risky if you didn't know them, but you had a wee bit of security playing with your brothers. We'd also go up to the hat factory in the industrial estate behind Clement Park where there was a huge area of flat grass. You'd go up there with a bottle of water and be there all afternoon, just playing football for hours. We'd play two-touch – Michael was absolutely ruthless when it came to two-touch, he'd do and say everything he could to put you off.
>
> Also, there was a football renaissance going on in the city in the early 1960s. Bob Shankly was appointed manager of Dundee in 1959, and then Dundee won the league in the 1961-62 season, when Michael was ten. In our summer holidays we would walk down to Dens Park from Lochee and see the players coming out at the end of training and ask for autographs, the likes of Gordon Smith and Alan Gilzean. Gilzean was a huge hero. Michael's later description was 'he strode like a colossus over the Tullybaccart' [17] because Gilzean was a Coupar Angus man. Dundee were the dominant team in the city at the time. Michael was a Dundee fan whereas I became a United supporter. Mum would take us to games – if it was Dens Park one time it would be Tannadice the next, or to see the Harp, the junior team. I can't exaggerate how important football was for us. [18]

One incident on a family holiday at Crieff in the late 1950s made a big impression on Nicky, but he only realised many years later that it had also profoundly affected his younger brother:

> We were on the lilo on the river [Earn] and Michael knocked me off, and I went down into what was a fifteen-foot pool, and I was struggling, I was drowning really, and I was just getting that feeling of 'Oh, well, this is it' when I felt an arm grab me, and it was a man, a one-legged man, who'd been watching us from the bank in his bath-chair. There were other people there but they all froze, I must have been making signs of being in difficulty, and this man managed to hop over and swim out and save me. A couple of years before Michael died, he told me, 'I think about that a lot, because I feel responsible for it, I'd

annoyed you and I always felt that that was my fault.' And that put a different complexion on it for me, because if it had ended badly he would have had to live with it, he would never have been able to put that away.

The one-legged man's name was Matt. He was from Crieff and his family were coal merchants. Michael was recounting this story one time when he was in Glasgow, and a woman was there who was from Crieff, and she said, 'That's a well-known story, about the time Matt saved the drowning laddie.' (Matt was dead by this time.) That happened in the 1950s

Niel Gow's Oak on the River Tay near Inver, where the Marra family often had caravan holidays. Beside the tree is the first bench inscribed with words from Michael's song 'Niel Gow's Apprentice'. After this bench was destroyed in a storm, a new one was installed in 2013. (See also pp.267, 272.)

but the story was still known. And it was clearly still in Michael's head, he would have worried away at it. Maybe he was thinking there might be a song in there. [19]

Despite winning a prize (*The Cub Scout Book of Cowboys and Indians*) 'for spellings' at the age of eight, it is fair to say that Michael and school did not agree. The zealous determination of some teachers to stamp on any spark of creativity did not help. Once, he was pulled up when writing a story about meeting Cilla Black on a bus in Lochee. He had written a piece of dialogue in which a bairn said, 'Look at her, she looks dead like Cilla Black.' The teacher red-lined the sentence and replaced 'dead' with 'very'. From then on, there was always likely to be trouble between Michael and the system.

That episode left a scar. Years later, in a school jotter in which he had copied out the lyrics of the songs on *The Midas Touch*, he got to work with a red pen, writing 'Careless!!' and 'Untidy' next to mistakes and underlining crossings-out. At the end, however, there is a big tick and the score '8/10'.

Look at her, she looks dead like Cilla Black.

BOOK OF
DIANS
—LORE

AGES
7 TO 11

FOR SPELLINGS.

Presented to

MICHAEL MARRA.

CLASS IV F,

ST.MARY'S LOCHEE.

JUNE 1960.

His last year at primary school was complicated by the fact that his class teacher was also the deputy headteacher, who was often called away on school business, leaving the class unattended and Michael free to play to the gallery of his peers. But it was at secondary school that things became really difficult. His disaffection was less with learning than with school as an institution, and this would grow into a lifelong distrust of all institutions. His extreme antipathy to being told what to do and when to do it was a defining characteristic which would re-emerge twenty years later when he found himself kicking against the demands of the music industry. 'I really have a big thing about control of my time, which many people may have, but I'm a bit of an extremist. I do not like anybody controlling my time or even deciding what topics we are going to be thinking about. That, very early, was a drawback at school.'[20]

Secondary school – Lawside Academy – was not a happy experience for either Michael or those charged with educating him. By his own admission he was every teacher's worst nightmare, an 'underminer' quietly and deliberately sabotaging everything he could. There was, for example, the occasion when he persuaded his classmates to bring an assortment of screwdrivers and other tools into school: under his direction, they proceeded to dismantle the classroom, taking the desks apart but leaving them with just enough support to stay upright until the next class arrived and tried to sit down.

Given this kind of activity, it is not surprising that his relationship with school was rocky. But what an indictment of formal education, that it could not accommodate a mind like Michael's. 'It wasn't as if I wasn't educating myself anyway. I could read and write.' He could, for example, consult the encyclopaedia his father had at home. 'They taught us at school about the discovery of the South Pole without mentioning Amundsen. That told me what was going on quite early, I thought: "Watch out." In my book at home, A was for Amundsen.'[21]

Another example of the agenda of orthodoxy that got his birse up was the Victorians' naming of Mount Everest in honour of the Surveyor General of India, Colonel Sir George Everest. 'Its real name in Tibetan means "mother of the universe". Imagine them sitting there saying: "Mother of the universe, that's not good enough. Let's call it after George Everest."'[22] Interestingly, George Everest, a Welshman, had objected to his name being given to the mountain, on exactly the kind of grounds Michael would have understood. But even he had been overruled.

Michael dreaded school, he dreaded the journey to school. A familiar pattern developed, as Nicky recalled: 'He would be late for school, sometimes deliberately. He would walk into the class and the teacher would say, "Marra, you're late again. What happened today?" Well, this gave him an instant stage, and he started these unbelievable stories about why he was late.'[23] But, to Michael, a great deal of what he was being taught was not believable; nor did he trust many of the people who were teaching him. Only occasionally was that mood of mutual antagonism displaced, as he later remembered:

> One morning, while reeling from two mind-numbing periods of mathematics, we were told that our English teacher was indisposed and that we were to make our way to Mr Ferrie's room instead. I had seen Mr Ferrie around the school and he seemed like a cheery, good-natured man, but we had never been subjected to him as a teacher.
>
> My usual fear and dread lifted when he told us he would read a poem by Robert Burns. What followed was wonderful because he didn't just read it, he produced a superb performance of 'Tam o' Shanter' while playing a recording of Malcolm Arnold's music inspired by the piece.
>
> I believe that there was not a boy in that class who wasn't captivated by his display of acting skills, his relish for the language and most of all his love of every syllable of the epic work. Love is the word. Here was a man with a noble purpose. He was excited and thrilled to be introducing us to the jewels of a giant who had been born among us.
>
> His performance discarded the need for thirty or forty questions about the text that would have wasted our time had we been looking at the page rather than associating a word with a facial expression. He could have been an actor – I've worked with worse – but he was a great teacher armed with superior material, and he had what was usually a riot of fourteen-year-old boys in his thrall.

> The next time I looked in my father's Kilmarnock Edition, it didn't look like German as it had before, and I have regarded Burns's work with professional envy ever since. [24]

Such experiences were exceptional. Michael even lost his appetite for finding things out for himself through reading. Books became inextricably linked in his mind with school. It would be some years before he rediscovered their magic. To be seen with a book was a mark of conformity, and the teenage Michael did not want to conform in any way. Chris Marra recalled:

> For a while he seemed to object to the idea of being 'clever'. It was a reaction to school. He rebelled against all that, became quite laddish for a while. But then he came out of that, and started reading again, and reading a lot. Hanging about with people at art college made a big difference to him. He felt failed by school, but school didn't fail him – he just didn't suit it. It's like saying that showbiz failed him – it didn't, it just wasn't his place.
>
> Church was another thing. He kicked against religion, and again he seemed personally let down. When I stopped 'doing' religion, it was pretty easy for me, but it seemed to leave a lasting impression on Michael. He would get quite angry about it. But then, he would have taken his religion seriously. If Michael was going to get into something he would get into it in a big way, so it was worse for him coming out of it. [25]

The rebel below Michael's unassuming exterior never vacated the premises. In later years he would channel his anger against injustice, establishments and institutions through his work or by supporting specific political causes. As a young man he was more inclined to direct action. One night in the early 1970s somebody chucked red paint over the statue of Queen Victoria in Albert Square. The culprit was never caught but rumours abounded. John Douglas, guitarist with the Trashcan Sinatras, was impressed enough by the story, as told to him by Kevin Murray, to write a poem about it. It is presented here as pure speculation, not as evidence:

> What brown poet's eyes could secretly vandalise
> Victoria's auld bronze coupon?
> 'Well, she's no queen here,' brown eyes had no fear,
> the deed's done, he's hame and fired the soup on.
> There's only six folk ken who did the Dulux then,
> seven if you count Victoria.
> Well, yer secret can bide for there's no clypes reside
> in the People's Republic of Dundonia.

*

Michael was in a band, formed with friends at Lawside Academy, called the Saints. With Michael on guitar they played at the Gaumont Cinema Saturday club, but everything changed when he was fourteen. Michael and the Academy reached an understanding: it would be to their mutual benefit if they parted. Or, to put it another way, he left and did not return. His mother, being a teacher herself, was hurt and disappointed, both in him and the school. There was an unspoken expectation from both parents that all their children should go on to further education. Mary: 'Mum would say to us, "Get a qualification, and then you can go off to be a musician or whatever. But you'll always have the qualification to fall back on."'[26] Mary and Nicky would themselves have careers in education, and Eddie also taught art, but there was to be no further school or college experience for Michael.

A succession of jobs followed over the next ten years. The first of these, acquired through his father's contacts, was as a message boy in the printing trade; he did this for a year as he was not eligible to start an apprenticeship until he was sixteen, and in that time learned every street and lane in Dundee. By running rather than taking buses for longer journeys, he saved his fare money and spent it on cigarettes instead. Without school qualifications an apprenticeship in printing was closed to him, so he worked for Burnett's the bakers for a while, then started as an apprentice electrician with Kilpatrick's in Albert Square. Later he would be a builder's labourer and a shipyard worker at Smith & Hutton. This last job saw him involved in a sit-in when, in 1973, the cancellation of contracts worth £1million threatened the yard with closure. Some elements of this story and the Timex strike and factory closure of 1993 eventually found their way into Michael's operetta, premiered at Dundee Rep in 2004 under the title *If the Moon Can Be Believed*.

Frank McConnell, with whom Michael would later form a hugely creative working relationship and close friendship, recounted the following story which Michael told him:

> Everybody in the yard had a nickname. Michael quickly became known as 'The Moth' because he was always hanging around the brazier. When the other men learned that he was a singer he became known as 'The Singing Moth'. One day a new hand arrived who made it very clear that he didn't like nicknames and that on no account was he to be given a nickname. He was known for ever after as 'The Man with No Nickname'. [27]

None of the jobs he did satisfied Michael or diminished his ambition to be a songwriter, but neither was he dismissive or unappreciative of the folk he worked with during this period. He observed and learned from them. He was wiry, not the 'burly Scot' of his self-caricature, so physical work was not about manhandling girders. 'I was taught how to find the centre of gravity, and never to double-lift. So, same as working with good actors, I worked with good labourers.'

Dundee and its people would always be a principal source of inspiration for him. When in later years he performed 'Australia Instead of the Stars', his celebration and lament for the spurned genius of Sandy Kidd, he would introduce it with an only partly tongue-in-cheek summary of the city's cultural history:

Before I sing this next song I'll have to tell you quite a few facts about my home town, which many people are not familiar with. My home town is Dundee, a very particular place. Mary Shelley writes in the foreword to her novel *Frankenstein* that her imagination first took flight on the 'blank and dreary northern slopes of the Tay'. So there's no argument about where that is, is there? Frankenstein comes from Dundee, we've established that. There was also a man called James Carmichael, a wonderful engineer who, in Dundee, invented reverse gear – you see, you're laughing, but this is actually true – and later became invaluable to the Italian army. So we got Frankenstein, reverse gear, and in 1690 a man called Patrick Blair, actually a doctor, Doctor Patrick Blair, became the first man to dissect an elephant. Now the elephant had died on the road between Broughty Ferry and Dundee – you keep laughing – anyway, Patrick had nipped out there with his scalpel and chibbed it. Anyway, he wrote a paper which is called *Osteographica Elephantina*, which I've actually seen a copy of in Dundee Museum. So: Frankenstein, reverse gear and the first man to knife an elephant for money. And then last year, the greatest of them all, the biggest thing ever to happen in Dundee – has anyone heard of Sandy Kidd? No? That's a very shocking thing, that. Well, Sandy's an inventor who worked in his garden shed for years, and he made a machine which produces thrust without opposite

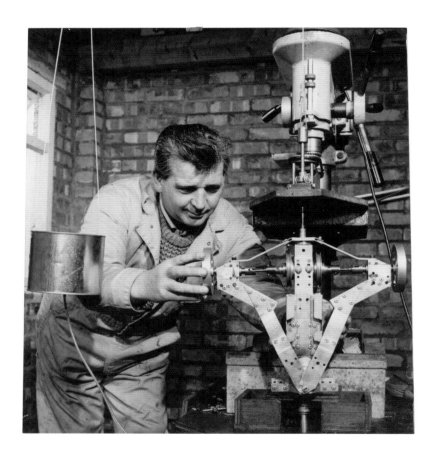

Alexander Duncan (Sandy)
Kidd, inventor of an
anti-gravity machine and
the subject of Michael's
song 'Australia Instead of
the Stars', at work in his shed.

He racks his brains
Till he finds out
His peers all show the romance
Of a ticket tout
With our hands on our hearts
And our hearts in our mouths
The bad news from here is
It's over and out
So we can stop telling lies
We know what we're like

I wish I'd seen
His garden shed
The man who made the spaceship
And scribbled in his bed
Is it all we can do
When we do raise our heads
To wave him goodbye
To Australia instead of the stars
We know what we are

The dog that was barking
To signal the end
From up Einstein's closie
We're growling again
And all the Queen's horses and
all the Queen's men
Would faint from the smell
of the treason we send to the
                              stars

And in this wilderness
of downward thumbs
When we've done our homework
There will be worse to come
And we've spent the 8 thousand
Such an unhappy sound
And we don't know the stars
From a hole in the ground
We'll get by selling cars
We know what we are.

Michael's handwritten lyrics for
'Australia Instead of the Stars'.

reaction. What this means really, in ordinary terms, you know when a spaceship goes up, all the fire comes out the back? Well, with what Sandy has produced it's just a machine which rises up, there's no fire. Anyway, he's interfered with the laws of physics, and he took his machine to Dundee University, and then they brought up the finest minds in England, and they ran some tests, and the only thing they knew about it was that it works, it works. He's made seventeen of these machines, small ones, and they've all worked. So Dundee University then called a halt to their research and said they'd spent £8,000 and hudnae reached the nearest galaxy yet. So, some Australians stepped in, very wealthy people, and also the Australian Government, and gave him the money to do his research down there. I mean, we've been laughing through all of this, but it's actually in the end a very, very sad thing, that he left the country and went to Australia, and there's currently one model being made in America and one in Australia. So, I wrote this song. And when the first flying saucer goes up and it has corks hanging from underneath it, we can all feel guilty. The song is called 'Australia Instead of the Stars', and I've thrown in the intro to *Neighbours* just to make you feel at home.

*

At the age of seventeen, Michael was keen to spread his wings. As he would later write in 'Big Wide World Beyond the Seedlies'[28], a song from *The Mill Lavvies*:

> There's a big wide world beyond
>   the Seedlies,
> They say it has a radiant perfume,
> So turn your back on the clickety-clack
> And make sure you zoom far away
>   from that loom.
> Way beyond the Seedlies there's a big
>   wide world,
> And that's a world you want to see,
> There's signs of life on the other side
>   of Fife
> And the Devil's tune on the dark side
>   of Dunoon.

In 1970, equipped with his guitar and his curiosity, he took off, making for London's folk clubs and venturing across to Amsterdam in the company of his pal Alfie Bremer, to take in a music festival. Michael busked by day and they slept rough by night. The first letter Chris Marra remembers receiving from Michael came from Amsterdam and described not only seeing bands like It's a Beautiful Day and The Flock, but also their 'house' in a bush in a park which they proudly showed to a curious Dutch policeman.

Michael loved the 1969
Humblebums LP so much
that when he went travelling
in Europe he took it with him,
writing careful instructions on
the back cover:

'If anyone should ever find this
record, listen to it six times,
dig it, and return it to the
address given.'

In London he shared a flat with a bunch of Blairgowrie girls who he was happy to let mother him. He enjoyed the cosmopolitanism of London and picked up enough casual work to pay his way while testing himself out as a performer in pubs and clubs. The sheer size of London offered a cushion of anonymity while he was practising and improving his skills. After eighteen months he returned to Dundee, and began to seek out music venues in and around the city.

Amongst these was the Dundee Folk Club, which had developed out of the Dundee Folksong Club and, after moving around a number of locations, had settled at the Woodlands Hotel in Broughty Ferry in 1965. The club was set up by Russ Paterson (father of the poet Don Paterson) and Willie Whyte, no mean performers in their own right, who ran a tight ship with an emphasis on quality control. One rising star of the folk scene, who came from Cupar, across the River Tay in Fife, and who would later have an important role in the direction Michael's career took, was Rab Noakes.

To Rab, a club night at the Woodlands was 'more like a concert, so you would go through this incremental process of nagging them until they would let you do a couple of songs, then if they liked you they would book you as a support act, and then eventually you would get your own gig.'[29] Rab played three solo gigs at the Woodlands in the course of 1970, but in April 1971 Russ and Willie brought nine years of club history to an end, owing to the rising costs of booking artists. One of the regular attendees, a singer and guitarist

called Gus Foy, took on responsibility for keeping the Woodlands as a music venue, and continued the policy of auditioning new acts to see if they were good enough.

Michael had been urged by a friend from Lochee, the singer Arlene Gowans, to try for a slot at the Woodlands. Bashful and unsure, Michael turned up one Sunday afternoon, looking – according to Gus Foy – 'like a miniature Wild Bill Hickok, with long hair and beard, and this guitar in a carrier bag'. He played a couple of songs which Gus didn't recognise. That was because Michael had written them. 'I asked how many he had, and he said "Hundreds."'[30]

I was taught how to find the centre of gravity, and never to double-lift...I worked with good labourers.

(Top) Michael at nineteen. Ian Lamb, who took the photograph, recalled: 'I did an interview with him in May 1971 and as far as I know that was his first press coverage. Not long before that a photographer called Daniel Kramer had released a book of photographs of Bob Dylan taken over some months, not available in the UK but I had a copy from Scandinavia and one of the photographs was of Dylan sitting up a tree, contemplating. When I did the interview with Michael at Clement Park there was a big tree in the garden. I said, "Would you mind climbing up the tree?" and I passed the guitar up to him. I thought it was a photograph that was right for him, it was right for the music, it was right for the time.'

(Bottom) Early gigs: receipts for Michael's appearances at Forfar Folk Club, showing a 16% pay rise in less than two months.

It was the start of a lifelong friendship. Michael and Gus put in many hours working up a repertoire of songs and, as well as appearing most weeks at the Woodlands, began to play as a duo in pubs and clubs across Fife and Angus. Michael was also doing solo gigs. Ian Lamb, who ran the Forfar Folk Club at the Queens Hotel, recalled the first time he played there, early in 1971:

> He got up and it was one of those magical moments when people realised they were hearing something special. He played a couple of songs on the guitar, but the thing that sticks in my mind was there was an upright piano in the Queens. He asked if it would be okay if he played something on this. He switched, and I think it was 'Your Song' by Elton John…. He seemed to enjoy the night and at the end he asked if he could come back. I said yes, any time, we're always looking for singers, and we were delighted he did. [31]

Shortly after this Michael headed down to London again. Ian Lamb and some friends stayed overnight with him on their way to the Weeley Rock Festival in Essex:

> I have a vague memory that there were quite a lot of us sleeping on the floor in one big room. Later, when he came back, he played a lot at Forfar. We couldn't believe that we were attracting such a talent because by this time he was headlining in quite a few clubs. Then we realised it wasn't

just the lowly Forfar Folk Club that drew him. There was a lovely young lady working behind the bar whose name was Peggy Peace. [32]

Peggy:

> 'I worked there, I was the barmaid. And he used to come in and leave his guitar. He was very timid, didn't say much when we first met, but we subsequently met in Dundee when I went to college to train to be a teacher.' [33]

Ian Lamb:

> 'He did seem nervous. What struck me was he was really quiet, he had an almost apologetic manner about him, as though he didn't want to impose but "Would it be possible…?" There was nothing about his manner to back up his incredible stage presence and musical ability… He was a thinker, you could conduct a really good conversation with him. I was a newspaper reporter, but Mick knew as much as I did, or more, about current affairs even at that age. There was a lot more depth to him than you would ever guess to look at him.' [34]

Michael had introduced his fourteen-year-old brother Chris to Gus Foy, who was greatly impressed by the youngster's guitar-playing. Along with singer Arlene Gowans, Dougie MacLean on fiddle, Jonathan (Jog) Ogilvie on drums and Michael also on guitar they formed

Hen's Teeth – 'pretty much a folk band' according to Chris Marra, 'or folk rock, you might say.' But there was a lot of interchange between musical genres at this time, and no doubt the Marras' eclectic tastes contributed to that on the local scene. Dundee also had plenty of venues where music could be heard, including the Hawkhill Tavern, the upstairs lounge of the Breadalbane (better known as the Bread or the Bothy) on Constitution Road, the Bowling Alley (the student union at the Bell Street Technical College) and the New Dines (Dundee University's student union). There was a kind of cultural surge happening in Dundee that few outside the city knew anything about.

Rab Noakes:

> There was that whole other Dundee that as a kid you don't come across, the more bohemian side around the Art College and up the Perth Road, you had to be introduced to it. I got to know it through Robin McKidd, who was an exemplar of that alternative scene, because he was quite well informed musically. Folk like Robin had record collections that included things like the Harry Smith *Anthology of American Folk Music*, they knew about those things before any of the rest of us did.

It was at this time that Rab began to notice and get to know Michael. 'I remember years later I sent him a photograph of me and Gerry Rafferty in the summer of 1971. We were doing a Stealers Wheel tour, just the two of us, and Michael replied saying, "Oh, I remember that look, we hitchhiked to the Salutation Hotel in Perth to see you play."' [35]

During this period, Michael's relationship with Peggy had deepened and strengthened. They were married on 18th November 1972. By this time Peggy was teaching at Auchterhouse Primary School, while Michael continued to pick up a variety of jobs. In the summer of 1973 he was working on a building-site at Inchture but, as soon as Peggy's school year was over, Michael gave up his job and they took off to explore Europe. They went by ferry to Norway, hitched their way through Norway, Sweden, Denmark, Holland, Belgium, France and West Germany, got a lift with a lorry driver across East Germany to Berlin, then headed to Amsterdam and home again.

1973 was also the year when Dougie MacLean left Hen's Teeth to pursue a solo career. This obliged the other members to consider the band's future. Also operating in Dundee at this time was a rock'n'roll outfit called Mort Wriggle and the Panthers, formed three years earlier by art college student Stewart Ivins. Although there appeared to be little in common musically between the Panthers and Hen's Teeth, they were linked by the fact that Jonathan Ogilvie played drums in both. Various members of these two bands amalgamated to produce a new line-up and a new sound. They were Stewart Ivins, Chris Marra and Gus Foy on guitars, Michael on bass and Jog on drums. They called themselves Skeets Boliver. [36]

(Above) Skeets Boliver
performing at the *Sunday
Mail* 'Popscot '76' competition.

(Right) Michael's Skeets
calling-card.

Stewart Ivins was the driving force behind Skeets Boliver, insisting on regular rehearsals and putting much energy into finding the band regular venues, such as Laing's Hotel on a Sunday night, as well as gigs further afield. When Jonathan Ogilvie left, his place was taken by eighteen-year-old Brian McDermott, who would go on to play with Danny Wilson and Del Amitri. Other Skeets members were brothers Allan and Peter McGlone. Allan would later play a very significant role as a sound engineer and producer of some of Michael's own records, while Peter became the subject of a song on the 2007 *Quintet* EP:

> Way back when before my hair was
>   gone
> I heard a little group was playing Casey
>   Jones
> It was a really silly place to put a
>   saxophone
> But Peter made them change their
>   minds

By 1976, Skeets Boliver were in constant local demand – 'we played for everything, including four-hour weddings,' Michael later recalled[37] – but were also performing in other parts of Scotland and picking up work in England and Wales. On occasion they played in front of unusually large audiences, as when they supported Bebop Deluxe at extremely short notice at the Caird Hall, after Steve Gibbons had to pull out following an accident.

There was also a recording contract with Thunderbird Records, won as a result of being runners-up in a *Sunday Mail* competition to find the best up-and-coming Scottish band. Two singles resulted. The first, released in 1977, was 'Streethouse Door' – at least, that's what it said on the label, but the sung version pretty much ensured that it would get no airplay. The writing credits were attributed to Michael, Stewart and Chris. The second single, 'Moonlight in Jeopardy', written by Michael, came out in October that year. But by then a relentless schedule of gigs was draining the band's energy, and the Skeets Boliver brand of music also perhaps seemed tired and old-fashioned alongside the explosion of punk in the mid-to-late 1970s. Michael himself kicked against the mainstream media's sometimes crass demands, as when a *Daily Record* photographer asked the band to jump off a bench so that they could run the headline, 'The Boys Are Jumping For Joy!': 'I said, "Nut!" The photographer said, "You're going to have a bit of bother in this gemme." Clever man.'[38]

After a particularly gruelling series of gigs in Wales in the spring of 1978 – lightened by a shared sense of humour and the irrepressible wit of their roadie, Boaby Barty – time was up for Skeets Boliver. Michael, wanting to concentrate on his own songwriting, was feeling hemmed in. 'There's such a thing as too much democracy in a band. I wanted to do it all. But they were great days.'[39] The band played a final gig at Bloomers on South Tay Street, Dundee, on Boxing Day that year.

The break-up was amicable and everybody was still speaking to one another. Michael considered that a victory. Those good relationships would prove vital further down the line, when he returned from what, in retrospect, we can call his London interlude.

voor haar
die tot
het uiterste
neen
bleven
zeggen
tegen het
fascisme

(Above left) Michael's
fake student ID card.

(Above, right) Michael in
Amsterdam and *(below)*
Peggy hitchhiking on their
1973 European road trip.

Notes

1   Interview with Sheena Wellington, 13th May 2017.

2   Peggy Marra: 'We visited Bailieborough in 2009. The first shop we saw was a beautiful ironmonger's called Clarke's.' For more on the song 'The Lonesome Death of Francis Clarke', see p.149.

3   Interview, 30th May 2017.

4   Sheena Wellington, *Travelling Folk* tribute programme, BBC Radio Scotland, 1st November 2012.

5   Interview with Nicky and Mary Marra, 13th January 2017.

6   Ibid.

7   Ibid.

8   Lorraine Wilson, *Take it to the Bridge: Dundee's Rock and Pop History* (2011).

9   Interview with Nicky and Mary Marra, 13th January 2017.

10   Interview with Matthew Marra, 26th April 2017. Alice Marra also remembered her father watching *Neighbours*, *Judge Judy*, *Pointless*. 'He loved all that rubbish. Maybe if your brain's working on the kind of level that his did, you need a bit of *Judge Judy*. But he didn't watch anything quietly. There was a running commentary all the time.'.

11   *The Scotsman*, 28th December 1991.

12   *Travelling Folk* tribute programme, BBC Radio Scotland, 1st November 2012.

13   Email, 9th March 2017.

14   This in fact happened in June 2002 when, every Wednesday, Michael on piano joined Jeff Craigie's Dundee band Hard Rain, with Angus Foy, Kevin Murray and Chris Marra in the line-up, to perform nothing but Dylan songs.

15   *The Scotsman*, 28th December 1991.

16   Interview with Nicky and Mary Marra, 13th January 2017.

17   A pass through the Sidlaw Hills on the road between Dundee and Coupar Angus.

18   Interview with Nicky and Mary Marra, 13th January 2017.

19   Ibid.

20   *Hermless: A Portrait of Michael Marra* (Billy Kay, Odyssey Productions), BBC Radio Scotland, 2004.

21   *Scotland on Sunday Review*, 21st October 2007.

22   Ibid.

23   Interview with Nicky and Mary Marra, 13th January 2017.

24   Quoted in Andy Hall, *Touched by Robert Burns: Images and Insights* (2008).

25   Interview with Chris Marra, 10th March 2017.

26   Interview with Nicky and Mary Marra, 13th January 2017.

27   Interview with Frank McConnell, 11th January 2017.

28   The Sidlaw Hills.

29   Interview with Rab Noakes, 21st July 2016.

30   Lorraine Wilson, *Take it to the Bridge: Dundee's Rock and Pop History* (2011).

31   Ian Lamb, interview with Alice Marra, December 2016.

32   Ibid.

33   *The Michael Marra Family Album*, BBC Radio Scotland, 1st January 2013.

34   Ian Lamb, interviewed by Alice Marra, 2017.

35   Interview with Rab Noakes, 21st July 2016.

36   The name came from a minor character in the stories of Damon Runyon. In 'Madame La Gimp' he is one of a number of guys impersonating the great and the good at a faked high-class reception: 'Next comes "the Very Reverend John Roach Straton," who seems to be Skeets Bolivar to me.' Note the change in spelling between the book and the band.

37   *Sunday Times*, 21st November 1993.

38   Undated letter from Michael to Nicky Marra.

39   *Sunday Times*, 21st November 1993.

Kitchen conversation

No.1

I wanted to ask Michael about songwriting, about where the songs came from, how they ended up in the form they did. And I wanted to ask him about where *he* came from. Origins and outcomes. It seemed to me that these things must be connected.

Actually, that was just a pretext. What I really wanted was to hear his voice again.

I thought I caught him glancing quickly away when I went into the pantry for something. I didn't close the door behind me.

I remembered him saying to me, back in 2006 when Marianne and I were about to get married, 'What are you giving her? You have to give her a song. I'll help you. It should be a surprise.'

I said, 'I don't have a song.'

He gave me a look. 'You write poems, don't you?' That was all: a kind of moral imperative disguised as a rhetorical question. I got on with it.

After a day or two I had some words and an idea for the tune. I phoned Michael. He said, 'Come round and we'll record it.'

Now this was problematic. He often came to our house but I seldom went to his. If I was there for very long, Marianne would wonder what we were up to.

'Tell her we're getting a new cooker, and you're going to help me move the old one,' he suggested.

The idea that Michael would organise or participate in such a manoeuvre made this the most unlikely scenario in the whole of Angus, but we went with it, and if Marianne was suspicious she never said anything. Over that day and a couple more, for an hour or two at a time, we worked away in his studio. He had me sing the melody, practising my phrasing over his piano accompaniment, then adding harmonies until there were three or four of me on the track. Then we worked on another couple of songs I'd brought along, because our ambition had expanded and we'd decided to make it an EP. He got me to notes I had no idea I could reach, to flush out previously undreamed of harmonies lurking among my vocal chords, and then he worked alone for more hours to mix in layers of instrumentation, *and* to write and record his own solo contribution, a waltz (because Marianne is a great one for the dancing) named in her honour 'Miss Mirren Mitchelson of Leslie'. He packaged it up, burned the songs on to a disc, and asked Matthew to design the cover from a photograph taken by Marianne which I'd surreptitiously borrowed. They even created a dummy CD got up like a Parlophone 45rpm record. And all this because Michael wanted me to make a song for his friend and my partner, soon to be my wife, and because he wanted to give me the gift of making it. The song was called 'This Thing is True'.

In an interview he explained the importance of songs as gifts: 'If you can write a song for somebody and give it to them as a present, if you are sincere about it and make this thing for another person, it will probably be one of the best presents they will ever get.'[1]

He was right. Of course.

James: You decided early on that you wanted to write songs. How did you know that?

Michael: Music was always very important in our home when I was a boy. We all loved listening to it and playing it. I was curious, even when I was six or seven, about how it was made. May I ask why that photograph of me is in there?

J: It felt appropriate. It's right behind where you used to sit.

M: I used to sit here in the kitchen. Now I'm in a cupboard. Where it can be quite dark.

J: It's not a cupboard, it's a room. It's called a 'butler's pantry'.

M: A butler? You are not selling this well.

J: Think of it as a metaphor. That thing you used to say about having your name in brackets. About being behind the scenes, off-stage, and everybody else singing your songs.

M: You probably didn't catch that.

J: Catch what?

M: My wry chuckle. It's true, though, I didn't know what Burt Bacharach looked like until I was in my twenties. I liked that, the idea of the song speaking for itself, the writer being invisible.

J: You were saying you were curious about how songs were made. Did you consciously set about learning how to make them?

M: Maybe not consciously, not to begin with. The learning process was listening and then playing, imitating and then trying to do my own thing. Once I'd heard The Beatles, that was me, writing my own songs.

J: Did you finish any?

M: Dozens. I had notebooks full of them, but later I destroyed the notebooks. That's part of the learning process too – recognising what's not good enough. There was one song I wrote when I was sixteen, 'Goodnight to Lovely You', that one survived and in fact nearly made it on to *The Midas Touch*.

J: Dougie MacLean sang that one at the Celtic Connections tribute concert to you in 2013. He said he remembered you singing it at Blairgowrie Folk Club. What's wrong?

M: Nothing. This is a weird conversation, that's all. Did anybody else remember it?

J: Marianne did. She must have heard you singing it around the same time as Dougie, maybe on the same occasion. And now Alice has recorded it on her album. And you're right, it's a survivor, it's good enough to have survived. How did you know, though, when you'd got something? I mean, when you thought, yes, this is going to work as a song?

M: I think that would happen when I was playing around with chords and something would click into place. It's the chord changes that lead you to new melodies. That's why most songwriters don't master playing the guitar or the piano: what they're most interested in is chord changes.

J: You like the idea of the invisible songwriter. So the fact that a lot of your songs are in the first person doesn't mean it's you in them?

M: The songs are never about me in that way. If I sing 'I', it's somebody else, a character I've invented for that song.

J: What about a song like 'Hamish'? 'I remember that time, it was an evening game / A European tie in the howling rain / Gus Foy pointed to the side of the goal and said / "There's Grace Kelly by Taylor Brothers' Coal"'. That's you, surely? You were there.

M: Aye, I was, but I was just one individual in the crowd. That 'I' could be anybody. The song's still about Hamish MacAlpine.

J: And you can make a song from any subject?

M: A song can be made from anything. From something you've heard or read about, or something you've seen happen. The same as for a writer. 'Where do you get your ideas from?' What sort of question is that? Nothing should be barred or out of bounds unless you, the writer, choose not to go there. But often, for me, there wasn't really a choice. Well, no, that's not right, there would be this huge range of choices and I would agonise over them and then panic my way into one of them. I would get totally obsessed with something and have to go after it, run it to ground. That's how it should be for any artist. It's not a commercial calculation, it's got nothing to do with money. Your job is to make it as good as possible. Hoagy Carmichael had a batch of songs marked 'Not for Commerce'. That's a real statement of principle.

J: You weren't motivated by money or glamour or fame. How did you know when you'd got something right?

M: By a process of elimination, to some extent. When you eliminate all the faults, maybe you're left with something that will stand up. But it's not for you to say if you've succeeded. That's a Dundee thing, though not exclusively. The last thing you do in Dundee is get above yourself or start believing in your own publicity. It's a great place for any artist to be based – you're always having to check yourself.

You know the story of Crichton Street? Back in the 18th century the city fathers wanted to build a street to give better access from the harbour into the centre of town. But in order to accomplish this they would have to go through the garden of a man called Dr John Crichton. He said they could do it as long as they named the street after him. So they did. But no Dundonian called it 'Crichton Street' for the next fifty years. They called it 'Vain Doctor Street'.

J: A lot of your songs have a dig at that kind of pomposity or pretension, but they're not negative. There's a democratic, human spirit at work in them. I would say the biggest thing that comes through in your songs is optimism.

M: Ian Hamilton Finlay was being interviewed by Melvyn Bragg once and he said he couldn't talk about Scotland because it was like a shadow across his heart. That's how he felt. I felt Dundee like a light across my heart. But not just Dundee, of course.

J: Ian Hamilton Finlay was a polymathic artist, like you. He enjoyed making things, he was always working with words, footering about in the garden, and like you he had a difficult relationship with authority and convention. His art is constantly challenging authority, celebrating the unconventional.

M: Well, there is plenty to celebrate in life that is unconventional, or that simply goes unnoticed. The tone of my songs might be dead-pan, but there's a lot of joy in them, and humour. If you're making people laugh then at least they're not booing you.

When I was working on something I would go through draft after draft. A song might take months. I was very hard on myself. You don't know where it's going to take you. Eventually I'd have to ask someone else if it was finished. Like M'Lach, for instance. If he said, 'That's no bad,' I knew I was getting somewhere. That's the height of praise in Dundee.

J: M'Lach is your brother Chris, right?[2] When I spoke to him he didn't see it quite that way.

M: Oh, you've been snooping around the family, have you?

J: Just trying to get a full picture, Michael. Chris said he'd go to see you and you'd say, 'I've got these new songs' and then you'd play them. And if there were certain ones that jumped out at him he'd say, 'I'd like to do that one'. But it wasn't a case of him telling you what was good or not good. Anyway, he said, you didn't really write anything that wasn't good. You might write something that was inappropriate or just didn't fit with what else you were doing at the time, but it was never a matter of quality. And sometimes what you had was just too dark – there might be a place for it somewhere, but not there. Does that sound about right?

M: It sounds like M'Lach, yes.

J: Here's something your other brother Nicky said: 'What marks Michael's music out is his originality.…You couldn't predict what was coming next with his songs and that was because he was a very deep thinker, he thought a lot about his work, and what came through was usually based on something he *wanted* to say.'[2]

M: Do I have to comment on Nicky's comments too?

J: No.

M: Good. Because there is a strong tradition of loyalty among us and I wouldn't want anybody thinking you were putting words in my mouth.

J: Neither would I, believe me.

M: Let's say that yes, what it comes down to is work. If you're lucky there's a song at the far end of the journey. But it's not just luck. It's hard work too. I was obsessive about work. I didn't respond well to praise. Praise doesn't do it, because there are always more faults that you have to eliminate.

J: Here's another quotation: 'There might be a month on one line just being wrong, and staring at it. The bulk of what they call inspiration will maybe give you two lines, enough to know it's worth the effort. The rest is the effort.'[3]

M: I can't disagree with that.

J: Well, that's good because it was you that said it.

Notes

1   'The Michael Marra Family Album',
     BBC Radio Scotland, 1st January 2013.
2   'The Michael Marra Family Album',
     BBC Radio Scotland, 1st January 2013.
3   Interview with Alastair McKay,
     Scotland on Sunday magazine, 1991.

Michael, aged about eighteen,
on Balgay Hill, Dundee.

London

I'm taking the next train home,
Following lines that I followed before...

'Taking the Next Train Home'

Michael's route to London – or rather, since he'd been there on his own initiative earlier, to the heart of its music industry – was facilitated in 1978-79 by Rab Noakes, who was already there. Rab offered to link him up with Bernard Theobald, Barbara Dickson's manager since 1972. Rab and Barbara knew each other from the Scottish folk club circuit and had toured together as members of the Great Fife Road Show. By the late 1970s Barbara was becoming a very big name. Rab introduced Michael to Bernard with some trepidation and the caveat that 'Bernard has his pluses but he also has his minuses'. To Michael, this was uncharted territory. He claimed, for example, that Bernard Theobald was the first person he ever knew who was a Tory.

Rab, Barbara and others around at the time are adamant that Bernard loved Michael's music and loved Michael too, and that he wouldn't have taken him on otherwise. But there were conflicting agendas from the start and eventually the differences between them became too great.

Could Michael have succeeded in the London music world which he found so unscrupulous, demeaning and soul-destroying? Barbara had no doubts:

Bernard thought if he could iron out the wrinkles in Michael then Michael could be the next big thing, the new whatever the next new thing was… And I think if Michael had been able to compromise, if he had really gone for it, he could have made it big time. But something in the whole process bothered him. I think he saw himself mutating into a can of beans, and he didn't want to be a can of beans. I think he thought he would lose control. [1]

Rab Noakes concurs:

There's a way you have to act in the music industry and it's difficult for many people but for Michael in particular it was hard, he just couldnae connect at that level, that kind of language and behaviour.

He got talked into changing titles of songs – 'Peddie Street' became 'Pity Street' for example – and sometimes you go along with that kind of thing and then later you stand back and realise you've given something away that you regarded as your own strength. And Michael, well, you know how thoughtful he was, he did not take anything lightly, he never skirted round the edges of things, he would always get into the nub of the matter… [2]

(Above) Michael and Peggy on
their wedding day. *(Facing page)*
They also made it on to the front
page of the *Evening Telegraph*.

(Above and facing page)
Michael and Peggy early
in married life.

Another song that had its title changed was 'When These Shoes Were New', which on *The Midas Touch* became 'Take Me Out Drinking Tonight'. Michael considered this to be undue interference: that was the last line but not the most important part of the song. Changing the title, in his view, shifted the emphasis. It was like doing wilful damage to the song's integrity. But reluctantly he agreed to it.

To be fair, Bernard Theobald was extremely complimentary about his new signing, telling the *Dundee Courier*:

> He sent me some tapes of his music and his songs really stood out head and shoulders above anything else I've heard recently.
>
> Of the hundreds of hopefuls who send me tapes of their material, Mike is the only singer I've picked up in this way.
>
> We're all very excited about him down here and I seriously put him on a par with Gerry Rafferty. Mike has enormous potential.

Despite Theobald's best efforts, however, which included negotiating a two-record deal with Polydor, the wrinkles refused to be ironed out. In the first few pages of Bob Dylan's *Chronicles* Dylan describes John Hammond signing him to Columbia Records in New York. 'I'm gonna give you all the facts,' Hammond says. 'You're a talented young man. If you can focus and control that talent, you'll be fine.' He hands Dylan on to the head of publicity at Columbia, who tries to build a profile of him for promotional purposes. The interview takes place across the PR man's desk. Dylan shies, balks, gives one-word answers, invents stuff ('How'd you get here?' 'I rode a freight train.') and generally does not like what they are trying to do with him and to him. Michael's experience at Polydor must have run on similar lines. He would have found it all so unnecessary. He was who he was: if they didn't like it, why sign him in the first place? For the folk on the other side of the contract it must have been equally frustrating.

'I was signed by Polydor because they actually wanted Gerry Rafferty, but they couldnae get him,' Michael said years later. 'That's why they signed me. A friend told me that, and I remember the first time that he said that, I thought, na, I don't think so, but the more I thought about it the more I thought, well, it makes sense. Loudon Wainwright maintained that he got his first record deal because Bob Dylan fell off his motorbike. And the more you find out about the music industry and how limited their imaginations are, then the more you realise these things are true.'[3]

He was commuting between his home in Newtyle, Angus and London, staying in a posh hotel when he was there – another cause, perversely, of his discomfort. Life on the streets of the city, in the pubs and music venues, could be stimulating, but he preferred working at home. He acknowledged and appreciated the quality of the musicians, singers and engineers he got to work with, whether on lengthy UK tours with Barbara Dickson or in the studio recording *The Midas Touch* (Barbara, Maddy Prior and Annie Ross all sang backing vocals), but then again, he had left a bunch of talented musicians, singers and engineers back in Dundee. The difference lay in the resources available to a label like Polydor:

> I got to work with a lot of great people. In fact that was the last record that I made where, if I'd said I want an orchestra for this, there was no question, they brought the orchestra in, things happened. There were funds involved. Ever since that album, every subsequent record has been a battle, fighting for everything, stealing studio time, conning musicians out of money and anything that it takes to get the record made. But that one, it was pretty luxurious. [4]

In retrospect he would play down the quality of the songs on *The Midas Touch*, referring to some of the lyrics as 'pretty dreadful' or 'embarrassing' – being, in other words, typically self-critical. In fact it's a very good first album, with two or three standout songs. Even Michael admitted that 'When These Shoes Were New' stood the test of time. As much as anything, the album was bound up with unhappy memories of what happened – or failed to happen – to the second record with Polydor. He kept running up against the problem that the material he believed was his best – that came out of his own background and formation – was deemed to be too Scottish, too parochial, too not what *they* wanted. This was not a sustainable situation, for anyone. The songs were recorded, a lot of time and a lot of effort were spent in the studio, but eventually there was a falling-out between Mike

Vernon, the producer, and Polydor, and the whole project was shelved. *Dubiety*, as it was eventually called, would not see the light of day until 2017.

Playing at Ronnie Scott's or, as support for Barbara Dickson, at London's Royal Albert Hall (on 3rd December 1980), were huge experiences, but – as he so often made clear – his preference was not to be in the full glare of the spotlight. Two good-luck telegrams sent to him before the Albert Hall gig seem, in retrospect, to sum up the tension he was feeling between home and the London music business. On the one hand friends wished him success in true Dundee style: 'MAKE SHARE ITS NO A KEACHIE CONCERT'. On the other, Barbara reassured him of her support: 'YOU'VE GOT THE JOB. DESPITE WHAT POLYDOR SAY I THINK YOUR ACE. THANKS FOR EVERYTHING.'

At various points he blamed the record company, his management or himself for things not working out. 'The first album was OK, but the second was going to be great. Polydor just knocked it on the head, though.' [5] 'I don't actually remember falling out with Bernard, it just became very, very obvious that we were poles apart.' [6] He was 'always awkward' with the music business, he 'threw a tantrum' and walked away. The break was inevitable, and it had to happen so that Michael could stay at home and get on with what he really wanted and needed to do.

Here are three different opinions on that period, which all lead to one conclusion:

Chris Marra: 'I think it almost broke his heart, to put all that work – fabulous producer, fabulous musicians, great songs – and then it's shelved and you can't use it. I think that lack of control was one of the things that stirred him on to doing his own stuff.'[7]

Rab Noakes: 'In some respects, maybe all that wasnae such a bad thing, because once it was done it was done, and a lot of what was developing in his mind was the music that became *Gaels Blue*, and that was the start of Michael finding his unique voice and his own way of working creatively, with all he knew and felt about his own home town and his own country.'[8]

Peggy: 'When you think back, it wasn't him at all. Glamorous photographs, hair done and everything, no, it just wasn't him. And he'd tried that, he'd done his best, and it was "Let's get on with the next thing."'[9]

Notes

1   *Hermless: A Portrait of Michael Marra*
     (Billy Kay, Odyssey Productions),
     BBC Radio Scotland, 2004.

2   Interview with Rab Noakes, 21st July 2016.

3   *Hermless: A Portrait of Michael Marra*
     (Billy Kay, Odyssey Productions),
     BBC Radio Scotland, 2004.

4   Ibid.

5   *Evening Times*, 8th May 1987.

6   *Hermless: A Portrait of Michael Marra*
     (Billy Kay, Odyssey Productions),
     BBC Radio Scotland, 2004.

7   *The Michael Marra Family Album*,
     BBC Radio Scotland, 1st January 2013.

8   Interview with Rab Noakes, 21st July 2016.

9   *The Michael Marra Family Album*,
     BBC Radio Scotland, 1st January 2013.

(Above and facing page)
Rare publicity shots, long
hidden from sight, of Michael
as he never really was. As Peggy
put it, 'Glamorous photographs,
hair done and everything, no,
it just wasn't him.'

Kitchen conversation

No.2

James: Can we talk a bit more about the writing process?

Michael: As long as you don't start that metaphor nonsense again. A man in my position does not need metaphors.

J: I'll avoid them like the plague.

M: Or similes.

J: Somewhere in an interview you said you had the 'songwriter's disease'. What's that?

M: You're never more than six feet away from a song. It's catching. I was watching and listening all the time to what was going on around me. Can you make a song from it? And the authenticity of a song comes down to experience. Some songwriters deliberately try to fall in love so they can write about it. The believability of a song or the singer singing it, that's what matters. You don't have to have a perfect voice or a certain kind of accent – these things might actually be a disadvantage. What you have to do is persuade the listener that the song is true, the way you're singing it is true. It's like being an actor. You can have the best script in the world but it's no use if the audience doesn't believe the actors.

J: There's a saying in Nicaragua that everyone is considered a poet until proved otherwise. Do you think that applies to songwriting too?

M: That's good. Yes, I'm sure of it. Anybody can write a song. Everybody in the world is entitled to be a songwriter. You don't need a qualification. You don't even need a musical instrument.

J: But it must help to have one. What comes first, then, the tune or the words?

M: The words, or I should say the subject-matter. The subject is the reason for the song coming into being, but it's like evolution, the words and the tune grow together. I never wrote the music first and then the lyric, or vice versa. I tried that once, and it was a horrible experience. Mainly because the music wasn't mine, but even if it had been…

J: How did that come about?

M: Well, money was involved, although as it turned out I never saw any of it. I got this job fitting words into tunes written by Björn from ABBA. This was in 1985, after ABBA had split up, Bernard Theobald heard that Björn Ulvaeus was looking for a new writing collaborator and suggested my name and I got the job. I was working on two different shows on the Edinburgh Fringe that summer. One was called *And as in Gilbert and Sullivan*, which was about Gilbert and, strangely enough, Sullivan. The other was a show called *Bathtime Bubbles* about American music between the wars, performed by Stewart Ivins, Pauline Rourke and me. I'd taken on too much and I wasn't looking after myself. I wasn't able to eat before or after performances, so I hadn't had a proper meal for a fortnight and I was getting sicker and sicker. In the final week I was in so much pain I thought I was on the way out. Instead of going to the

doctor, I decided I'd better get the Björn thing done so my family would have some money. I went up to Dunkeld, where my mother had a hide-out. He'd sent me three tunes with dummy lyrics, and I had to fill in the words, but it was hard work because everything was so precise. All he wanted from me were lyrics that mathematically fitted the music. There was no subtlety. I wasn't used to working with other people's music, I was really much more comfortable working on my own, and I was very particular about phrasing. Every night I'd go to the phone-box beside Niel Gow's cottage and call Sweden, play the tape and sing the words down the phone to Björn. But his English didn't seem very good to me, I thought it was if he'd learned it from listening to Elvis records. My Swedish was, well, very basic, I probably didn't have the accent for it, and he didn't seem to appreciate my humour either. He kept saying, 'You are departing from the tune.' Eventually I finished the job, I threw some words together, changed the melody to a better one and said, 'That's what you're getting.' And then I went to the doctor. And I wasn't dying, I had an ulcer.

The songs were never used. I should be grateful. But I hate that attitude to music: you're under contract to write songs, but you don't actually care what they're about.

The phone box at Inver, scene of
Michael's unhappy collaboration
with Björn Ulvaeus.

The Next Thing

Throw in one of your special smiles
The one that shines for a thousand
*   miles*
Drive on the left and remember honey
Dip your eyes
Racing from Newburgh through the
*   night*

'Racing from Newburgh'

Back in Newtyle in 1981 – 'the green fields of Angus are not the sort of place where one would expect to find one of Scotland's most talented rock songwriters', one journalist wrote[1] – Michael's immediate problem was how to earn some money. There was no profit in lamenting the failure of Polydor to promote *The Midas Touch* properly or to put out the second album, but without a recording contract his songwriting efforts were effectively stymied: 'I have spent a whole year writing songs which are just lying on the top of my piano rather than going to the presses. But I'm an eternal optimist and perhaps another contract could see the songs put onto record.'[2]

In the meantime, while he was plotting how to put together and produce what would become his next album, *Gaels Blue*, Michael took whatever work he was offered. In the first half of 1981 he was guest performer on several episodes of BBC Scotland's *Afternoon Show*; 'M. Michel Marra et son Broadcasting Band' appeared with the Gary Clark Band at the Angus Hotel, Dundee; the Bonar Hall, Caird Hall and Dundee Rep became regular venues, with Michael playing solo or in collaboration with some of his old musician friends. And out of those renewed links came a new, flexible but also dependable ensemble.

'What's blue, got twenty-six legs and only plays once a year?' Michael asked local journalist Toni Scott. 'The Gaels Blue Orchestra.' The line-up for a Bonar Hall concert on 6th December 1981 included Donny Coutts on drums, Ged Grimes on bass, Gary Clark and Chris Marra on guitars, Derek Thomson on keyboards, Dougie Martin and Gerry McGrath on vocals, Allan McGlone, Mick McCluskey and Peter McGlone on saxophones, Mark Fletcher on trumpet and Frank Rossiter on trombone. Also appearing were 'special guests' Saint Andrew and the Woollen Mill (Andy Pelc, Stewart Ivins, Eddie Marra and Gus Foy). All these would play regularly with Michael over the next three decades. His Christmas show at the Westport Bar and subsequently at Fat Sam's became an annual event.

*

Michael's first foray into musical theatre happened in 1982, as the following fresh but defiantly droll biography reveals:

MICHAEL MARRA was born in Dundee in 1952 and lived in Lochee until he was seventeen. At school he formed a group called the Saints and appeared at the Five Ways Club, a centre for elderly people: and the Gaumont Cinema Club on a Saturday morning, learning to combine the wild badness of rock and roll and the desire to become a good and decent citizen and therefore produce a fine upstanding degenerate. Later folk scene groups were Hen's Teeth, Mort Wriggle and the Panthers, and Skeets Boliver with whom he started making records. In 1979 he signed with Polydor Records to produce two albums, one was released and the other was never completed. He toured Britain extensively with Barbara Dickson, his last Glasgow appearance was at the Apollo Theatre, and London performances include Ronnie Scott's and the Albert Hall. Marra recently did a thirteen week series for BBC Scotland, singing a song per week and revelling in the fact that it looked like he was busy. More recently he has been working with Saint Andrew and the Woollen Mill, the Dundee group, in a musical production of Stagecoach, the John Ford Western, playing the part of Doc Boone, this was his first acting role and there was no really big trouble.

While rehearsing this show Marra mentioned that he had a solo performance the following day and the actress who was playing Mrs Mallory said, 'Oh you do that at the piano do you, just like Hoagy Carmichael?'

'Yes,' said Marra. 'Just like Hoagy Carmichael'[3]

Appropriately, Perth-based company Stagecoach sponsored this show, supplying an open-top bus in which the cast, in full cowboy regalia, toured a rainy Dundee.

'There was no really big trouble': that is

pure Michael. And the reference to Hoagy Carmichael, one of his all-time songwriter heroes, suggests that however tight things were financially, Michael was enjoying being back on his own territory.

He was constantly organising shows and concerts such as, in January 1983, three nights of what the press called 'riotous cabaret' at Dundee Rep, under the umbrella title 'Dundee Adolescent Showtime'. The third night was entitled 'That's Lightweight Entertainment' and was written and presented by 'Pat Santos' (a.k.a. Saint Andrew) and 'Rock Newtyle' (Michael). The various acts included 'Philippe Du Biety' (Trick Cycling Champion of ALL Belgium) and a wrestling match between Brutal Wilhelm Sykes (a.k.a. saxophonist Peter Benedetti) and Tiny Tim O'Rourke (a.k.a. Michael) to the accompaniment of Manakross De Pletty (a.k.a. Bob Quinn) playing 'Cavatina' on classical guitar. In May that year Michael supported Jack Bruce and Friends, again at the Bonar Hall. And during the month of June he exhibited thirty of his drawings at Dundee Rep. (This was his second art show: the first had taken place in Cupar, Fife a year or two earlier.) 'After I made my first album I did a couple of tours supporting Barbara Dickson,' he explained in the press release. 'There's always a lot of hanging around on these long tours so I bought myself a small sketch pad and a packet of felt tip pens and started drawing simply as a way to relax. Now I find it quite compulsive.'

*

Oh you do that thing at the piano do you, just like Hoagy Carmichael?

Yes. Just like Hoagy Carmichael.

(Facing page) Peggy,
Michael and new baby,
Alice. *(Above)* Alice and
Matthew, early 1980s.

(Above, left to right) Allan McGlone, Michael, Stewart Ivins and Saint Andrew in an early manifestation of The Woollen Mill.

(Right) Michael and Stewart Ivins, late 1970s.

(Facing page) Tickets and flyers for various 1980s shows.

EUPHONIA
A Charity Concert in Aid of
The Samaritans Dundee

STARRING
MICHAEL MARRA
THE GAELS BLUE ORCHESTRA
SAINT ANDREW
BATHTIME
KEVIN MURRAY
CHILLI PEPPERS
THE HEADSQUARES
THE QUIET'S OVER
CHRISTOPHER MARRA

Sunday 5 May 1985 8pm
Bonar Hall, Dundee
Ticket £3.00

The Samaritans Dundee Branch
would like to say a
BIG THANK YOU
to all Artistes Appearing
Groucho's — The Other Record Shop
Mitchells Self Drive — Baillie Marshall
and all others who helped
including those who purchased this ticket

DU BIETY PRODUCTIONS PRESENT

MICHAEL MARRA
and
THE GAELS BLUE ORCHESTRA,
featuring RAB NOAKES,
and introducing
THE TAY ROPE WORKS SKING SECTION
PLUS
ST ANDREW and the WOOLLEN MILL.

BONAR HALL, PARK PLACE, DUNDEE
SUNDAY 19 DECEMBER at 8pm
TICKETS £3.00 FROM GROUCHOS, R.G.FORBES & CENTRAL BOOKING OFFICE

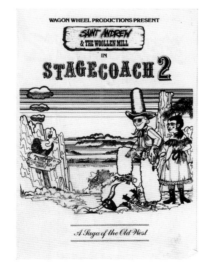

WAGON WHEEL PRODUCTIONS PRESENT
SAINT ANDREW
& THE WOOLLEN MILL
IN
STAGECOACH 2

A Saga of the Old West

Les Promotions Pathétique
présente

M. Michel MARRA
et son
BROADCASTING BAND

ET

M. Gary CLARK
et son
BAND ORDINAIRE

Compère ANDRÉ Big Boy PHC

Hotel Angus — Sunday 29 June 7.30

Admission 20 francs (£2)

Students must be signed in by a member
of the General Public

77

One constant feature of Michael's career was the sheer amount of hard work he undertook, often for very little financial reward. The 1980s were particularly tough years financially. Peggy stayed at home to look after the children for five or six years after Matthew was born, so the family was reliant on Michael's ability to earn money. His intense creativity was accompanied by bouts of guilt and even gloom, despite his claim to be an 'eternal optimist'. The lyrics of his song for Peggy, 'Peggy Peace', written in a notebook in the mid-1980s, give a hint of this:

> Maybe the Good Lord will send us
>   a great big single
> Go a long way to removing a deal
>   of the heat
> Maybe we could even feed and
>   clothe our children
> Think about it honey. Gee Whiz it
>   really would be neat.
>
> Pretty Little Peggy, Pretty Little
>   Peggy Peace
> I hear you keep a monkey, house
>   trained and up on his feet
> Ah, what's a little thunder, what's
>   a little rain
> And what's a little loss of sleep?
> I love you and you love me Peggy.

In the same notebook are these lines:

> Fame, a bull within an aging frame,
> Who tickles at my feet and then,
> Like a thief in the night,
> It's hiding round corners and avoiding
>   the lights.

> Fame, tugging at my sleeve again,
> Just a little sip and then I'm heaving
>   in the race.
> With all of my might
> It's like a horse drawn dream to beat
> a dog drawn life explained.
> Give a drink of water to my little
>   piece of fame.
> Light shining in my sleep at night
> When I'm just about to feel all right
> It's eager to tease,
> And I'm staring at the ceiling at a
>   quarter to three.

And again, in the following scribbled-down thoughts there appears to be an echo of Frank Loesser's daily 'rendezvous with failure'[4]:

> My beautiful little girl and my beautiful little son may live to regret at some point in their lives having a reprobate father, however, after thinking about it they will go on to do whatever they do just to spite him and do it, no doubt, exceedingly well. Just the same as I did, or rather as I mean to.

*

Some time in 1984 Michael put out a cassette album of songs under the title *Dubiety*. Some of these would eventually appear on the 2017 downloadable collection of the same name. Four of them – 'Gaels Blue', 'Monkey Hair', 'The Altar Boys' and 'General Grant's Visit to Dundee' – made their first 'official' recorded appearance on *Gaels Blue*, released on vinyl on the Mink Records label (Michael's own) in 1985.

Arguably, *Gaels Blue* marks the moment

when Michael Marra regains control and establishes, with astonishing confidence, his true voice not just as a songwriter but as prime interpreter of his own songs. It is a notably home-grown product: the musicians were Gaels Blue Orchestra stalwarts and other friends, including Kevin Murray on guitars and mandolins, and all the tracks except 'Gaels Blue' (recorded live at East Kilbride) were recorded at Dundee's Inner City Sound Studios. The sleeve design was by 'Pat Santos' (Saint Andrew) and the photograph of Michael by Stewart 'Stewartie' Sutherland. Allan McGlone was the sound engineer (as well as playing saxophone), Michael was composer, arranger and producer, and the sleeve bore the legend 'Made in Scotland'.

Chris Marra, who played on just one track on the album, was in no doubt about the significance of Allan McGlone's involvement: 'Allan was a big fan of Michael's stuff but he was also a really talented engineer, good at getting things done.'[5]

A note on the cover of the album paid special thanks to McGlone, and to Peggy Peace and Margaret Comerford Reilly (Michael's mother) who 'came to my assistance when I both stumbled and fell whilst making this record'.

'Racing from Newburgh' was for Peggy, but the whole album was a labour of love. It was also a statement of defiance: success was to be measured not in commercial terms but by the quality and integrity of the words and music. And it was an uncompromising commitment to working in Scotland.

Notes

1   Andrew Collier, *Sunday Standard*, 14th June 1981.

2   Ibid.

3   Handwritten entry in notebook.

4   See below, p.153.

5   Interview with Chris Marra, 10th March 2017.

Kitchen conversation

No.3

James: When we were talking about your ill-fated collaboration with Björn Ulvaeus, you mentioned language and accents. Let's move on to the Scottishness of your work. I met a young fan of yours recently, James Kirkpatrick, he's a student at Dundee University, a songwriter and performer himself, and he told me that this is something he really admires about your songs: 'He captures Scottish life in a way that no other performer I've heard does. He gets right down to the inconsistencies, the highs and the lows, all the things about Scotland that don't quite add up, and that is something special.'[1] Back in the 1980s, one of the problems at Polydor was that they had a completely different attitude. They didn't like where a lot of your songs were, literally, coming from.

Michael: If I came out with a Scottish word they used to complain about it. I used the word 'wee' in a song and they didn't like that, so I wrote another song called 'Like a Frenchman (I Said Oui)' as a protest and they didn't notice the pun. They even put that one out as a single.

The generation before mine, you had to go to elocution classes if you wanted to get on in the music business, and some of those attitudes still existed. My Scottishness was a problem for them. Using Scottish references in my songs annoyed them. They tried to tone me down. Well, that just annoyed *me*, and the more annoyed I got the more I wanted to annoy *them*. I'd been reading John Prebble's book *The High Girders*, about the building of the Tay Bridge and its subsequent collapse, and that inspired me to write a song which became 'General Grant's Visit to Dundee'. Ulysses S. Grant visited Dundee in September 1877 at the end of a very long tour of Europe after having been President of the United States of America. Dundee was the last stop on his tour and it is fair to say that he was not fascinated. In fact the only thing anyone could remember him saying was, 'That's a mighty long bridge,' which it was – the longest bridge in the world at the time. Once I had the line, 'What a mighty long bridge to such a mighty little ole town', the rest followed. I sent it to London and they hated it, it was too Scottish. So after that I wrote a whole album of Scottish songs.

J: Which became *Gaels Blue*.

M: Eventually. It was heavily influenced by a record Randy Newman made in 1974 called *Good Old Boys*. In those days they called it a concept album, which sounds pretentious but just meant he had a thread running through the songs, which were all about the Deep South, from the point of view of people who lived there. And that really changed the way I thought about writing my own songs.

J: There's a definite connection between a song like 'Louisiana 1927' and 'General Grant's Visit to Dundee'. They're history lessons in miniature, in the voices of people on the receiving end of that history.

M: I think John Prebble managed to deliver that too, only on a bigger scale.

J: Academic historians were very sniffy about Prebble. They said he didn't do his research properly, he wrote a mixture of fact and fiction and created a whole set of questionable myths about Scotland, and the Highlands in particular.

M: They were probably jealous of his sales. All myths are questionable. That's what they're for. For me, John Prebble's books opened up a whole lot of questions about where I was from. That wasn't a bad thing.

J: But you were also celebrating Scotland and, specifically, Dundee – but not in a 'wha's like us', uncritical way.

M: Why wouldn't you write about your own place? And if you do, why wouldn't you be as honest as you possibly can be? But there are traps about. If you are announced as a Scottish performer in Canada, for example, or Australia, that carries certain expectations. I was allergic to all that. It was hard enough dealing with the real Scotland without having to battle with the non-existent one. Dundee was sometimes painted out of the picture altogether. Or if it was noticed, it was in order to give it a kicking. It was as if the people there didn't deserve any respect.

J: Is that what the song 'Gaels Blue' is about?

M: In a way. It's really about Scottish soul singers, and that they have the same passion and commitment as anybody. You can be from Dundee or Elgin and have soul, just as you can in London or Detroit. It's the same, but it's also different.

J: There's one line that seems to sum that up: 'We've been weighed up and found to be true'. But then a wee bit later you kind of undercut that: 'Though we never had the Chevys or the Baptist Church / We had a choice of colours for a broken crutch – we'll do.' That's very Dundee.

M: Well, there you go then.

J: Just as a wee aside, more than thirty years after *Gaels Blue* came out, your friend the Skye composer and accordionist Blair Douglas made an album with the trilingual title *Stay Strong / Bithibh Laidir / Rester Fort*. There's a song on it, that you sing, for the people of New Orleans after the devastation of Hurricane Katrina in 2005. He wrote it in French, 'Rester Fort, La Nouvelle Orléans', and it carries such a distinct echo of Randy Newman's 'Louisiana 1927' I can see why he got you to sing it.

M: It's a great song of solidarity. There are always going to be events of that kind. It's how people respond to them that makes them tragic or heroic – or both.

J: Going back to Scottish history, the first song on *Gaels Blue*, 'Mincing wi Chairlhi', was inspired by the Battle of Culloden. Could you talk about that?

M: Culloden was a different kind of disaster from the Tay Bridge one. We're still living with the consequences of Culloden. The song takes the form of a postcard home from an Italian nobleman who had no idea why he was there other than it seemed like

a great idea at the time when he talked about it in the pub in Paris with his pal Chairlhi. Bonnie Prince Charlie was a PR man's dream, all front and no substance, but everybody followed him into this huge pit and we're still climbing out two hundred and fifty years later. I wanted to write about that whole episode but with a bit more realism than you find in many of the folk songs that deal with it. And I discovered that could upset some people. I was playing in Cumbernauld and before the gig somebody sent me a death threat. I didn't realise there were any Jacobites left but there were, and not only in Cumbernauld. I think it was the word 'mincing' that they found offensive. The song isn't meant to be flippant, though, it's about the dangers of where you can end up if you follow a charismatic leader.

J: You'd been doing a lot of reading about Scotland, and not just history.

M: *Gaels Blue* is a very literature-led record. Good books had an effect on me. They made me want to work harder. I would latch on to something in a book, one of the characters maybe, or the way they think, and find I was putting myself in their place, and sometimes a song came from that. It's the experience thing again. One of the books that made a big impression on me was Lewis Grassic Gibbon's *Scots Quair* trilogy, and two songs came out of that, 'Happed in Mist' from *Sunset Song* and 'Monkey Hair' from *Cloud Howe*.

J: Whenever I listen to 'Happed in Mist' it strikes me that it pays the highest kind of tribute that one artist can pay to another. It is completely respectful of the novel but it also raises the tragedy of the events it describes to a new level. In *Sunset Song* there are thirty or forty pages about Ewan Tavendale, Chris Guthrie's husband, enlisting in the army, leaving the land to go off to war, coming home on leave a changed man, being cruel and unloving to Chris, then returning to the Western Front and to his death. Your song captures all that bitterness and sadness in three minutes.

M: I had other tools at my disposal than the ones Lewis Grassic Gibbon had. I made a different thing with them.

J: That's still a lot to cover, from the cutting down of the woods to Chae Strachan coming back from the trenches to tell Chris that Ewan wasn't killed by the enemy but shot for desertion, yet it doesn't seem packed or rushed. I had a careful look at the text of the novel and it's amazing how you reshaped what Gibbon gave you, and how you redeployed some of his words. 'A blink of fine weather' becomes 'a blink of light'. The word 'flowed', which he uses to describe the parks ready for harvest, moves the song from Scotland to Flanders. The title and opening words come from Ewan's reminiscing about the Mearns the night before his execution. Chae in the novel tells Chris, 'Better always to know what truth's in a thing,' but you have Truth and Honour's henchmen arresting Ewan. It's very powerful.

M: It's a powerful part of the novel.

J: The other song, 'Monkey Hair', is written from Chris's perspective. You managed to pull in a thread from *Cloud Howe* about the argument between evolutionists and creationists, but more importantly it refers to Chris's fears about having another child who might be slaughtered in a future war, as Ewan was, and her determination to have a choice about becoming pregnant. And that's the really striking thing about the song, it's expressed from the point of view of a woman.

M: Which is why Arlene Gowans sang it on *Gaels Blue*.

J: You did sing it yourself, though, for example when you were touring with Mr McFall's Chamber in 2010. And also on what would have been your second album, *Dubiety*, which has just been released more than thirty years late.

M: Hmm.

J: What?

M: If I had been asked, I might have had something to say about that.

J: About the album getting released?

M: Even by my standards, that's a long gap between intention and outcome. But 'Monkey Hair', it really needs a woman's voice, that song.

J: Your daughter Alice once asked you, not really expecting you to have an answer, which of your songs you thought was your best, and you said, without hesitation, 'Monkey Hair'.

M: I think it stands up, even after all these years.

J: And now Alice sings it. She's made it her own, in a way.

M: That seems to me like a good outcome.

Notes

1   Interview, 9th February 2017.

(Above) Michael in
contemplative mood and
(following pages) with
Frank McConnell, in character
for *A Wee Home From Home.*

Another Stage

O what remains when our mouths are
  filled with dust?
What lingers on when all has fled
  but bone?
What stays after a long life?
  Something must
More than words cut out of a stone.

'Humphy Kate's Song'

It took Michael a long time to extri-
cate himself from the management and
publishing contracts he had signed with
Bernard Theobald's B.A.T. Music Ltd. In
fact the terms of those arrangements still
tie Michael's songwriting to the company.
A complete list of the songs published by
B.A.T. Music, sent to Michael in February 1987, runs to 127 items. These include
all the tracks on *The Midas Touch*, what
would have been *Dubiety* and *Gaels Blue*,
plus dozens of others – many of them songs
that never appear to have been recorded
except as demos, with tantalising titles
such as 'Mysterious Ways of the Buroo',
'The Things I Do When I'm All Alone',
'Gallons of Coffee' and 'A Straight Man
Yearning for Laughter'. Also on the list are
all the songs Michael wrote for *Stagecoach*
and for his next big venture, the music for
Billy Kay's play, *They Fairly Mak Ye Work*,
which was directed by Alan Lyddiard and
staged by Dundee Rep in 1986.

The play grew out of Billy's programme
on the Dundee jute industry, part of his
Odyssey series for BBC Radio Scotland. As
Billy wrote in the theatre programme notes,

89

> Whilst wishing to be associated with the current renaissance in Scottish art and music, I am actually a recessionist and have only joined to see if that's where the real money is.

the material he gathered was rich beyond all expectation:

> …the unique subculture that emerged from the reversal of the usual social roles between the sexes, with the women working and the men 'bilin the kettle'; the difference in status between spinner and weaver; the inescapable pervasive influence of the staple industry over everyone's life in the city; the political protagonists, Winnie and Neddy – Churchill and Scrymgeour – as different as chalk and cheese; the role of the Prohibition party in a town not famed for its sobriety; the relationship between Scots and Irish; the grinding poverty and the women who resisted it with little more than their concept of their respectability as armour.

Among the many folk Billy Kay interviewed for that programme was an octogenarian former millworker Sarah Craig. Her life became the basis for the play but with many fictional and historical elements woven into a story that ranges in time from 1913 to 1931. All of this provided fertile ground for Michael to arrange new versions of traditional songs (including Mary Brooksbank's 'Jute Mill Song', from which the play's title was taken) and to write new ones. Among the latter were 'Here Come the Weak', a rallying-cry for underdogs everywhere which subsequently appeared on Michael's album *On Stolen Stationery*, and the sublime 'The Lass wi the Flax in her Hair'. In his contribution to the programme notes, Michael reflected on his own family history:

The task of composing music for *They Fairly Mak Ye Work* was made doubly interesting for me given my own family's close involvement with the jute industry. My maternal grandfather James Reilly worked as a batcher in 'Cleggies' Low Mill in Benvie Road and my grandmother Bridget Reilly was a spinner in Grove Mill, Lower Pleasance. Three of their daughters, Mary, Rose and Kathleen, were also jute workers. Mary was a spinner with Thomson Shepherds, Rose worked as a reeler in both Grove and South Mills, and Kathleen was a weaver in Moncurs Calendar Factory in Ure Street, 'Cairdies' and Baltic Works. If it wisnae for the Reillys… My paternal grandfather Nicholas Marra was one of the founders of the Jute and Flax Workers Union.

In that paragraph, Michael summed up why the play touched so many lives throughout Dundee and why consequently it was such a phenomenal success. It broke box office records when it opened in April 1986, and was revived for a second sell-out run in August and September. A perceptive review by David Will in the political magazine *Radical Scotland* commented:

> Marra is almost invariably described as a Dundonian Randy Newman and I can't describe him more effectively. His music for the play is full of biting wit and a range of styles whose eclecticism precisely mirrors that of the interplay between past and present in the play. He opens the play with a stunning

version of Mary Brooksbank's 'Jute Mill Song', in which the traditional and contemporary are fused in a questioning poignancy, which insists that the audience reacts to the song rather than just get swept away by its troubled beauty. [1]

Michael knew that he was involved in something special with *They Fairly Mak Ye Work*, and also that it – and he – belonged to a wider community-based cultural movement happening across Scotland. He couldn't, however, resist adding a note of caution from that special, reductive Dundonian perspective:

> Whilst wishing to be associated with the current renaissance in Scottish art and music, I am actually a recessionist and have only joined to see if that's where the real money is. The music from this play is available on cassette. [2]

*

July of the following year, 1987, saw the realisation of an eighteen-month project involving Dundee Rep, the Dudhope Arts Centre and a range of local groups, arts organisations and individuals across the city of Dundee. Over the course of a weekend, Dundee Community Festival presented what was then, and probably remains, the largest and most ambitious community theatre event ever staged in Scotland. *Witch's Blood*, adapted by John Harvey from the 1946 William Bain novel, told the story of Dundee from the 1660s to the 19th century.

(Above, and facing page)
Michael in the role of a
condemned man in *Witch's
Blood,* the Dundee community
play for which he also wrote
and performed the music.

Michael in rehearsal with
Witch's Blood director
Alan Lyddiard.

Directed by Alan Lyddiard, it had a cast of three hundred, an audience of thousands who were bussed around a number of city locations, and culminated in a finale in Dudhope Park. The music was written and arranged by Michael, and performed by a choir and a 45-strong orchestra, both drawn from across the city. Michael himself put in an impassioned performance as a blind beggar, singing the song 'O Penitence' which would appear on *On Stolen Stationery* in 1991. (So too would 'Here Come the Weak' and 'Humphy Kate's Song', the great thematic anthem which runs through the play, co-written with John Harvey.) Despite atrocious weather conditions on the weekend of 18-19th July the play was a resounding success, and a second version, *Witch's Blood II*, was produced in July 1988.

Michael collaborated with John Harvey on various other projects over the years, creating songs and music alongside John's scripts. They worked together, for example, on Communicado Theatre's 1988 show *Bicycle to the Moon*, and on *Love and Pocket Money* (1990) and *parallel | parallels* (2008), both productions of Frank McConnell's dance company, plan B. And, in 1997, John, Michael and playwright Linda McLean were commissioned by the Benchtours theatre company, each to write, independently of the others, a monologue for a character who has reached a crisis point of some kind. The three characters and their monologues were then brought together in a play called *The Corridor*, which premiered at the Traverse Theatre as part of that year's Edinburgh Festival Fringe, and subsequently toured Scotland and Ireland.

*

It was while working on *They Fairly Mak Ye Work* that Michael first met Frank McConnell. Frank, who was born and brought up in Glasgow, had been a PE teacher, but in the early 1980s was living in Fife where he had retrained as a dancer and choreographer. In the late summer of 1986, when he had not long started working at the newly created Dundee Rep Dance Company, he bumped into Michael outside the theatre: 'He immediately struck me as an unusual man. With little knowledge of who I was, he tried to persuade me to be part of a sketch in which I would play Rab fae Maryhill, pretending to ice-skate to "anything by Black Sabbath". It was a great idea which I believe has never seen the light of day.'[3]

Two days later, with Frank having seen *They Fairly Mak Ye Work*, they met again. 'The moment I heard Michael sing I knew I wanted to work with him.'[4] (Years later, Michael told Frank he would never have got involved with him if he hadn't known he could dance.) Although he knew nothing about the craft of songwriting, Frank recognised the quality of the songs in *They Fairly Mak Ye Work*.

In January 1987 Frank was performing in Dundee Rep Dance Company's production of Neville Campbell's *A Dance for Africa*, for which Michael had composed music 'at the other end of the spectrum – a soundscape of dry desert effects, occasional helicopter noise and so on.'[5] For Frank, this simply reinforced his eagerness to work on a project with Michael as his musical collaborator.

Their first partnership was in *A Wee*

Home From Home, an exploration through dance, dialogue and music of Frank's home city. The show was first performed in 1988, as a Communicado Theatre/Frank McConnell production, and was revived twenty years later, in 2009, by Frank's own company, plan B. A man returns to his childhood tenement home after long absence, and through a mixture of dark humour and nostalgia confronts his memories of education, religion, sectarianism, football, industrial decline, alcohol and other Glasgow truths and clichés. It was one of the projects Michael most enjoyed working on: its quality, he felt, stood the test of time.

Pat Kane sings 'Mother Glasgow' so beautifully, and I'm very grateful to him, but that song confuses me now. The danger's in the tune… It's a bit seductive.

(Facing page, and over)
Michael in *A Wee Home From Home*. As one critic put it, 'he created a dark violence which completely dominated the stage.'

Frank McConnell:

When Michael got into something, he worked like a demon. With the exception of one tune, he wrote all the incidental music plus nine original songs for *A Wee Home From Home* in the space of two and a half weeks, while we were also doing rehearsals. To give you an example of how he worked, the *Daily Record* at this time had a regular feature entitled 'Amazing but True'. We built a series of vignettes into the show under this heading, like the famous story of Charlie Tully scoring a goal against Falkirk from a direct corner kick which was disallowed, and then doing it again from the retake. There had also been an article in the same paper in which a minister made the statement, 'We will not enable our children to make their way to heaven by allowing them to dance.' My mother was from South Uist and Michael had a strong understanding of the Roman Catholic-Presbyterian divide between the southern and northern islands of the Western Isles. I gave him information about my upbringing and about my mother, including that she attended church at Our Lady of Perpetual Succour in Broomhill. Michael managed to distil all this information and more, from different places and contexts, into the lyrics of the song 'Mother Glasgow'. To begin with, Gerry Mulgrew, who was directing the show, couldn't see where it would fit and was going to leave it out. Fortunately that didn't happen. [6]

The song became one of the show's highlights. When Pat Kane saw *A Wee Home From Home* at the Tron Theatre, he sent Michael, by letter, an incisive analysis of the show, and asked him for the tune and lyrics of 'Mother Glasgow'. The song was a huge success for the Kane brothers' band Hue and Cry when they released it on their 1989 *Bitter Suite* album. But Michael was conflicted about the way Pat Kane changed the phrasing and tenor of the song, effectively reinterpreting its deeply critical take on the sectarian divide in Glasgow. In an interview with David Belcher a couple of years later he admitted as much:

> It's become 'I Belong to Mother Glasgow'. It worked on the show and made sense when *A Wee Home From Home* was on the telly near Christmas. On the telly you had violent images of Orange bands, a wine bottle smashing on a fence, the Union Jack in the colours of the Irish tricolour. Pat Kane sings it so beautifully, and I'm very grateful to him, but that song confuses me now. The danger's in the tune...It's a bit seductive. [7]

He elaborated on this theme elsewhere: 'It is not a song that says "I love Glasgow, it's a nice place". It's a complaint, it's a song about the wonderful gift of communication that Glaswegians have that's been twisted and I still hear educated people coming away with this bigotry that you just don't get in our part of the country, but I hear it often in Glasgow. It makes you feel ill. And "Mother Glasgow" is about that, the waste of great communication.' [8]

A Wee Home From Home made a big impression on both of Michael and Peggy's children. For Alice, its songs remain firm favourites among all her father's work. She first saw it when she was about nine, then again when it was revived, and loved that so much was packed into it despite the simplicity of the set and the fact that it was just Michael and Frank on stage throughout. The show had a similar lasting effect on Alice's brother Matthew:

> I'd have been seven when I first saw the theatre production of *A Wee Home From Home* in 1988. The age of reason, Michael called it, and I still have the birthday card he made marking it as such. I was old enough to take on board some of the themes in the show, but only came to understand others when I was older. Musically, however, the songs got hold of me immediately. I'm often struck by the rolling opening piano chords of 'Dear Green Place' upon driving into Glasgow from the north-east, and catching glimpses of the cranes, wharves and slipways referenced in the song. Possibly even more definitive of the production than the better-known 'Mother Glasgow', the melancholy mood is reprised at the show's conclusion, after all the violence has passed. A dark undercurrent runs through songs like 'Hielan Umbrella', and even the seemingly sweeter moments such as the title song and the aforementioned 'Mother Glasgow'. There is humour also: 'You'll Never Take Me To The Top Of The Hour Alive' satirises local radio, while

the breathless Andy Stewart medley is absurdly sinister. The show's climax arrives with the haunting 'Tango De Glasgow', in which the minor key verses and euphoric chorus give way to guttural howl, a nightmarish echo of John Lennon's dream sequence in 'A Day In The Life'.

Maybe the music resonates that little bit more because the songs have never seen a physical release, and were very seldom performed in a solo setting. The whole programme seems to occupy its own place, stylistically, in Michael's catalogue, and in time. The musicality present may show Michael at, or nearing, his creative peak, and I'd hope that these songs find a way to remain in people's consciousness, as they have in mine.

A Wee Home From Home – 'the best show I was ever in', he said later – gave Michael an opportunity to work on his stage presence as much as on his acting skills. A review of the show's 2009 revival noted, 'There are few words outside the songs… but what words there are Marra, in particular, delivers with a deadpan timing that skewers any suggestion of nostalgia or sentimentality.'[9] Another critic later observed that he 'uncloaked the menace', but not through the music: 'By standing still and doing, apparently, nothing he created a dark violence which completely dominated the stage. Few actors have that gift.'[10]

The show also enabled him to indulge in one of his favourite pastimes, 'creative' writing. Here is his biography from the 1989 programme:

Michael Marra was born in Hyndland St, Partick on February 14th 1949. Educated at St Peter's Primary and St Aloysius he was then transferred to Skye High in Portree where both his parents taught Norwegian. A keen sportsman he entertained hopes of playing for Glasgow Celtic until forced out of the game by a serious head injury which almost rendered him deaf. Turning to music instead he took up the saxophone and worked happily until he suffered a serious mouth injury while playing both Rock and Roll in the Maxwellton Bar, Paisley. Having decided that there might be good money in contemporary dance he formed the Red Shoes Ballet Co. and danced cheerfully until forced offstage by a serious leg injury. Frank McConnell, an old school chum, stepped in and very kindly gave him a job on this tour for which he had to learn to play the piano. Michael's hobbies include pretending to be drunk and abseiling – though never at the same time.

A Wee Home From Home was the first of many collaborations between Michael and Frank. In 1989, Frank moved on from Dundee Rep and set up his own company. Integral to plan B, as he named it, was a creative philosophy that appealed to Michael's desire to push beyond boundaries. Frank:

The company is called plan B because it always resists relying on a formula. Each project would start with something original and try to break new ground, for example with cross-discipline collaboration, which was far less common in the 1980s than it is now. Michael was very open to this kind of experimental process, and he showed amazing generosity as a creative collaborator. I know he was quoted as saying that he needed total control of his work, but that didn't fit with my experience of working with him. He never brought to a project the kind of egotism that meant that he would have to see his own contribution highly visible in the end product. [11]

*

Michael's work ethic was always impressive, and even when he put himself under immense pressure by taking on too much he made a point of delivering the best that he could. In 1987, the same year he worked on *Witch's Blood*, he was asked to write words and music for a show celebrating the centenary of the acquisition of burgh status by Tayport, on the south side of the river opposite Dundee. He struggled to find enough material but still managed to turn out ten or twelve songs. Frank McConnell remembers the event with mixed feelings:

> The final song had lines about seeing the stars through a telescope set up by the University of St Andrews in Tayport, which went
>
> And so, goodbye, farewell, adieu
> This ferry port cries out to you
> A message on the River Tay
> From Tayport to the Milky Way

The song had a beautiful tune. Michael would sometimes wait weeks or even months for the right word or phrase, but in this case the lyrics really didn't do justice to the tune. I remember in rehearsal the cast singing such nonsense with such pride. I glanced over at Michael and his gaze went straight to the keyboards in that devilish way he had. [12]

Frank can recall only two occasions when he and Michael fell out, and on neither of them was the falling-out very serious. The first time was when an opportunity arose for Frank, working with the Kingussie-based traditional dance company Dannsa, to perform for the guests invited to Prince Charles's garden party at Holyrood Palace in Edinburgh. Frank, as he puts it himself, 'in my poverty and lack of wisdom thought I could make a lot of money from these bastards'. Michael found out, and made it clear, though without personal malice, that the republican in him was not amused.

The second occasion was when Frank and Michael were touring the Highlands and Islands, and Frank had forgotten to collect tickets for a very early morning ferry, which meant that they had to queue for an hour or so at 5.45am. Michael did not let this go for the rest of that day's journey, but later wrote a letter of apology, explaining that in similar circumstances Peggy would have ended his bad behaviour by simply and firmly saying, 'Michael, be quiet.'

Frank learned two important lessons from Michael. The first was that 'my job as an artist was to observe'. The second was more direct: ' "Frank – get on wi yer work," by which he meant stop doing the admin and fundraising and be creative.' [13] This was a lesson that Michael learned himself. When, over the years, he was commissioned by Dundee Rep, plan B, Communicado, Wildcat and other companies it meant that those administrative and budgetary concerns were not primarily his to worry about – unlike when he was trying to make records. His working relationship with Dundee Rep was especially productive, and led to notable successes such as *The Mill Lavvies* and *If the Moon Can Be Believed*. The sheer volume of songs and music he wrote in collaboration with many different partners is quite staggering. A list of theatre productions for which he wrote songs and music, appears at the end of this book: it is almost certainly incomplete.

In 2007, Perth Theatre staged *The Demon Barber*, a play written, designed and directed by Graham McLaren. McLaren asked Michael to compose the music. There was a nice symmetry to this engagement, given that old school playground conversation in which Stephen Sondheim's name had come up, and the fact that Sondheim wrote his own music and lyrics for *Sweeney Todd* back in 1979. The set represented a teetering three-storey building in Georgian London – from pie-shop at street-level through a gorily red-painted barber shop on the first floor to the attic. Into this top section was squeezed a three-piece band: Michael on piano, John Sampson on trumpet and Bill Murdoch on accordion, all in white face paint and bowler hats. As one reviewer put it, 'the gravel-voiced singer

finds himself somewhere between Kurt Weill and Tom Waits, his score capturing the raw danger of a lawless London.' [14]

'The theatre is very good for songwriters,' Michael once said, 'because if you're writing for the theatre they usually want the song by Friday. Left to my own devices, I would probably take months to write a song, but if someone is telling you, with a raised eyebrow, that they want it by Friday, you'll get it done, and it will probably be the same song.' [15] But precisely because of its tight timescales and other people's dependency on his turning in finished work on schedule, theatre could also be stressful and exhausting. In an interview in 2008, Michael admitted that he 'didn't do theatre for a long while because I was doing so much I made myself sick of it. I eventually realised I was doing it for the pay cheque rather than enjoyment, so I started choosing what I did very carefully.' [16]

Notes

1   *Radical Scotland* 22 (Aug/Sep 1986).

2   Programme notes, *They Fairly Mak Ye Work.*

3   'An Unusual Man', in *Resolis Remembers Michael Marra* (Resolis Community Arts pamphlet, 2014).

4   Interview with Frank McConnell, 11th January 2017.

5   Ibid.

6   Ibid.

7   *Glasgow Herald*, 12th February 1991.

8   *The Michael Marra Family Album*, BBC Radio Scotland, 1st January 2013.

9   Robert Dawson Scott, *The Times*, 19th November 2009.

10   Jennie Macfie (STV, 29th January 2013), review of *All Will Be Well* tribute concert at Celtic Connections.

11   Interview with Frank McConnell, 11th January 2017.

12   Ibid.

13   Ibid.

14   Mark Fisher, *The Guardian*, 12th November 2007.

15   *The Michael Marra Family Album*, BBC Radio Scotland, 1st January 2013.

16   *The Courier & Advertiser*, 11th October 2008.

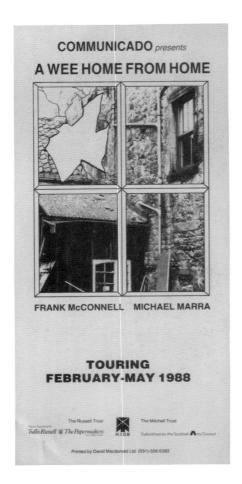

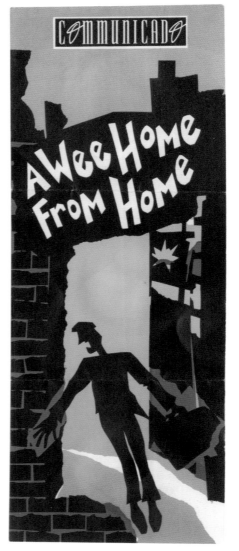

Promotional material for the
original and revived productions
of *A Wee Home From Home*.

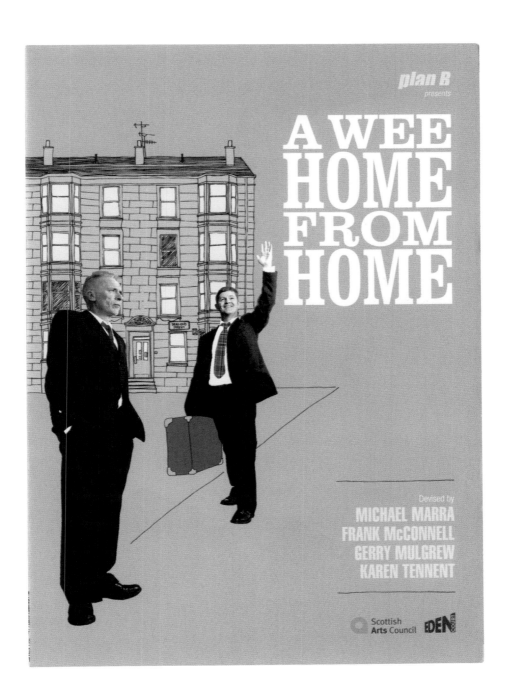

Kitchen conversation

No.4

James: It's no great secret that you used to get very wound-up before a gig, but then you would walk on and do it, apparently completely at ease. You gave a bit of advice to Craig Coulthard about that. He'd sent you a copy of his first CD and said he was going to be doing some gigs. You sent him a letter in which you wrote, 'Breathe deeply for a while before you go on and feel confident about your material, you are entitled to do that because your stuff is good. Leave your real self in the dressing-room and enjoy the gig. I am assuming of course that since you are a songwriter you are therefore neurotic like myself.' Is that how you prepared for a gig?

Michael: Performance is an act. You're like an actor, and that's what an actor has to do: become someone else. I admired anyone who could do that, but it wasn't a straightforward process for me. On days when I had a gig this whole neurotic process would begin at eight in the morning and go right through until long after the gig was over. It was to do with shyness, but also it was about wanting to perform well for the people who'd paid to hear you. You're on a tightrope all the time you're out there in front of them. So it can't be this neurotic person doing that – that wouldn't be fair on anyone involved. You have to *be* the tightrope walker.

J: That's quite a drastic way of dealing with – what would you call it? – stage fright?

M: It was stage fright to the power of ten. I really did find it terrifying. I always thought that sooner or later I would blow it, and then I'd never be able to go on stage again. And it didn't have anything to do with the size of the venue or the number of people. I did a gig in Shotts once. I've been to more enchanting places and there were only seven people in the audience but I didn't know that until after the show. The quality of your performance is not determined by the number of people who've paid to hear you. It shouldn't make any difference and in fact I think I performed well that night.

J: You often opened with 'Mac Rebennack's Visit to Blairgowrie'. Was that a kind of therapeutic way in?

M: The piano's working, my fingers are moving, the voice is okay – we might just get away with this. It was reassuring, yes.

J: You must have done thousands of gigs. Did it not get easier?

M: Never. In fact it got worse. To the extent that we had to develop a system so I didn't know I had a gig until a couple of days beforehand – just long enough to prepare but not long enough to get too sick about it. Peg kept the diary. She wouldn't let me in on the secret until forty-eight hours before I was due to play.

J: I remember one time Iain Anderson was interviewing you on Radio Scotland and he said something like, 'And you're playing Aberdeen next week', and I could hear the slight panic in your reply because you didn't know about that.

M: It happened quite a lot. People would say, 'I'll see you on Thursday, we're coming to your gig,' and it was news to me that I had one. I told my family and friends, 'Don't say that, Peg will keep me right.'

J: One time I came to see you at the Sage in Gateshead playing with Mr McFall's Chamber, and an hour before it started you were trying to eat a sandwich, or trying to keep it down, and I said hello but you kind of waved me away, and I backed off. I'd been warned. Andrew Mitchell told me when you were on the *Houseroom* tour with The Hazey Janes that he decided to take your mind off things by discussing your collection of short stories, *Karma Mechanics*, which he'd just been reading. Big mistake. You growled at him. I think maybe you gnashed your teeth a bit too.

M: It wasn't personal.

J: He realised that afterwards. He also realised that your own children were leaving you alone. In fact Alice told me a story about when The Hazey Janes were backing you at a Christmas show at Fat Sam's in Dundee, and you had to go on first to do a solo set before they joined you. She said it was quite a long way from the dressing-room, so she walked you down, and all the way you were going through this whole I'm-going-to-throw-up routine, but she got you down the stair and said, 'Have a good one,' and then went back up and stopped and stood and watched you. You didn't know she was watching and there you were, standing and pacing, pacing and standing at the stage entrance, you had your head in your hands and then all of a sudden you took a deep breath, turned around, and in one second changed into this completely different person, apparently the most relaxed man in the world walking onstage.

M: I'm sorry she had to witness that.

J: She'd seen it before, but never when you were alone, when you thought no one could see.

M: All that fear, when I stepped out on stage, it became something else. It was like entering a heightened state of being. The time went very fast but it felt good. I was in familiar territory.

J: When you watched other people performing, did you think that was how it was for them?

M: I would be right with them, willing them to do well, but often I stayed away. I didn't want to transmit the fear I felt for them.

J: Your brother Nicky says he was once on the Dundee team in a Scots language radio quiz, it was the final and it was being broadcast from Stirling and you and Peggy were in the audience. He said your face was tortured all the way through because you didn't want anything to go wrong for him. He reckoned he was far more relaxed about it than you were.

M: He probably was. For some people – and I don't mean Nicky when I say this

– being on stage is the safest place to be. It's when they come down that the trouble starts. Whereas I always felt if I could stay in my room writing all the time, I'd be fine. I could get lost in there and it didn't bother me.

J: Incidentally, speaking of writing, what do you think about Bob Dylan getting the Nobel Prize for Literature?

M: They're not really my thing, prize-givings.

J: Or Bob Dylan's, apparently. He didn't go to the ceremony in Stockholm. Some people thought that was disrespectful.

M: Then they don't know much about him.

J: Patti Smith was there. She sang 'A Hard Rain' as a tribute to him, accompanied by a full orchestra. She got stuck on one of the lines, had to stop and apologise and start that verse again.

M: That's my worst nightmare.

J: She was very gracious about it. She said it was because she was so nervous. The audience were gracious too. They applauded her graciousness. Later she wrote about it. She said she hadn't forgotten the words, it was the enormity of the occasion, she just couldn't draw them out.

M: She's a bra' lass. She and I played at the Burns an' A' That Festival at Culzean Castle in 2003. That was one of the great pleasures of my life. There was an orchestra on that occasion too. We were both a little on edge but when it came to performing 'Sweet Afton' together, that was a beautiful thing.

J: She said something once in an interview with *Rolling Stone*: 'In art and dream, may you proceed with abandon. In life, may you proceed with balance and stealth.'

M: Aye, that pretty much sums it up. I like the positive meaning she gives to 'stealth'. And to 'abandon'.

J: Just to go back to Dylan for a minute, you said on many occasions that he made a big impact on you, the way he sang, what he wrote songs about, how nothing seemed to be off-limits to him. Did you ever see him perform live?

M: No, I never did. Matthew got tickets for us to see him in Aberdeen but in the end I decided not to go. Sometimes it's better to keep some distance between yourself and those you admire the most. You might be disappointed if you get too close.

Songwriter

the starry nights that never end
the kiss that sparks the rage against
  the light
let there be no doubt that
true love is something no one ever,
should ever be without

'True Love (Something No One Should
Ever Be Without)'

A cassette tape of the music from *They Fairly Mak Ye Work*, recorded at Inner City Sound Studios, was released on Michael's own label, Mink Records, in 1986. There would be a five-year gap between this and his next album, *On Stolen Stationery*, which came out in 1991 on the Eclectic label, with Michael's portrait of Clayton Moore (the actor who played the Lone Ranger) as Richard III gracing the cover.

The opening track of *On Stolen Stationery* is an instrumental tribute to his mother, Margaret Reilly. Three of the songs were originally written for *They Fairly Mak Ye Work*. 'Niel Gow's Apprentice' was written for Dougie MacLean: 'We were in a group together when we were boys and it was called Hen's Teeth,' Michael said, introducing the song years later. 'When the group split up Dougie travelled all round the world. I spent most of my time in one room.'

'The Bawbee Birlin' was co-written and sung with Rod Paterson. Rod's explanation of its origins goes as follows:

Methil
Bob Dylan
U.S. Grant
Africa
Seedlies
Reynard
Angela Gunn
Chairlhi
Pins
Niel Gow's Apprentice

Dr. John
For To Be Or No To Be
Frida
Francis
All Will Be Well
Macushla
Englishman
Scribbled
Green Grow
Baps and off

To ALLAN with THANKS Michael Marra

Set list, with sketch and
dedication added, for Michael's
gig at the Edinburgh Folk Club,
11th July 2001. The dedication
was to Allan McMillan, the
Club's photographer.

One night I told Michael how some years earlier I had woken one morning with a new song fully formed in my head (a verse and chorus to the tune of Niel Gow's 'Farewell to Whisky'), and that I'd been trying ever since to finish it by sleeping a lot. He was horrified. The idea of not finishing a song was his worst nightmare. Next morning I found, scribbled in a dog-eared note-book, the second and third verses of 'The Bawbee Birlin'. Not so much a collaboration as a bale-out. [1]

There is praise of Queen's Park F.C. for developing some of the basic techniques of modern football in 'The Wise Old Men of Mount Florida':

The wise old men of Mount Florida knew
If the game was to flourish some changes were due.
When the science of football emerged from the dark
It was due in the main to the men of Queen's Park.
Crossbars and corners,
Free kicks and throw-ins –
The scientific game.

The football-as-life theme is enlarged upon in one of Michael's best-loved songs, 'Hamish', which had been recorded by Leo Sayer back in 1983, after the two men met in London and Michael sang it to him. Let Michael explain the origins of this one himself:

A great footballer called Ralph Milne, who played for Dundee United for over a decade, asked me to write something to celebrate the testimonial year [1983] of his team-mate, the great United goalkeeper and entertainer Hamish MacAlpine. I admired Hamish although I was a Dundee supporter but we are not Glaswegian about these things, and then one night I attended a match at Tannadice Park, which is where Dundee United play. The newsreader Peter Sissons pronounces it 'Tanna-dee-chy', isn't that cool? Anyway, Dundee United were playing against F.C. Monaco, and present among us, the people of Dundee, in the grand-stand, was the wonderful Hollywood star Grace Kelly. She was there with her man, I can never remember his name. Anyway, she was wearing a white turban – which is unusual in Dundee – but unfortunately she was sitting behind an advertising hoard-ing which proclaimed 'TAYLOR BROTHERS COAL'. It was what we cry incongruous. I had no camera so I went home and made this song. It's called either 'Hamish' or 'Grace Kelly's Visit to Tanna-dee-chy'.

Then there is 'Under the Ullapool Moon', written to mark the Wester Ross town's bicentenary in 1988. Michael had had a gig at the Ceilidh Place, Ullapool and afterwards, sitting in the bar with the bicentenary events co-ordinator Joan Michael, he asked if he could write a song for the occasion. A few months later he sent Joan a cassette on which was a recording of him performing the song somewhere in Central Scotland. It's a downbeat song about a woman who escapes an abusive relationship in Cumbernauld and finds something more hopeful in Ullapool. Joan Michael was delighted with it. It was never an 'official' song but he did finally sing it in Ullapool, years later, probably, Joan thinks, when he and Liz Lochhead were touring their show *In Flagrant Delicht*.

'Rats' is an unsettlingly atmospheric celebration of the dubious qualities of those 'seeknin, lowpin, skulkin, greasy, maggot-vomitin, hough-spewin, mingin, bastartin' rodents. Michael's growling voice-under is perfect for expressing the revulsion in the words.

'Like Another Rolling Stone' is one of Michael's truly great songs, a beautifully understated encouragement to face difficult times, pick up the pieces and keep going:

> Don't let your sail blow over,
> Don't let your ship go down,
> Batten down the four-leaf clover
> And tell yourself you're glory-bound.
> …
> Don't let your heart get weary
> Don't let your lip go down
> Pander to the bright and cheery
> And make the optimistic sound…

'Make the optimistic sound'[2] is a good piece of advice in almost any circumstances. The song never gives up on hope, even in the lines leading up to the final chorus: 'And when you feel the best bit's over / Remember how you come into town'. Those lines might feel valedictory, but the chorus says otherwise. It's a simultaneous celebration of independence and mutual support – the list of things you might or might not be without is itself both liberating and reassuring:

> Not a comb nor a hammer
> Nor a feather nor a flight
> Not a hoe nor a spanner
> Nor a fiddle nor a fife
> Nor a hand on your shoulder
> In a bitter and a biting cold
> You could be out on the street and on
> your own
> Just like another rolling stone

'Like Another Rolling Stone' connects, in its quiet wisdom, with another masterpiece from *On Stolen Stationery*, 'Hermless'. Again, in concert Michael explained it better than anybody else can:

> This song was my suggestion for the national anthem of Scotland, and it's one of my songs, and that would appear to be a very impertinent thing to do, especially in Dundee as, you know, we take a pride in our modesty. But, I must stress, at the time there were only two suggestions, and I didn't like either of them really. Both of them were kind of military, or based on hatred of our neighbours, and I find that unacceptable, although we're not alone in that, because I did a study of national anthemry the world over, and we are not alone, you know generally they are pretty duff. I think the South African one is beautiful, it's celebratory and it's up and you can tell it's full

of love, so I like that one. The Dutch one has a great tune. But apart from that they're all pretty dodgy, I think. They're either based on extravagant claims about themselves, or just plain simple hatred of their neighbours. In fact if you ever get a chance to read the Algerian national anthem, have a drink before you do. Anyway, this one is very simple. The chorus goes 'Hermless, hermless, there's never nae bather fae me. I ging to the lehbry, I tak oot a book, and then I go hame for ma tea.' Okay? Take great care over the word 'lehbry', it has a Latin root but it is definitely Dundee, that one.

Anyone who could propose, for a national anthem, a song containing such utterly unthreatening words as

Wi ma hand on ma hert and ma hert
  in ma mooth
Wi erms that could reach ower the sea
Ma feet micht be big but the insects
  are safe
They'll never get stood on by me

had to have his tongue in his cheek as well as his hert in his mooth. One verse contains the lines

There's Tam wi his pigeons and Wull
  wi his mice
And Robert Maclennan and me

which is a beautiful honouring of three quiet men that most folk would barely notice. Sheena Wellington recalls Michael telling her, around the time he wrote 'Hermless', that 'Robert Maclennan' was a reference to the then interim leader of the newly formed Social and Liberal Democrats (a merger of the Social Democratic Party and the Liberals), who 'rose without trace and then disappeared'. Actually, he now sits in the House of Lords as Baron Maclennan of Rogart, but who would know?[3]

One of Michael's younger fans, performer and songwriter James Kirkpatrick, considers it a great song because it 'turns a word that could be construed as derogatory – "Och, him, he's hermless" – into a positive attribute: this is someone who is incapable of doing you harm. I like that optimism mixed in with averageness. And I love the idea of a whole country full of people who will do no harm.'[4]

The strange thing is, when you hear 'Hermless' being belted out by hundreds of voices together, it is not just a wonderfully uplifting affirmation of non-violence, it is incredibly *powerful*, like all the best peace songs. Which, no doubt, was exactly what Michael intended.[5]

*

In 1992 Eclectic re-released *Gaels Blue* on CD and cassette. Meanwhile Michael was busy working on the songs that would form the next album, *Candy Philosophy* (released in July, 1993). But nothing happens in isolation and during this period the Marras were having to cope with illness and bereavement. Back in 1974 Michael's father Edward had had a lung removed after being diagnosed with cancer. He lived for another thirteen years and, according to Nicky, was a changed man, more outgoing, fun-loving and sociable than he had ever been. He died on 23rd October 1987. Six months later, Michael's eldest brother Eddie was told he had liver cancer, and despite his youth and new drug treatments he died on 19th September 1990, aged only forty-two. The two and a half years between his diagnosis and his death were harrowing for the entire family, and had a profound impact on Michael.

SONGS FROM EUROPE [6]

My brother Eddie was an artist, three years older than me. I remember the last time I saw him, when my mother and me went to the rest room. We'd put one red sock and one green sock on him, because he was like that when he was alive. He'd go out in different coloured shoes.

When we got outside the rain came down like you'd never seen it – rain that wasn't taking time to fall. I remember running towards the car and I burst out laughing. That's terrible, I know, but it just seemed like it was the end.

The period before that, for about five years, was almost non-stop grief for our family. My father died just before Eddie's illness began. Everything had been so intense, it was like all your emotional reactions were multiplied. When Eddie actually died there was an element of relief. Except for the fact my mother's house was where you went back to after the funeral. It didnae look like it would get over that.

After the funeral we needed a break from one another, the chance to grieve in different ways. Eddie was the eldest, then Mary, Nicholas, me and Christopher. We were always close. Our family grew up in Lochee in Dundee, which is kind of an Irish community with lots of Poles, Italians and the occasional Scot. Marra means sailor. We were supposed to have come off the Spanish Armada to the coast of Ireland.

Eddie was a beautiful draughtsman. He was always drawing as a child. Drawing is a good thing, it calms you down. Back then I never did it because his work was so good. It's the same with guitar-playing with me. Christopher is so talented you withdraw a bit – or keep it close to your chest.

Eddie also played the piano and understood the theory of music. For me it was one note at a time, I was too slow. When I was a boy he taught me how to play 'Go Now' by the Moody Blues. He taught me how to play it in E Flat. That key has been home for me ever since.

I suppose he was quite shy in some ways but he had loads of pals at school. He suffered badly from asthma, but he always did football, always everything everybody else could do. It just seemed ten times harder for him.

After I turned eighteen we'd go out to the pub together or the match. He was at art school. I was a labourer in a Dundee boatbuilders. The company went down and we occupied the place. I always remember one of the guys painting a beautiful sign on the bow of the last boat saying 'The Doomed'. It was originally called *The Bountiful*.

We found people to take the yard over and it became Kestrel Marine. But I left around 1972 to begin my life as a professional musician. Eddie went to Florence on a scholarship. Later he came back to teach in Fife. I was in London for a short time, then I came home as well.

Eddie played in a Dundee band called Saint Andrew and the Woollen Mill throughout the 1980s. He took a close interest in my work – to the extent of telling me how terrible it was when he didn't like something. 'That's really, really poor,' he'd say.

I think he liked *Candy Philosophy*, which we were working on when he died. It's a cheerful album. He liked the track called 'True Love'. But when his death came, work on the record kind of fell apart.

You're pushed for time after a death like that. You know what you want to achieve but suddenly it's later than you think. I used to waste time moaning and complaining about things that hadn't even happened. I'd put a lot of energy into worrying about getting hit with a debt I'd forgotten about.

But when the funeral was over, I had this big surge of energy, most of which was to do with songwriting. I also decided to spend all my time writing love songs. Only love songs. My initial reaction after the funeral was hate. But Eddie spoke a lot before he died about the importance of mercy and forgiveness. So then I decided

that's it, love songs.

They can take very different forms as you know, a certain amount could be what people would call political songs, but it amounts to the same thing.

I wrote numbers called 'Knee Deep in Daisies' and 'This Wonderful World'. I even did one about someone bullying people in the playground. In the end, originally, he got a hiding. Then I thought, 'Naw, you cannae finish it like that, he'll have to go to counselling.' So I made him go to counselling at the end of the number. He becomes a much better person. Three years ago he would have been bombed out!

I can't remember all the songs. Some demo tapes were later burned in a fire which broke out in digs where I was staying in Carlisle.

This desire not to waste time also made me do something I've never done before. I have never, ever asked for a gig. It seems less than modest. But just after the funeral I got a call from Ricky Ross asking if I would do some dates with Deacon Blue.

The offer was just to play in Britain. He mentioned that they were going to Europe first but had no plans to take anybody with them. I thought: 'I want to play Paris, I really do…'

How would I get the chance? No one from Paris was ever likely to ask me. Anyway, Ricky being a nice guy, I thought: 'Well, maybe he doesn't *know* that I don't ask for a gig…'

So I said: 'Let me do the European tour with you… I'll be as unobtrusive as possible. I won't cost you anything. I'll go to the bakers at the end of the day and get all the cheap rolls like they do in Amsterdam…' Ricky bent over backwards to make it happen.

I walked straight into a song in Holland at the very start of the tour. There was a young girl following Deacon Blue. She'd been to every gig, every single gig. The guys introduced her and I was just horrified. I took it like a parent. She kept referring to the fact that she expected people to think she was, you know, mental. That made it worse for me.

I never see anybody in the audience, but thereafter I saw her at every gig. The song is called 'The One and Only Anne Marie'. It's awful melancholy, but it's a good song.

The way the tour went it seemed the songs came one after another. It seemed the place was littered with songs. For twenty years I've written in a room with a bit of paper, the piano and that's it. But I wrote two songs in one night in Paris as well as playing.

After Paris I came to Scotland and did a gig at the Tron. Then I flew back to catch a train to Milan. That's when I met Martina Navratilova in the street outside the station – it seemed like all these experiences were for my benefit. All these songs.

I met a woman from Czechoslovakia. When they took the Wall down she'd driven to Vienna just to prove she could do it. She was a doctor and was disgusted by her colleagues, who'd shot the craw to the West and hadnae

come back. So I did a song called 'Moravian Girls'. Again it's lasted the pace.

I write a lot, there's usually a lot of dross. But every single one of these was right.

At the same time there was definitely something wrong. I was getting the gigs done, but was becoming ill as I went. I didn't want to eat. I couldn't sleep. I just wanted to work all the time. Every song was carrying into the next part. I was finishing things as I was moving…

We ended up in the Alps for a few days off. I was in quite a bad way… So I sat and wrote a really, really nasty letter to this person who is a representative of the music business. It was a complete tirade, I was blaming every single music business executive for the negative side of music over the years of my life.

The business can be very frustrating. Certain songs, I want to finish them, record them and put them out. These songs I was writing in Europe are for the next album, after *Candy Philosophy*. Everything's held up… Normally it's held up by the music business. I wish it could be like a newspaper when you can have it on the streets the next day. That's one of my complaints about the business.

Also, when I was in London years ago, the music publishing company was only interested in a little tiny part of what I did. They wanted me to go over and over that part. When I didn't do that, they abandoned me. But I kept giving them my good stuff because in the contract it said you must submit your best endeavours. It was almost a sense of honour. But I ended up losing the rights to all these songs.

Anyway, this person I wrote the letter to got all this stuff in the ear. I was getting a bit unbalanced. Here I was in these mountains. I should have been completely exhilarated. But it was terrible.

We got to Germany and the fascists were marching in the streets. They burned down a hostel while we were in Bonn. I wrote a song called 'Lieblings in the Absence of Love'.

That would then have been exactly a year since Eddie's death. I then wrote a song directly for him called 'Dear Hank Williams'. I didnae want to stop. It should have been a sensible time to say: 'Let's leave it at that.' But I knew I was working well. You might get a wee while when nothing works at all, so I thought: 'No, I'll carry on.'

We toured Britain and there was a huge explosion across the road from where we stayed in Belfast. Then, on Christmas Eve, Lorraine McIntosh, the singer in Deacon Blue who is also married to Ricky Ross, told me she was pregnant. I just thought about this baby, you know, moving through Germany, where there was riots and burning, and then going to Belfast through the bombing. I came home and on Christmas Day I wrote the song 'Pax Vobiscum'.

I made a quick demo of it. That's how understanding my family are. On Christmas Day it was: 'God bless the absentee.'

At that point I decided to relax. This baby song just made a correct point. It was like a full stop on the thing.

But the illness caught up with me after Christmas. I went to work in Uist, teaching young people to write songs in Gaelic. I was driving along the road with Calum, the son of the woman who was looking after me. He saved the day and ran to a cottage to get help. I remember very little. Only waking up and seeing all these nuns. It was an ulcer. The priest brought me a bowl of carrageen, which is a local white jelly made from seaweed. It's full of iodine. When the Indian doctor came to see me, he said: 'Aye, keep giving him the carrageen.'

I can't afford to get ill again. But I'm still obsessive about working. We went back to *Candy Philosophy* and finished it quickly. I wanted to get on and form a group to learn all these songs from Europe. There was no time to waste.

*

If *Candy Philosophy* is, as Michael said, a cheerful album, it is knowingly so. The cover photograph by Calum Colvin is bursting with colour, a collage of bright toys, sweeties, dolls, bits of jigsaw puzzle and cocktail umbrellas, with Michael, welcoming arms outstretched, in showman's bow-tie and shiny blue jacket against a backdrop of beach holiday snaps. Michael's musical contributions are credited to Colm Calvin, Chick Singer, Fabio Lino and a host of other invented names, but his alter egos are easily outnumbered by the other musicians and singers involved. The production and arrangements are rich and multi-layered, the outcome of fruitful collaboration with, especially, Allan McGlone and Chris Marra.

The crowing of a cockerel heralds the first track, 'The Land of Golden Slippers', which is an upbeat mix of metaphors, Biblical allusions and the promise of 'a daytrip to Skye'. The mood of irreverence and sheer fun spills over into other songs, such as Michael's homage, in French, to 'le vieux loup du rock' Johnny Hallyday: 'Salut! Johnny Hallyday, je vous salue'. 'True Love', 'Painters Painting Paint' ('I know what I like and I like emulsion / high rollers made from Vikings' beards') and 'King Kong's Visit to Glasgow' are in similar vein, but it is not all unalloyed happiness. 'Don't Look at Me' takes a hard look at male irresponsibility, while 'The Violin Lesson' exposes Michael's deep-seated worry about the tendency of formal training to flatten the innocent joy of childhood:

> the boundless dwells in every soul
>   and very few awake
> the old professors sentence us all
> to carry on this grave mistake

'To Beat the Drum' was written for the workers at the Timex factory in Dundee, who were embroiled in a bitter dispute which ended with the factory's closure in August 1993. 'The Guernsey Kitchen Porter' is about the exploitation of low-waged employees in the hospitality industry. Written as part of the soundtrack of a BBC television series, *Hard Cash*, it had first appeared in 1990 on a tie-in compilation record put together by Richard Thompson. 'Australia Instead of the Stars' is a bittersweet song in praise of Sandy Kidd, whose scientific genius was so poorly valued in Scotland that he took it to Australia. [7]

The final two tracks, 'O Fellow Man' and 'This Evergreen Bough', seem to complement each other but also to tug in different directions: in the first, the aspiration to human fellowship is undercut by greed and selfishness; in the second, which takes the Irish love-song 'Macushla' for its cue, a sentimental hope of heavenly love and peace is restrained by living reality. [8] And yet both songs have an optimistic edge to them. It is as if Michael sees the possibility of success even in failure:

> we all sometimes
> lose control of the ball sometimes
> unless we pass it on to our Fellow man

Here, once again, Michael is using football as an analogy for life. Or he proposes the coming of light even as he fills in the darkness round about:

> oh lay me down to dream tonight
> that all will be mended soon
> and all will be right
> if you're smiling now
> in the arms of this evergreen bough

As ever, Michael doesn't give you the world straight and he doesn't give you songs without making you think about why he has given them to you.

*

In the summer of 1996 a live album, recorded at the Tron Theatre in Glasgow for Radio Clyde, was released on Eclectic. *Pax Vobiscum* featured five of the songs written when Michael was touring Europe with Deacon Blue, four from *Candy Philosophy* and one from *On Stolen Stationery*. There were other songs too. Michael wrote 'Julius' as a tribute to Dougie Martin, lead singer in the Dundee band The Poor Souls in the 1960s. 'Dougie had a sheepdog called Julius who never got to go to any of his gigs,' he explained. 'Margaret Reilly of Cado Belle had a dog called Paddy who sat at the mic stand at every show. So this is Dougie seen through the eyes of his own dog, Julius.'

'Chain Up the Swings' is a searing critique of Christianity as practised in parts of the Western Isles:

> Six days I will be sober
> On the seventh I'll take a drink
> I'll sit by the window with a tin of beer
> And watch them chain up the swings
> I will think about the power of love
> A most agreeable groove
> And wonder what on earth they're
>   thinking of
> Who only disapprove

This song grew out of his time teaching young songwriters in South Uist. The strict adherence of the Presbyterian majority in the Western Isles to Sabbatarianism was what led to the playground facilities being chained up on Sundays. In Roman Catholic South Uist, Michael noticed that none of the boys playing football wanted to wear anything other than the green and white hoops of a Glasgow Celtic top. He came up with a fantasy solution to this problem, which was that in order to distinguish between the players of opposing teams, special Fair Isle-patterned balaclavas were knitted by mothers, grannies and aunties, to be worn by one side or the other for the duration of a game!

Musically, 'Chain Up the Swings' grew from another, quite different source as Matthew Marra explains: 'So much of what he did was experimental, and the songs grew out of the experiments. We've got tapes and tapes of him just playing, working out tunes, feeling his way around things, and then maybe getting hold of something that's a bit special which he can turn into something completely different. You can hear the evolution of a lot of his songs on those tapes.'[9] In this instance, in the mid-1980s Michael made a demo of a piece written for Abdullah Ibrahim, the South African jazz pianist and composer who influenced Michael's own piano style. This was possibly around the time that Ibrahim played Dundee's Bonar Hall in February 1984. The sketch went on to become the basis for 'Chain Up the Swings'. That a song about religion in the Hebrides should be part-rooted in Cape jazz is testimony to the astonishing range of Michael's musical explorations.

'Beefhearts and Bones' is a grimly humorous take on separating couples, which uses song references with devastating accuracy to point out the failings on both sides. Michael would introduce this song at gigs in his customary dry manner:

This song is on the hilarious subject of divorce. I'm sure you've all had plenty of laughs out of that. I got a bit fed up with my pals who all seemed to be getting divorced at the same time, and round about the same age too. They mostly had the same faults as well. I learned that the procedure is that when a couple are splitting up one of them tells you one side of the story and you are invited to despise the other party. It's boring. I was not willing to join in that kind of game, but I am interested in the subject, so I wanted to write a song about a couple who are splitting up. This particular couple are childless, just so it's not too tragic. And because they have no children the most important thing they must do is divide their record collection, and that's when the trouble starts. I noticed while I was writing this song that I was giving the woman all my favourite records. It didn't seem fair somehow, so I went back to the start and I gave the man the Captain Beefheart album, which I thought was very nice of me.

Sometimes when doing a gig Michael would pair this song with another, 'She Said, He Said', which covers a related subject, dating through self-promotion. This is how he would link the two:

I've always blamed the man in that song ['Beefhearts and Bones'] for the trouble between the couple. Which is daft really, because they don't exist. They are a fictitious couple but for some reason I've always blamed him, even to the point that recently I was wondering how he was getting on. I thought, if he did exist, this man, he probably was the kind of fellow who would place an advertisement in a newspaper in order to get another woman, after he'd split up with his wife. You know these columns you get, headed 'Perfect Partners' or 'Cupid's Stunts'. In Dundee we have something called loneliness, and we have these columns in the newspapers full of people who are able to describe themselves in eighteen words or less. I think anybody who can do that is dangerous. So I see big long lists of dangerous people looking for each other. And you don't get to see the interesting bit, you don't get to see what happens when they meet, which is a pity, I think. And it helps if you know all the jargon, if you know the terminology. WLTM: Would Like To Meet. GSOH: Good Sense Of Humour. NS: Nasty Sadist. You know the kind of thing? Keep an eye out for EDKIAB: Enjoys Drowning Kittens In A Bucket.

Pax Vobiscum finishes with a flying version of Chuck Berry's 'The Promised Land', as if to affirm the debt Michael and most of the musicians on stage with him owed to rock'n'roll and black American music in particular.

*

'Somewhere around my fortieth birthday,' Chris Marra says, '– so this would be in the mid-1990s – we started talking about doing another album. This eventually became *Posted Sober*. It took nearly five years to make. I think we went into it saying, the same way you go into every one, let's make it painless but it never works out like that. People wonder how you can take five years to make an album, but to be fair we did loads of other things – a whole lot of stuff for television, a Saint Andrew album, the Mackenzie album, *Camhanach* – and also we wanted to make Michael's next one as good as we possibly could.'[10]

Among the numerous projects to which Michael was committed in that same period of the late 1990s was another major theatre production: he wrote the songs for, and acted in, Chris Rattray's *The Mill Lavvies*. This hugely popular play was first performed at Dundee Rep in 1998, when it had two runs. It was revived in 2002 and again in 2012, just a month before Michael's death. Set in the early 1960s in a Dundee mill where most of the workforce are women, the action takes place in the mill's male toilets and dips into the lives of five men whose banter, tricks, petty cruelties and occasional kindnesses to one another reflect the changes going on in society around them. Chris Rattray's scenarios and dialogue are in the tradition of John Byrne's *The Slab Boys* trilogy, Roddy McMillan's *The Bevellers* and other plays set in male, working-class workplaces, but there is a particularly Dundonian underdog take on life in *The Mill Lavvies*. Michael's songs are beautifully crafted to tap into this theme, and it is not doing an injustice to the strength of Rattray's writing to say that they are the highlights of the play, partly

because they slot so seamlessly into the narrative, enhancing and never disrupting it. Some of these songs, which teeter on the edge of pathos but never quite topple in, are rightly regarded as top-drawer Michael Marra creations, 'Big Wide World Beyond the Seedlies', 'Broom Crazy' and 'Gin Eh was a Gaffer for to Be' among them. 'Oh Meh Goad', in which Erchie, the janny, is urged by his workmates to supply them with ever more surreal non-rhyming limericks, is a comic masterpiece. Perhaps the most memorable song, though, is 'If Dundee was Africa', a geography lesson in sound-pictures. At one point in the play, Erchie wants to know where North Africa is but, since he is unable to read or write, one of the other men has to find a way of explaining its location to him without the aid of an atlas or globe. He does so with this song:

> If Dundee was Africa,
> And Fife was Antarctica,
> If Arbroath was India,
> And Perth was Peru,
> In that darkest of continents
> How happy Eh'd be,
> Cause that would mean Aiberdeen
> Was deep in the Mediterranean Sea,
> And a'body would agree
> That's a no bad place for Aiberdeen
>   to be.
>
> If Dudhope was Zambia,
> And the Hulltoon was Gambia,
> If Fintry was Egypt,
> And the Stobbie was Chad,
> If the Ferry was Mozambique,
> The Ferry would mebbe seem no bad.

Eh'd wheel meh wheelbarrow up
    Kilimanjaro,
What a bra' view there would be –
A' thae icebergs in Teyport
When it's bilin in Dundee.

If Dundee was Africa,
The south is whaur the Tey flows to
    the sea,
In the east it's the Blackscraft,
In the west it's the Sinderins,
And Erchie, as any fool can see,
Tak it fae me, North Africa's Lochee.

The *Mill Lavvies* songs were released on a CD by Mink in 1998, with Saint Andrew assisting with the recitation of the limericks.

*

What was it like for Chris Marra, working with his brother in the studio? Was it difficult? Challenging?

No, never challenging. It was always things outwith what we were doing that were the challenges. Sometimes Michael took these extra jobs, like television work, when he was in the middle of a block, which is a really bad idea. The pressure that put on him was just awful, because we were then working to a deadline without any material. You can't say to someone like Michael, 'Quick, write something,' you just have to go at his pace. But working with him in the studio, it was always great.

One of Michael's maxims was 'Finish everything'. Even if the thing's a lot of shite, always get it done.

Nobody saw him doing it. That would be him on his own, completely. I never saw him write anything, never saw him come up with a lyric, he would always go away to work on his own. By the time I got to hear anything, usually he'd have done a demo, and the lyrics would be written out in pen. Start off in pencil, finish in pen. He really hated working with other people on songs. He did it once or twice, but he did not like it at all.

For *Posted Sober* we had fifteen or sixteen songs selected right at the very start. They were already written, finished by the time we saw them. Maybe there were a few others in the running but they were ready to go too, it was just a question of which ones we would keep.

You can see the progression in his songwriting all the way through his records. He just kept getting better. By the time you get to *Posted Sober* the material is very rich. Even a song like 'Posted Sober' itself, which he wrote pretty quickly as I remember, I don't think that was in the first batch of songs for the album, he just came up with it and let us hear it, and it was right. Which is why it's just him singing it solo with the guitar. We didn't want to muck about with it. [11]

More than thirty musicians and vocalists are credited on *Posted Sober*, which was released on the Inner City Sound label in 2000, to universally positive reviews. Once again, the skilful hand of Allan McGlone is evident, steering this eclectic and

North Africa's Lochee

If the hale toon was Africa
South Africa is ~~doon faur the sea~~ Stauith Tay flows into the sea
In the East is the Blackscroft
In the West is the Sinderins
And North Africa's Lochee

If Ann Street wis Gambia
And Fintry Tunisia
If Kenya was Polepark
And Zimbabwe was Stobbie

And Fife was Antartica
Perth wid be Ecuador
And Arbroath was India

If the hale toon was Africa
Oh how happy eh wid be
Because dat would put Aberdeen
Deep in the Mediterranean Sea

Eh'd wheel meh wheelbarrow
Up Kilamanjaro

(*Preceding page*) An early draft
of the lyrics of 'If Dundee
was Africa': not only the title
but also the geographical
references changed greatly
in the final version.

(*Above, and facing page*) Michael
in *The Mill Lavvies*, for which
he also wrote the music.

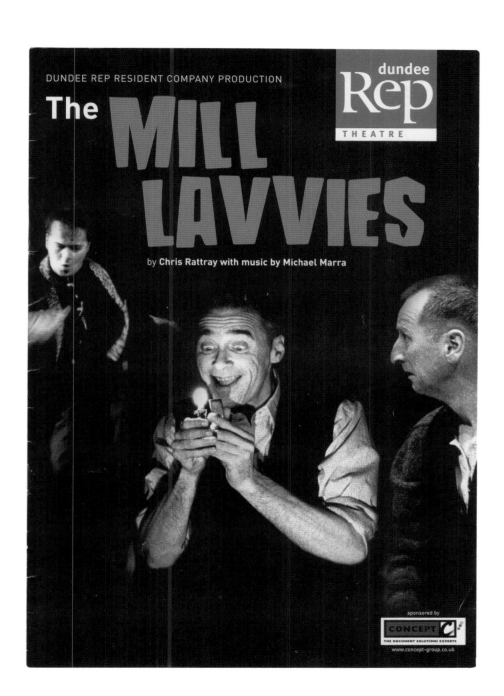

possibly unruly ensemble through four-teen songs of tremendous variety. Chris Marra was right: the material is unde-niably rich, the production values high. Every song is a gem in its own way, and yet it really holds together as a collection, one track seeming to lead naturally to the next however different it may be. The mood swings from the upbeat optimism of 'Letter from Perth' and 'All Will Be Well' to more sombre reflections on cause and effect ('Every now and then a policeman is born / And a silence fills the air' are the opening lines of 'The Butterfly Flaps Its Wings'). 'Constable le Clock' expresses a yearning to impede the progress of time ('Do not swing sweet pendulum / And let the cuckoo stay asleep', and the insistent refrain 'Arrest this moment'), while 'Rey-nard in Paradise' captures a real event and transforms it into a philosophical fable. 'The Lonesome Death of Francis Clarke' and 'Frida Kahlo's Visit to the Taybridge Bar' both seem to turn the clock back and offer redemptive outcomes to stories that did not, in reality, end that well.

Michael made extensive notes about each song, and his own explanations, shot through with his usual sharp wit, are prob-ably the best way to give background to some of them here. They also demonstrate the enormous respect and appreciation he had for the musicians who played on the album, some of whom he had worked with over many years.

Albert White Feather
Dedicated to Val Dean.

This one started the day after I saw the Grand Canyon. I was travelling with my host Rod Cameron and Val who is a bluegrass musician from Kansas and we stayed at a Navajo Motel in Cameron, Arizona. There was a sign outside the general store which read 'YARD SALE, ALBERT WHITE FEATHERS PLACE SATURDAY'.

I liked how you were expected to know where Albert lived and I asked about the Yard Sale concept. After Val had explained what it was he spoke again saying, 'Don't you go thinking that Albert is in any kind of trouble just because he's having a Yard Sale. People have them for all kinds of rea-sons, maybe just to make space.'

I admired his concern for the rep-utation of a man he didn't know and since the plumbing at the Navajo Motel was of such a high standard, I decided that Albert probably had to make room for a new piano which he could now afford because he was so good at his job.

The number is in the key of E Flat which is home for me and there was no editing involved in the rhythm section work. Brian McDermott on drums counted through the silence and Gregor Philp did a fabulous job with the bass part which was not written as a standard blues. I wanted Jim Morrice the sax player since I heard him at 'The Gig' in Blair [12] twenty years ago. Jim also plays bass clarinet on this track, it's a beautiful sound which I love from the old Brian Wilson days and from working with Dick Lee and Hamish Moore. It's worth having Frank Rossiter in the studio even if there are no trombone parts, for his turn of phrase alone. I admire his technique, strength and humour and he is a good man to have by your side in a tricky situation. Jason Sellars plays the trumpet and he is a very talented young musician from Dundee. He and his brother Tony are a great force for music here. These boys are not only great musicians but are also extremely well mannered, well groomed and generally a credit to their mother, the kind of boys you can take to your Producer's house. Derek Thomson plays the piano and is one of my all time favourite musicians, his intrinsic whimsy was perfect for this tune. Derek was quick to point out that he thought the whole thing was a good idea when he said, 'That's where the real money is after all, the jazz comedy poetry gemme!' Allan McGlone plays alto sax and drums as well as controlling the space and spacing the controls. Christopher played a Gibson and was very patient with an arrangement that originally looked like a suicide note. Worth noting here that when Arthur Koestler died, they found six drafts of his suicide note. Proper writer.

The Butterfly Flaps Its Wings
Some years ago I was performing in a radio show to celebrate Hugh MacDiarmid's birthday. The gig was in Queen Street in Embra[13] in the big room with the good piano. I fell in with Norman MacCaig in the green room, other performers came and went but at one point there was a wee silence and a woman said an angel had just passed over. Norman laughed and said that when that silence happened in Russia people said it was because a policeman had just been born.

There's an element of what I like to think of as CHASO THEORY. I read an account of a breach of the peace in the local paper, a bit of it went, 'Mrs McGoldrick told the accused to behave himself. The accused stated that his intention was to put Mrs McGoldrick through the wall. Chaso ensued.' It may have been only a typing error but for me it became the basis of my entire outlook. I got a prise for spelling at St Mary's Lochee after all.

Brian McDermott and Ged Grimes are the basis of this track along with the Blackbird who sang in the tree outside the studio, he was a hero in the tense times. He has now launched a solo career off the back of these summer sessions. Joy to have Derek Thomson back with Frank Rossiter to boot. Frank blew a note at the end which had us all gasping for breath. It's C minor all the way with one or two lay-bys, in fact there is only one conventional bridge on the whole record, in 'Francis Clarke'. Christopher plays Hammond Organ and all the guitars, and the groove is related to Pax Vobiscum in the songwriting as therapy section. Jim Morrice plays flute.

Botanic Endgame
Once I had a gig at the Dungannon

Ice Bowl with Deacon Blue and I was staying in a place called the York Hotel in Botanic Ave. I had come up from Dublin and had a night off so I went for a walk. When I returned to the Hotel the reception was deserted and there was a hold-all lying on the floor, the hold-all was ticking. I went through to the bar and shouted to the barman, one Seamus Flynn, I said, 'There's a bag in reception,' and left the premises waiting across the road in a highly agitated state. Eventually Seamus came out looking for me and he was laughing. He said, 'It's those fucking halfwits at the Chess Club.'

Ged originally tried a JuJu kind of bass thing which was very groovy but came into conflict with the lyric. I hope Allan still has that bass thing as we could do something else with it. Helen Forbes played the whistles perfectly, first take, every time. Fiddlers are Mike Ward and Michael James, and Kevin Murray is playing mandolin. Mike has a rare shop on the Perth Road in Dundee. It's called VS (Vintage Strings) and every plucker can satisfy their plucking needs there. The great John Huband goes for a simple groove and Stewart Ivins plays the moothie. I think M'Lach mixed acoustics as well on this one.

Reynard in Paradise
Football statos could tell you the date, I heard it 'live' on the radio and eventually saw it on television. A fox ran on to Celtic Park during a league match between Celtic and Aberdeen. It seemed a strange choice of venue for a personal appearance although I had seen a fox in Mount Florida station and that's right beside Hampden Park, the national football stadium. I thought maybe he'd come from the country because his family were being persecuted by huntsmen in red costumes, that he had tired of the rural way of life and come into sophisticated Glasgow for a change. Whatever, during the song the fox revises his opinion of mankind having seen Aberdeen playing Celtic. I played my Epiphone Texan with the bottom string dropped to D and the same with the top string, DADGBD. This song is dedicated to Bernard MacLaverty with grateful thanks for his beautiful work.[14]

Frida Kahlo's Visit to the Taybridge Bar
Homage to the great Mexican painter. I tried to make a drawing of Frida in which she was happy, healthy and single. The drawing didn't work so I made the song in which she dies and goes to Heaven but they can't get the Pearly Gates opened so Saint Peter asks her if she would mind spending the interim period in the Tay Bridge Bar in the Perth Road, Dundee. Christopher used his Martin and my Epiphone for the luxurious guitar sound, Derek played the piano and I was delighted when Patsy Seddon agreed to the session on harp C+. I worked with Patsy on the Mackenzie album Camhanach and I'm a great fan of the Poozies, a great group. Ged

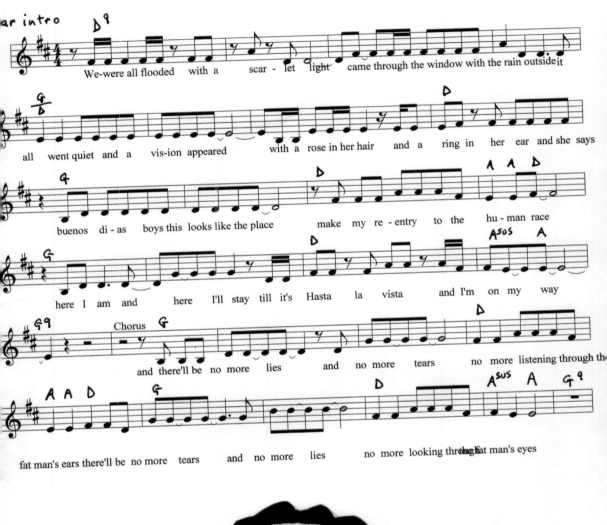

We-were all flooded with a scar-let light came through the window with the rain outside it all went quiet and a vis-ion appeared with a rose in her hair and a ring in her ear and she says buenos di-as boys this looks like the place make my re-entry to the hu-man race here I am and here I'll stay till it's Hasta la vista and I'm on my way

Chorus

and there'll be no more lies and no more tears no more listening through the fat man's ears there'll be no more tears and no more lies no more looking through that fat man's eyes

Grimes is Mister Groove playing bass and percussion very tastefully indeed, as usual. I didn't get a chance to thank Ged personally for all his help on this and other records, he is a very inspirational man whose standards are an excellent example to all young musicians, long may he groove. Harmonies were provided by one of my favourite singers of all time, Rod Paterson. I've admired and worked with Rod for many years now and hope to continue to do so for many more. I like the image of Frida dancing with Jimmy Howie the distinguished painter and terpsichorean, they make a handsome couple.

All Will Be Well

Some years ago I worked on a show with Frank McConnell composing music for Frank's company, plan B. We worked in Rosehall in Sutherland, a beautiful place, it was summer but ultimately I found the piece depressing and I worked on a waltz simultaneously to keep my spirits up. After the show had been done I decided to make an optimistic song and it lay about for a long time until Christopher said that he thought it was good and then we gave it a bit of attention. I recorded a version with Luke Ivins, a very talented young Dundee singer, but we didn't make much progress with getting it out and then Christopher and Allan chose it for this record. Brian and Ged played drums and bass, Christopher played guitars and glockenspiel and we had a welcome return from Gary Clark

playing electric guitar and singing like a linty. Lloyd and Christopher sang the other harmonies. Derek played Fender Rhodes and Frank played trombone. I like the thought of Derek and Frank on a tour bus.

Violins were Guido de Groote, Dervilágh Cooper, Michael and Alison James who also played viola with Jenny Sutherland (grandchild of Robert Garioch, who wrote the wonderful 'Ower Weel' [15]) and Rosemary Townhill played cello. This song is dedicated to my sister Mary who recently started a new life as herself.

Frank McConnell's recollections add some extra detail to the origins of the song 'All Will Be Well'. He had been invited by the Dundee Rep Dance Company to choreograph a piece with the working title *All Will Be Well*. While visiting a friend in the Western Isles Frank had seen what was apparently a quotation from Winston Churchill on the kitchen wall: 'Withhold no sacrifice, grudge no toil, seek no sordid gain, fear no foe. All will be well.' Given the Churchill connection with Dundee, Frank thought it would be appropriate to work this quotation into the piece, for which Michael was to write the music. (After obsessive research in Dundee Central Library, Frank subsequently established that most of the phrases were not coined by Churchill but came from obscure Victorian hymns and similar sources.)

Frank McConnell:

The whole company went to Rosehall

in Sutherland on a two-week retreat. In retrospect, I can see how ironic the title was, as I was far from being well and was in fact heading for a depression. I was asking the dancers to do some weird stuff, asking Michael to write in unusual tempos like 7/4 and 5/8. It was all quite pressurised and a stressful time for all concerned. After this there was a three-month break before we started to rehearse the piece. I looked at it and thought, 'Oh my God, this is a piece about someone trying to have a nervous breakdown!' Michael too had found the whole experience depressing but nevertheless from it all he picked out the kernel of a lyric and a tune which became 'All Will Be Well'. [16]

The final song on the album, 'Scribbled Down Drunk (But Posted Sober)', is a deceptively simple package which, like the envelope in its first verse, proves to be stuffed with detail. It's an American short story, but delivered in Michael's unreconstructed Scottish voice over four verses and three choruses. Before singing it at gigs he would explain that it was indeed composed when he was in the United States: 'I'd been trying to get a haircut in Las Vegas but I couldn't find a proper American barbershop. You know what hairdressers look like now, they're like abbatoirs of style. I didn't want that. So I went to this wee town called Hurricane in Utah, to get a haircut. And although it was Hurricane, Utah it could have been Winchburgh or Thurso or Wick, the kind of place you leave when you're about thirteen.'

Christopher played a Gibson and was very patient with an arrangement that originally looked like a suicide note.

Worth noting here that when Arthur Koestler died, they found six drafts of his suicide note. Proper writer.

(Preceding page) Sheet music for 'Frida Kahlo's Visit to the Taybridge Bar', with decoration by Michael.

Michael at the famous Blüthner
piano in his studio at home
in Newtyle.

Michael's composite portrait
of Gordon Maclean, creative
director of An Tobar on the
Isle of Mull.

By the end of the song, the woman whose story it is has a gun in her handbag and a yearning for 'a time when it all made sense', but 'She's never going back to Hurricane Utah / To the tree and the swing and the picket fence.' It's the perfect coda to an album which invites the listener into many different lives, and doesn't close the door on any of them.

*

Michael had played gigs on the Isle of Mull several times, and in 2002 Gordon Maclean, creative director at An Tobar, the arts centre in Tobermory, invited him over to run a songwriting workshop for young people. The idea was that the songs would be based on the songwriters' dreams, and prior to Michael's arrival Gordon encouraged those intending to participate in the workshop to keep a journal of their dreams. The first workshop session was to take place at Tobermory High School rather than at the arts centre, and involved some two dozen pupils from the senior classes. After an hour or so break-time arrived, and Michael slipped outside for a cigarette. When the class reassembled twenty minutes later, Michael was absent. Gordon Maclean found him leaning over a fence, smoking intensely. 'I cannae go back in there,' he growled. The rest of the workshop took place at An Tobar, where Michael, freed of his antipathy to the school environment, immediately won his students over with his never patronising and always encouraging attitude to their work and ideas. The outcome was a fine collection of songs entitled *Tobermory Songdreams*.

In April 2003 Gordon commissioned Michael to return to Mull and spend several weeks there on a set of new songs as part of An Tobar's Interface project. Previous commissions had gone to Mr McFall's Chamber and the clarinettist Karen Wimhurst, and to the harpist Corrina Hewat. Michael wrote and recorded six songs and the EP, *Silence*, was released on An Tobar's own Tob Records label that summer.

After a launch concert on Mull, Michael went on a short tour of the Highlands, accompanied by Kenny Fraser on fiddle and whistles and Gordon Maclean on double bass. Michael spoke to journalist Kenny Mathieson about the project:

I went over [to Tobermory] for two weeks in the first instance, and the day I arrived was the day the war in Iraq broke out. I didn't write anything while I was there. I felt I was on the edge of writing something big about the war.

My brief was *Extremes*, and here I was on this very beautiful island, and the war was going on. I couldn't really get that out of my mind, but I ended up writing nothing at all about the war. It was very strange. It was such a big issue that it was impossible to ignore, but in the end I just couldn't find a way in.

I came home after the two weeks, and I started thinking about the gossip I had heard on the island, and began to work up some material from that. I was struck by two things in particular. One was the fact that gossip seemed to me very necessary in a place like Mull, but the other thing that I noticed mostly through gossip was racism, and specifically anti-English feelings.

I felt that was particularly overt on Mull, and I thought I would throw that at them. It's like the Glasgow thing – if you try to write about sectarianism at all, it is either going to have to be really great, or it is going to have be very subtle, like planting a thought. It's not looking to confront or cause trouble, it's more like saying do you realise that you are doing this?

One of the songs ['Gossip'] has a section about a cultural awareness class, which is to teach the local bairns about English culture. I've done it in quite a light-hearted way, but my hope is that people will maybe question their own attitudes through that.…

I went over last year to do a songwriting workshop in Tobermory, and one of the participants there was an English guy called Ben Potter.

He was 22 and had gone back to Tobermory High School to do his Highers. He was a nice guy, and seemed very happy, so I wasn't expecting him to come up with much, because we all know that songwriters are introverted, horrible, nasty fowk like me!

He came up with a song which was about a woman he had split up with, who had gone back to New Zealand. He sent it to her, and she got on a plane and came back to Tobermory, and the two of them moved down to England.

By chance, I had just heard the Mackenzie album [*Fama Clamosa*, Macmeanmna Records, 2002] and they had featured a very old Gaelic song from Dalmally by a guy called Donald MacNicol who had asked a woman called Lilias Campbell to marry him.

She had refused, but he wrote this song, and they were married, so presumably the song had changed her mind. I was struck by that connection across a couple of centuries and more, and made a quick wee song ['Lily'] just to mark the way it had worked for Ben in the same way.…

The record is called *Silence*, and I'm chuffed with the cover. I kept seeing people in the paper every day with hygienic masks on because of the SARS virus, and I fancied getting one of them and drawing the bit of my face you couldn't see on it.

In Tobermory I couldn't buy one, though – I think there had been a run on them! Instead I got a serviette and drew the missing bits, and taped it to my face. It's very striking, and I'm thinking of trying to persuade Liz Lochhead to let me do one for her. We are doing a new version of our show *Flagrant Delicht* soon, and we need a poster. [17]

There is a certain world-weariness in the songs on *Silence*, along with frustration, anger and sardonic humour – you can feel the war rumbling in the background. But there is optimism too – faith in tradition and music in 'The Bard is Well', and in the power of gifting a song to someone in 'Lily'. There is also an appeal to love and

Artist Doreen Cullen, an admirer of Michael's work, included many cartoons featuring him and his beret in her correspondence with him, and was also responsible for creating a life-size papier-mâché model of him.

kindness in the last song, 'The Fold', the psalm-like qualities of which are wonderfully enhanced by the chapel-choir arrangement and Michael's harmonium-playing. Michael himself liked the song because it was that rare thing, a hymn with a middle-eight. Gordon Maclean recalls that Michael didn't want his own voice on the finished track, but only sang as a guide for the female chorus. However, on playing back the recording it was clear to Gordon that the interplay of voices further enhanced the song's extraordinary atmosphere, so Michael's stayed:

> Sometimes when the night winds
> blow and
> Whispers make their way
> When reputations can be lost or found
> And a kind word leads to solid ground
> O mercy then befriend us
> To temper all we're told
> Lead us to the fold

*

Mull, Rab Noakes believes, became a very special destination for Michael: 'an amenable creative and spiritual space for him to be.'[18] Gordon Maclean thinks that might be true, but also knew that islands made Michael wary: you depended on a ferry as your means of escape. Once when he and Michael were driving in the south of the island, they spotted a small house with three doors. 'That's smart,' Michael observed. 'Plenty of escape routes.'[19]

Island life definitely provoked ambivalent feelings in him. Years earlier, in the spring of 1992, when he was away in South Uist teaching songwriting, he had written a letter to his brother Nicky, who was himself a teacher:

> I'm glad to hear you're alive and working which is just about what I am. I have been missing Peg and the bairns something awful for the past wee while and am looking forward to getting home a week on Saturday. Most of the classes have been good but I can't bear teaching any longer, I don't know if I'm doing any good and spend most of my time worrying about it all, no wonder teachers are all looneys. I enjoy feeding the sheep and am on the lookout for lambs just now which is a responsibility I take very seriously as everybody else is out all day. The McPhees are a lovely family and look after me very well but if I didn't know I'd see Peg next week I'm sure I'd go insane. You're either an island person or not and although it can be incredibly beautiful I find myself pining for traffic jams. Privacy is a luxury also, if one person kisses another the whole island gets aroused. Mental.[20]

On the other hand, and perhaps particularly as he grew older, Mull did offer some kind of sanctuary, a sense that by crossing the sea you were escaping *from* something, from being constantly traceable and available. In any event, four years after *Silence*, in the summer of 2007, he was back at An Tobar to record another mini-CD for release on Tob Records.

Quintet is exactly what the blurb on the sleeve says: 'five songs about five musicians played and sung by five musicians in five days.' Gordon Maclean provided the technical support, Michael did the artwork for the cover, and besides himself the musicians playing were Dick Lee on clarinets and backing vocals, Aidan O'Rourke on fiddle, Gordon on double bass and various percussive instruments, and Steve Kettley on saxophones, bass drum, Vietnamese jaw harp and backing vocals. The musicians celebrated were Peter McGlone (the song 'Peter' had been a wedding present for him years before – 'I was skint at the time,' Michael claimed), Mac Rebennack (Dr John), the Shetland musicians Thomas Fraser and Peerie Willie Johnson, and the English folksinger Martin Carthy. Most of these songs had long been in Michael's live repertoire but they had not been recorded before.

Gordon Maclean recalls:

> Michael was always quick and easy to work with, a complete professional. He was a one-take kind of guy. We'd recorded some backing vocals and then I'd forgotten to switch the microphone back to take just his voice, and I had to ask him to sing all his solo parts again. He growled at me and then got on with it. His vocals on those five songs were all done in one take. [21]

Michael was fascinated by the story of Thomas Fraser, a fisherman and crofter of Burra Isle in Shetland who died aged fifty in 1978, leaving behind a legacy of thousands of country and blues songs which he had recorded on a reel-to-reel recorder. His astonishing guitar and vocal style marked him as a brilliant and authentic performer of the American song tradition epitomised by Jimmie Rodgers and Hank Williams, despite his never having set foot outside Shetland. Some years after his death a selection of his recordings became available, and between 2002 and 2005 three CDs were released. Michael's song 'Thomas Fraser' is a heartfelt tribute to the determination and musical courage of a painfully shy man.

'Schenectady Calling Peerie Willie Johnson' celebrates another Shetland musician. Michael often included it in his performances and the story behind it, as told by him, deserves to be repeated in full:

> This is a song that comes all the way from the Shetland Islands. I loved it immediately, the first time I arrived there. I got off a ship, I went in the filling-station, I bought a map of the Shetland Islands. If you buy such a thing, you get the United Kingdom in a tiny wee box at the bottom. It's worth the voyage. Anyway, I went up to Shetland to do a gig, and after I'd finished the gig I was introduced to a fascinating man called Peerie Willie Johnson, who is a guitarist. Some of you may know his work, he's a wonderful player. And Peerie Willie was telling me his life story, and he told me that when he was young his pal Tommy Anderson made a crystal set, you know, a primitive radio. And they used to gather round this crystal set in Lerwick, and because there are no mountains in the Atlantic Ocean they were able to pick up a radio

station from New York State which was called Schenectady. Remember that word? You used to see it on the dial with all those beautiful words Stavanger, Allouis and Athlone, and Schenectady was one of them. So that was how Willie heard the music of Louis Armstrong and Duke Ellington and Count Basie for the first time, and Django Reinhardt and his favourite guitarist Eddie Lang, who played with Joe Venuti. And he'd learned all the traditional music, but when Willie heard these guys it changed his style, which eventually became this beautiful mixture of traditional music with very groovy chords indeed, and he had a great style of playing.

So, I loved the idea of the crystal set, you know, and music coming across oceans and travelling the world like that, so I started writing a song about him, on the boat to Aberdeen. And then when I got home, I had to take the family on holiday to Tunisia, and I kept working, I kept trying to get this song done because I had a gig in Aberdeen, and I wanted to do it when I got back. So while I was in Tunisia I was in this little town called Hammamet, and there was a wonderful house there called Casa del Mediterraneo, which had been commandeered by Rommel during the Second World War. So I went to visit the house, it was gorgeous, and in the corner was a beautiful Steinway grand piano. I asked the guide, 'Do you mind if I...?' He said, 'Be brief.' I said, 'Okay.' So I sat and I practised this song on it,

and then when I came back to Dundee I went into the Tay Bridge for a quick pint, and I just happened to drop into the conversation, 'I was playing Rommel's piano the other day.' Well, you know what Dundee is like – we take a pride in our modesty – so that was followed by silence. Nobody said anything. And then a real hero came to my rescue, it was actually Chris Rattray, and Chris Rattray said, 'Ah, Rommel! I'll never forget his immortal words at the start of the North African campaign.' And they did it to him as well. I felt sorry for Chris, so I said, 'Oh yes, Chris, and what were those immortal words?' He says, 'Right, lads, get in the tanks.' The amazing Chris Rattray.

Anyway, it brings me back to the song. Although, do you know a group called the Boys of the Lough? Wonderful group. Well, a few years ago there was a tragedy in the group and they had to get somebody to fill in for one of the members for a world tour, and they asked Peerie Willie Johnson to do it, and during the American leg of the world tour one of the gigs was in... Schenectady. I find that truly beautiful. So there you go, here's the song, it's much shorter than the introduction.

The story behind 'If I Was an Englishman' is also instructive in several ways:

At the time that the Scottish Parliament opened, I was in America. I was at a wedding in San Francisco, and one of the other guests was a great man,

DR. JOHN

at

WEDNESDAY
20th JUNE

8pm · 12 Midnight

Tickets £4.00

Courtesy coach will leave the
City Mills Hotel Car Park at 7.30 pm

RESERVATIONS Tel. (0250) 2802

(*Preceding page*) Poster for Dr John's legendary Perthshire appearance which inspired Michael's song 'Mac Rebennack's Visit to Blairgowrie'.

(*Above*) Dr John the Nite Tripper's cheque for '£ove + £ife' made out to Michael when they met in London.

(*Right*) Michael expanding his keyboard skills.

Martin Carthy, I'm sure some of you know his work, he's a wonderful fellow, Martin, and he's always encouraged me. And we were talking at the wedding about the fact that the Parliament had opened, and Martin had recently been awarded an MBE, so we were kind of teasing him, you know, and poking fun as you do when your pals get an MBE, we were saying things like well, you're actually a member of the British Empire, any chance of you slipping me some civil rights or … stuff like that, generally we were having a laugh. But Martin was talking about the fact that he reckoned that English people were going to have a harder time celebrating being English than the rest of us do celebrating being ourselves. He reckoned that Scots had a readily recognisable culture which they always employ and enjoy, and he didn't know if English people had that. And I was thinking about all the stuff I know, all the great things that have come out of England, because I enjoy touring there, I do it quite a lot, I play in hundreds of little towns and none of them ever remind me of the British Government. So I actually quite like it. So I had this idea for a song, it's called 'If I was an Englishman'. I didn't actually write it that night because I found out to my surprise that I was unable to read or write. So I waited till the following day.

The outcome is a song that celebrates England's radical tradition in politics and art:

> If I was an Englishman I'd sing and
>   dance and play
> I'd dig out all the old ones and beseech
>   you heed their say
> Their visions of a better life in a land
>   as bright as day
> I'd do my William Morris dance and
>   I'd be on my way

It goes on to namecheck some of the Englishmen Michael most admired, including Thomas Paine, Stanley Spencer, Harold Pinter and Martin Carthy himself. One verse, with typical Marra humour, places two unlikely heroes from the common people way above their social superiors:

> If I was an Englishman I'd raise my
>   voice and sing
> I'd enter in the House of Lords and
>   make the rafters ring
> I'd sing of all those noblemen of
>   cabbages and kings
> I'd do my Arthur Mullard dance and
>   turf them in the bin
> I'd do my Norman Wisdom dance and
>   turf them in the bin

The last track on *Quintet* was the song Michael frequently used to kick off his gigs, 'Mac Rebennack's Visit to Blairgowrie'. The unlikeliness of Dr John ever doing a show in the Perthshire town is the theme running through the song, but in fact it happened, in the early 1980s, and Michael was there, and kept the poster to prove it. 'People didn't really think it would be him, that it must be a tribute act... but there he came, walking through the pub and, as anybody who was there will tell you, it was fabulous.'[22]

Years later, in London, the two men met, and after being told the story of the song Dr John wrote out a cheque to Michael as a memento of the encounter.

*

In 2006, at Edinburgh's Bongo Club, Michael had played a couple of his songs in new arrangements with the string section of Mr McFall's Chamber. Formed in 1996 by a number of players from the Scottish Chamber Orchestra and Scottish Ballet, this always innovative and entertaining ensemble mixes classical with a wide range of other styles – jazz, progressive rock, cartoon classics and folk among them – with great skill and plenty of humour. Music journalist Rob Adams had noted immediately that Mr McFall's and Michael were natural partners, that they should get together more often and that there was potential for 'a full-scale Marra-McFall's collaboration'.

In 2009 this happened, again at the Bongo Club, with a set of ten songs and a fantastic display of versatility from the ensemble, playing – among other instruments – guitar, violin, cello, accordion, harmonium, mandolin, double bass, electric bass and musical saw. The following year an extensive tour across Scotland and Northern England was organised, and from this came a live CD, *Michael Marra with Mr McFall's Chamber* (Delphian, 2010), featuring eleven Marra songs, two by Burns ('The Slave's Lament' and 'Green Grow the Rashes') and Michael's spoken introductions. As Robert McFall put it in the CD booklet, 'Marra's songs are keenly focused. His congenial introductions, as well as being entertaining, are often vital scene setters.…We hope that the inclusion of some of the introductions will also help to recreate the atmosphere of those performances.'

The album as a whole certainly does that. Robert McFall's arrangements (for all but three of the songs – the others were arranged by David McGuinness of Concerto Caledonia, with whom Michael had also played the previous year) manage somehow to be both sumptuous and subtle, and the diverse instrumentation enhances Michael's unaltered and unmistakable vocals. Perhaps most striking is Su-a Lee's immaculate playing of the musical saw on three tracks, especially on 'The Lonesome Death of Francis Clarke' where its mournful sigh is perfect for the song's atmosphere of snow and ice. Michael's explanation of how this song came about varied from gig to gig, and the following is an amalgamation of various introductions that he gave over the years. It begins with his customary assertion that his songs had nothing to do with him personally, but this was at least one exception that proved the rule:

I went into the Tay Bridge for a quick pint, and I just happened to drop into the conversation, 'I was playing Rommel's piano the other day.'

I had been marvelling about Loudon Wainwright's work.[23] He'd been writing about his family and writing very personal stuff, and I found that kind of overwhelming, because I never do that. If ever I use the word 'I' in my songs, it means there's a character that is speaking, it is never anything to do with me, who must be left out because it causes trouble. Now Loudon writing about his family – and he wrote about it so honestly and so well that there is benefit to other people – I thought how would my family react if I was to bare some of our trouble in order that other people might learn something from it? And the subject was going in the huff. My great-uncle was a man called Francis Clarke, and he was my grandmother's brother on my father's side. The family came from a place called Bailieborough in County Cavan in Ireland. They came across [to Dundee] and Francis served his time in the boatyard as a shipwright. That was his trade. He worked on the building of the *Discovery*, and then when that ship was finished he got a job on board the *Discovery* as the ship's carpenter, which is what a shipwright becomes when a ship sails. He travelled all over the world, had many great adventures, and eventually he died and was buried in the Yukon Territory. And the sad thing is that at the time that he died, the family were in the huff with him, they werenae speaking to him. Your families probably don't behave like that, but mine, on my father's side, could

represent Scotland at the Olympics – and probably Ireland on a technicality – in heavy grudge-bearing. Anyway, because they were in the huff with him there were no stories – you would imagine that if you have an adventurer in the family the stories should come down but there were none. I wouldn't have known about him at all but a few years ago my Auntie Molly told me about him, she said the reason they never spoke about him was because he'd had an unhappy marriage, and unhappy marriages were not as popular in those days as they are now, so they just never mentioned him. I thought it was a pity. So I wrote this song just to say hello to him, and maybe to warn people against going in the huff. Actually I put a verse of absolute fantasy in, where he meets a very beautiful woman, but I just put that in so that something nice would happen before he froze to death.

The last recording made by Michael and issued during his lifetime was the EP *Houseroom*, another collaboration, this time with The Hazey Janes, the band in which his daughter Alice and son Matthew play. This was a further production of Tob Records and came out in 2012, following a recording session of several days at An Tobar. We will return, later, to the six songs on this disc.

Michael's recorded output, between *The Midas Touch* in 1980 and *Houseroom* in 2012, was not large. This chapter is only a summary of that output, and hardly touches on the hundreds of songs that Michael wrote

MICHAEL MARRA

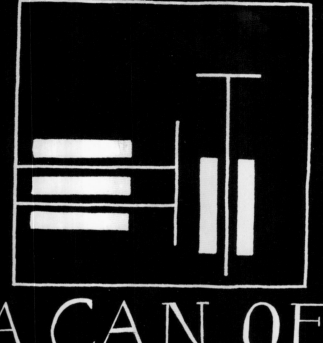

'A CAN OF MIND and A TIN OF THINK SO'

VENUE 25

ACOUSTIC MUSIC CENTRE
16 CHAMBERS ST. EMBRA.

AUGUST 29.30.31
12.30AM £3 (£2)

but never recorded, or seldom performed, or didn't think good enough to perform. Many of these exist only as demos or even just as handwritten lyrics without tunes. Like Thomas Fraser, Michael left a huge sound archive on cassettes and other tapes. Most of it is still to be explored. Given that he set himself the most exacting standards, and was reluctant to put anything permanently into the public domain if he was less than completely satisfied with it, it is likely that hidden jewels remain to be found in that archive.

Notes

1 Email, 21st May 2017.

2 After Michael's death, his family established the charity Optimistic Sound, with the campaign objective of bringing a Big Noise Orchestra and the Sistema music programme to Dundee.

3 Interview with Sheena Wellington, 13th May 2017.

4 Interview with James Kirkpatrick, 9th February 2017.

5 'The first time he sang it, the whole audience stood up.' (Note from Peggy Marra).

6 As told to Joan McAlpine in *The Scotsman*, 13th September 1993.

7 See above, p.35.

8 Allan McGlone's recollection is that 'This Evergreen Bough' was a late addition to the album, and was written for Eddie Marra.

9 Interview, 27th April 2017.

10 Interview with Chris Marra, 10th March 2017.

11 Ibid.

12 Blairgowrie.

13 The old, much missed BBC studios.

14 See p.224 for more on this song.

15 An extract from Garioch's 'Owre Weill' reads:

> 'Something's gane wrang: my heid's no sair.
> I'll see the doctor, and he'll say,
> He's no been taen this wey afore;
> the man's owre weill to wark the day.'

In 2017 Jenny Sutherland (Hanson) played as a member of the Gaels Blue Orchestra on Alice Marra's album *Chain Up the Swings*.

16 Interview with Frank McConnell, 11th January 2017.

17 'Michael Marra – Listening to the Gossip', in the Highlands & Islands arts magazine *Northings*, 11th June 2003.

18 Interview with Rab Noakes, 21st July 2016.

19 Interview with Gordon Maclean, 17th May 2017.

20 Undated letter to Nicky Marra.

21 Interview with Gordon MacLean, 17th May 2017.

22 *The Scotsman*, 5th October 2007.

23 Loudon Wainwright III demonstrated his own admiration for Michael's songwriting by performing his version of 'Hermless', which he sings as 'Harmless', live on numerous occasions, and including it on his 2014 album, *Haven't Got the Blues (Yet)*.

Kitchen conversation

No.5

James: Can we discuss something else that used to give you a lot of anxiety?

Michael: It doesn't sound promising.

J: You never broadcast the fact that you couldn't read or write music. Why did you keep that mainly to yourself?

M: For practical reasons. It might have cost me employment, especially in the theatre or with orchestral stuff or composition for film music or even straightforward production work. It's expected of you in those worlds. The tape recorder was always the stave to me, and Kevin Murray was always an ally and confidant when I had to come up with proper piano parts or melodies. Any time I was asked to produce written music it threw me into a panic which made my behaviour and the task more difficult. I loved the shapes of clefs and notes and tails and so on but it didn't have anything to do with what I played. I just played.

Over the years I had to find all the ways round this problem. Fortunately most good musicians work by listening first, then contributing emotional playing. When I worked with the Scottish National Orchestra it took me a month to get my piano part on manuscript, it was checked by Kevin before being given to Kevin McCrae, who is a composer and also plays the cello, to arrange the orchestration. Playing with the SNO was not a problem because I knew the music, they had to read their parts but I just knew it between my head and my fingers. That's the only way I can explain it.

Once I started work on a book of songs with a man called Sandy Stanage, an excellent musician emotionally who had the formal music training as well. We never completed the project in the end, but he sat with me and watched my fingers and wrote it on the stave, it looked beautiful and I felt proud that my playing made such bonnie shapes and patterns but he could have been writing down 'Ten Green Bottles' for all I knew – an excellent number by the way, from a minimalist point of view.

It all goes back to when I used to play the piano in Eddie's room in our house in Clement Park. I thought then that if I played notes which sounded all right under what I was singing, then nobody would know that I couldn't play the piano. That was my starting point: if I chose the right ones then I wouldn't be found out. So I had a purpose – to make songs – and got on with it. It was the same with the guitar, the purpose was not to be a guitarist like Chris or Kevin, just to make songs and then a clear recording of them, and then they would exist.

Some people find it hard to believe that people like myself and Irving Berlin know nothing about music. He was worse than me, I wrote songs in every key but he only worked in F# which is the black notes, really. He still made some of the best songs of the 20th century.

J: Frank Loesser, too, who wrote the songs for *Guys and Dolls* – another hero of yours, I think. His dad Henry was a piano teacher but he never taught Frank. Frank taught himself. He was composing songs when he was six. Henry said by the time Frank was fourteen he could play any tune he heard by ear.

M: He was a wonderful songwriter, truly great. Frank wrote 'Inchworm'. When I was a child I knew that that was an important song. It really was very dramatic and beautiful. It was written in counterpoint which is a hard thing to do. I loved it.

J: You and Frank Loesser have a lot in common. He was expelled from High School without getting his diploma, and later he was expelled from college after failing everything except English and gym. He did a whole lot of different jobs to make ends meet but all he really wanted to do was write songs. He later said of that period that every day he had a rendezvous with failure.

M: That's an honest statement.

J: And when he became successful, he would work with musical secretaries to make sure that the scores really conveyed the music as he conceived it. So you were not alone in having difficulties about writing music down.

M: Some people might think it's laziness of thought or deed, or omission – that's one of my favourite sins, omission. I mean, I admire the fact that even though you try your best, it's still a sin.

J: Robert Louis Stevenson thought omission was an art, not a sin. He said if he knew how to omit, he would ask no other knowledge.

M: I like him already. Do you know him?

Michael at the first public
exhibition of his artwork
in Cupar, early 1980s.

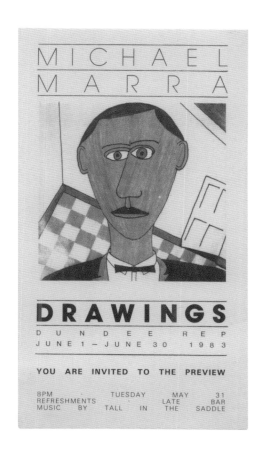

Invitation to Michael's
exhibition at Dundee Rep, 1983.

Artist,
Playwright,
Actor, Writer

There's nothing worse than a miser
  with a paintbrush
Little bitty red, little bitty blue

'Ceci N'est Pas Une Pipe'

Michael was an artist – in the widest sense of the word – in everything he did. He saw the world through an artist's eyes, and grasped it with an artist's hands. Andy Pelc, one of his closest friends and collaborators, who when not being Saint Andrew lectured in Textile Design at Duncan of Jordanstone College of Art, puts it like this:

> Michael was a 100% creative person. That's what he was about, all the time. It could have been music, it could have been a boat made out of old bits of wood in his back garden, it could have been a pencil drawing. The idea of him doing nothing, sitting outside with a cup of tea on a lovely afternoon, *not* talking, *not* thinking, *not* doing something, no, that wouldn't be him. He wasn't hyperactive, he just had to be always flexing that creative muscle. I think he felt he should always be busy, always be working. If you didn't work that's when it all ended. That was his life, it was what he was brought here to do. He wasn't incapable of relaxing,

of poking a fire with a stick, but there would always be something going on in his mind.[1]

As well as songwriting and musicianship, Michael wrote short stories and plays, acted, drew and painted, took photographs, manipulated the images he made, made collages, constructed objects, whittled sticks and invented things. Conversation, too, was a form of art for him. He enjoyed the company of visual artists and engaging with their ideas: he liked hanging out in their studios. His brother Eddie was an accomplished painter; he had a lifelong friendship with the prolific Dundee painter Vince Rattray (1954-2000), to whom he attributes the lines 'She was a woman to whom life had been cruel / And she lived with a fat man of the naïf school' in 'Frida Kahlo's Visit to the Taybridge Bar'; and he counted Andy Hall, James (Jimmy) Howie, Francis Boag, Calum Colvin, Eddie Summerton and many more as friends. He saw ordinary people as artists even if sometimes their art was unintentional. There were occasions when, had they known this, some might have been upset by the idea, as Frank McConnell explains:

> Michael absolutely loved visual art. It was he who introduced me to George Wyllie's work. We'd been performing *A Wee Home From Home* in the run-up to Glasgow City of Culture in 1990, and when the show finished about 2pm we went off to Anderston Quay to see George Wyllie's paper boat. As we were walking down from Charing Cross to the river, I clocked

a policeman standing in the middle of the road and from his manner, position and the time of year I realised that an Orange Walk was imminent and if we didn't get across the street before it arrived we'd be prevented from crossing. We could hear the flutes and drums playing so I told Michael to speed up and we ran down to St Vincent Street and got over the road just in time. Then from the safety of the other side we waited to see the Orange Walk, as Michael had never experienced one before. But instead of the full-on version of an Orange Walk it was all women in white crocheted bunnets, white silk blouses and black, knee-length skirts. Some were wearing sashes, some were in dark glasses, and not a man among them, and from the writing on the drums the participants seemed to belong to an organisation called the Order of Ruth, which I had never come across before. After we'd watched them go by, we carried on and had a look at George's paper boat! It was typical of Michael that his first experience of the Orange phenomenon should have been so, well, untypical.[2]

Years later Michael found a new platform for his own creativity when he began experimenting with digital photography. He produced a series of witty and insightful digital portraits of friends, some of them familiar faces to the public, in which he manipulated and merged details to reflect aspects of their characters as he saw them. It was the challenges as well as the opportunities that the new technology offered that interested him. An exhibition of the portraits was held at the Bank Street Gallery in Kirriemuir in October 2008. Today some of them look a little dated technically, but Frank McConnell believes that Michael was making the best use he could of the tools available to him at that time.[3] Frank, who was one of his subjects, recalls that he had the images printed by KallKwik in the Overgate, Dundee. A shop unit next door became available, and Michael, along with Kevin Murray and some others, seriously thought about raising funds to rent it for a month or two so they could call it 'Phuck Rite Oph'.

This anecdote points to a fundamental aspect of Michael's artistic outlook. It was obvious to Andy Pelc that:

> Michael was basically a rebel when it came to art or anything else. He was the rebel of the family. He was *into* art but almost anti-art in any formal or academic context. Anything that involved classical, formal training, he would reject that. I have it in my head that Michael might have applied to go to art school. But if he did apply, if he had been offered a place, I don't think he would have accepted it, or he wouldn't have stayed. He would have hated being told how to go about 'doing' art. In the same way, if you wanted Michael to, say, watch something on television, the worst thing you could do was tell him, 'Watch this programme, you'll really like it.' That immediately erected a barrier. He would take umbrage at you telling

him what he should watch or would like.[4]

Andy, quite independently, concurred with Frank's belief that Michael was ahead of his time in making the most of the available technology. When the first Saint Andrew album, *The Word on the Pavey*, was re-released in 2008, Michael and Mick McCluskey (former Mafia band-member and author of books including *Dundee For Beginners* and *The Dundee Scheme-hopper's Survival Guide*) made video animations of 'This World is Phuhl o' a Number o' Things' and some of the other tracks. Andy Pelc again:

> These wee animations Michael put together were admired by, among others, David Mach. He was a contemporary of mine at Art School and he'd seen the animations and was asking me what software was being used. It would have been very basic software. By now, with the technology available, Michael would probably have been making films. The key thing, though, is that even with more sophisticated tools at his disposal Michael would have been looking to keep that naivety in there. The minute it started to look slick he wouldn't have been so interested. He loved the idea of instant creativity – of making something out of nothing. I think that actually explains a lot about him as a person, that he would make something out of the smallest wee thing. He would get angry about the smallest thing. He would make a musical piece

about the smallest thing. I liked his stuff when it became a bit quirkier, a bit less controlled. But the earlier work was also very good, and of course it started as a kind of therapy, to while away time when he was on tour. He did like the idea of drawing. [5]

*

Back during the days of touring with Skeets Boliver and Barbara Dickson, Michael had found that a lot of hours were spent sitting around waiting for things to happen. To help himself relax before gigs, he bought himself crayons and felt-tip pens and started drawing – often very detailed, multi-lined images that needed a lot of concentration and a fair bit of colouring-in. The influence of modern masters like De Chirico, Matisse and Picasso is evident in his drawings and paintings, but his unique perspective meant that there was something identifiably Marra-like in nearly all of his output, which included a large number of cartoons and drawings enhanced by captions, speech-bubbles or other text. There was also always a sense that he wanted to break down boundaries between different art forms. He noted that wherever painters are working – whether they are artists or painters and decorators – there is usually music too, coming out of a wee radio or a big blaster. Music, as he put it on *Candy Philosophy*, is the sound of painters painting paint. Why wouldn't visual art have a powerful presence in a music studio?

In 2009 Michael wrote the foreword to *The Mearns Distilled*. In this book Andy Hall and Francis Boag presented their complementary images of Kincardineshire which, being Lewis Grassic Gibbon country, held a special significance for Michael. In a few short paragraphs he manages to combine an appreciation of what visual art tries to do (and how it sometimes fails) with a sweeping evocation of that land and seascape:

Place any two independent artists in a room together and they will produce trouble or love. I have seen both, and if those artists have a similar approach to their work, things can go from badinage to worse. I have witnessed metaphysical fights to the allegorical death over metaphorical punctuation and they have not been productive.

However, painter Francis Boag and photographer Andy Hall are two very different artists who have made the positive move of placing their work together like avuncular scientists for the common good and the result for the rest of us is beauty and joy.

I have admired their paintings and photographs individually for many years and their eyes have shared many landscapes in different ways with different people, but the skill and talent they display comes into its sharpest focus among the shores, parks and hills of the Mearns where they have both spent most of their working lives.

Kincardineshire can be harsh, it can also be beautifully mysterious, lush and occasionally heavenly. From the North Sea shore which lapped Joan Eardley's ankles, Dunnottar where I imagined I saw Hamlet tapping his feet to Scott Skinner's music, past the mesmeric red-clay furrows which laced Lewis Grassic Gibbon's literary boots, to Cairn o' Mount for a dream-like overview, Francis and Andy have made a cycle of songs from dawn matins to sunset and their endeavours combine to produce harmonious hymns to a landscape which they obviously love.

Here's to James Leslie Mitchell, chance encounters and harmony itself.[6]

At the launch of the book, which took place at the Grassic Gibbon Centre at Arbuthnott in August that year, Michael, Peggy and other members of the Marra family met Rhea, the daughter of James Leslie Mitchell (better known by his pen-name, 'Lewis Grassic Gibbon'). Rhea was then nearly eighty years old. Her father had died in 1935 when she was not quite five, and she had lived all her life in Welwyn Garden City where her parents had settled. It was a very big moment for Michael. Francis Boag, according to Nicky Marra, felt that the meeting was a squaring of the circle – Lewis Grassic Gibbon, Michael, his *Sunset Song* songs and Rhea.[7]

*

Place any two independent artists in a room together and they will produce trouble or love. I have seen both, and if those artists have a similar approach to their work, things can go from badinage to worse.

Michael and Saint Andrew
creating in Newtyle.

Portrait of Michael
by John Byrne.

LONG BEFORE TABLE CLOTHS AND GRIDIES PEOPLE HAD TO EAT FEASTS AND THAT.

SO ME WENT TO SEE MERLIN

HE WAS BRAW.

CREATURES EXISTED WHO NEVER BOUGHT MATCHES

WHEN DAYS WERE ROTTEN

Gwen WAS NICE.

A facility with words was obviously integral to Michael's songwriting craft, but his interest in language went far beyond that. Once he was back into the habit of reading he read widely and deeply – and slowly, with intense concentration, whether it was a newspaper, a novel, a poem or some other material. If somebody had taken the trouble to write a book, he thought it was incumbent on him to take the trouble to read it carefully. He preferred short fiction to long, and admired the work of Raymond Carver, Jonathan Safran Foer, Flann O'Brien, Alice Munro, Damon Runyon and Bernard MacLaverty among others. Any writer who could open a window with a fresh view on the world for him was worth reading. Andy Pelc:

> He was highly intelligent, highly articulate. He was fascinated by language, and what you could do with it creatively. If you got a word wrong, he would let you know in no uncertain terms, and probably later announce it in friendly company, suggesting that you repeat your mistake for the benefit of those assembled. Language was a key element in all he did. The Saint Andrew albums were never just Dundee things, there was as much general Scots language in them as specifically Dundee, and they sold as well in Glasgow as they did in Dundee. [8]

Inventing names, as we have seen, was a favourite occupation. He loved word games, puns and rhyming slang: a flock of Meryls (Streep/sheep), a queue in the Hamiltons (Accies/baccies) and suchlike.

His term for beans on toast was 'thousands on a raft', usually shortened to 'thousands'. A 'yink' was the next level of foul smell above 'stink', and might be further qualified by the adjective 'vicious'. Any word beginning with 'st' would be canonised: St. Andingstone, St. Eel and St. Igma, for example. The endless possibilities of words played straight into the playfulness of his personality. It came out in songs like 'Baps and Paste', in which three Dundee women insult each other's housing schemes while eating their 'packed lunch' at the berry-picking near Blairgowrie. The chorus alone is a tour de force of linguistic versatility:

> Baps and paste and coarn doag,
> peace on Earth and earth on piece,
> butcher's hough and tinkie's gochles,
> wha can tell the difference?

But words were also serious business. He wrote the libretto – as well as the music, of course – for a comic operetta, which began life as *Nan Garland*[9] and eventually, in 2004, became a Dundee Rep production with the title *If the Moon Can Be Believed*:

> He had his head down for nine months straight and in the end Peggy ordered him to go out and see people. '"Go and eat where the humans eat," she said. I was lost, in the forest, immersed in it. That's a wonderful thing though – it's the best job in the world.' [10]

Michael's interest in writing drama led him to adapt his short story 'Saint Catherine's Day', already largely written

BAPS AND PASTE

BAPS AND PASTE AND LEMON CURD
BAPS AND ROE AND TINKIES GOCHLES
MULK AND ROLLS FRESH THIS MORNIN'
STOLE FAE BROUGHTY FERRY

(1) WHA COULD BEAR TO BIDE IN BEECHIE
FOWK KEEP DONKEYS IN THE BATH
EH HAE BETTER THINGS TO DAE
THAN HOSIN' DOON A DONKEYS ERSE.
SHE HAS BETTER THINGS TO DAE
THAN HOSIN DOON A DONKEYS ERSE
WHAUR ON EARTH WOULD YOU KEEP THE COAL
IF THE CREATURE OCCUPIED THE BATH.

CHORUS: BAPS AND PASTE AND COARNED DOAG
PEACE ON EARTH AND EARTH ON PIECE
BUTCHERS HOUGH OR TINKIES GOCHLES
WHA CAN TELL THE DIFFERENCE.

(2) EH DREAM ABOOT A MOOSE IN WHITFIELD
UP TO MY EARS IN JUNKIES PISH
CORRUGATED IRON CURTAINS
SITTIN IN THE LOABY GUDDLIN' FISH.
SUCH A SCENE IS LIKE A DREAM
SKINT MEH KNEES ON A SUBMARINE.

CHORUS. BAPS + PASTE ETC.

(3) IN MID EH SAW A BIG ALSATION
FAG IN ITS MOOTH A FEW TATTOOS
BARKIN AT THE LAUNDERETTE
AND ON ITS FEET WERE POINTED SHOES

SPOKEN AN ALSATION WI' POINTED SHOES?
EH! AND IT HID BRYLCREEM ON ITS EARS
WHIT! EH THOCHT THAT WIS THE SPEECH THERAPIST
CREHIN OOT TO THE FAITHFULL.

CHORUS BAPS + PASTE ETC.
FIRST FOUR LINES OF (1)(2) and (3) SIMULTANEOUSLY

FINAL CHORUS.

© MMARRA
1994.

171

(Preceding page) Michael's handwritten lyrics for 'Baps and Paste'.

(Above) Richard Conlon (left) and Ewan Donald in Michael's play *Saint Catherine's Day*.

(Right) Flyer for Michael's operetta, *If the Moon Can Be Believed*.

as a script, for the stage. With Dundee Rep and Glasgow's Oran Mor partners in the production, the play was performed in early 2011 in Dundee and as part of *A Play, A Pie and a Pint* in Glasgow. Joyce McMillan's review was a fair appreciation of what was an extension of different yet connected parts of Michael's artistic life:

> *Saint Catherine's Day* is a slightly surreal musical comedy about a day in the life of a Daniel O'Donnell-style Irish ballad singer called Columba Carnoghan, who starts out at the St Agnes of Prague Eventide Home – where his geriatric fan-base can hardly contain their excitement at his presence – and proceeds through a disastrous radio interview, to a strange encounter with his showbiz hero, an older singer called Casey Collins. Like Brian Friel's great monologue drama *The Faith Healer*, Marra's play concerns itself with the strange borderlands between fraudulent showbiz tat, and genuine, transforming inspiration; and that tension is brilliantly captured in Richard Conlon's superb central performance as Columba, part cynical showbiz chancer, part seriously-talented man, with a wicked wit and a beautiful voice. The show also features an inspired Ewan Donald, playing every other character from Columba's ever optimistic manager to the killer queen of radio presenters, Agnes Brash; and Marra himself on keyboards, as singer, narrator, and the weary-but-brilliant voice of creative wisdom, in all its contradiction and complexity. [11]

Although *Saint Catherine's Day* and *If the Moon Can Be Believed* are not by any means the best-known of Michael's work, he felt prouder of them than of almost anything else he produced. They demonstrated his ability to create and control complex pieces of art way beyond the demands of a single song, and as such he felt that they were real and substantial achievements.

*

Despite his pre-gig nerves, Michael was a natural performer – or, at least, someone who was drawn to performance. On stage, he preferred to stay out of the limelight if his main contribution to a piece of theatre was playing the music he had written for it. But no alert director could have failed to spot the acting talent lurking in the wings during rehearsals. Over the years he had many roles, some of them cameos, some more integral to the whole piece. He took these parts seriously, however small. His friend Rod Paterson recalled:

> In the early 1990s, Michael appeared in Communicado's Christmas show *Bicycle to the Moon* in the character of a wolf, and stayed at my flat in Edinburgh, which was free during rehearsals and the show's run. Unexpectedly, I had to use the flat, and turned up one evening at the door. He took a while to answer and, when he let me in, I discovered newspapers spread on every horizontal surface – all the floors, shelves, worktops, window sills were covered. He was teaching himself to tread lightly and silently, as a wolf might. [12]

His theatre acting credits included, in 2006, a role in the National Theatre of Scotland's inaugural production *Home*, which saw ten different pieces performed in ten towns and cities across the country. Alison Peebles, who had worked with Michael at Communicado, created and directed the Aberdeen event, which was staged in an abandoned tenement at 48 Logie Place in Middlefield, repopulated by some of the characters who might once have lived there. Michael was one of a mixed cast of professional and community actors – that itself would have stirred his interest in being involved – and the role given to him was that of a fisherman whose livelihood and sense of himself have been destroyed by the overfishing and consequent decline of cod stocks. The *Daily Telegraph* described his 'deeply affecting monologue' as a 'perfect way to bring the NTS home to Aberdeen.'

He also appeared on television, in 1990, in the filmed version of John McGrath's *Border Warfare* trilogy, in which he played parts as diverse as John Balliol, Manny Shinwell and the Duke of Queensberry. He acted alongside Robert Carlyle as 'Jackie Dallas' in an episode of the series *Hamish Macbeth* in 1995, and again the following year as 'Mr Craig' in Caroline Paterson's short film *The Lucky Suit*. In 1990 he played the part of 'Alex the butcher' in *The Big Man*, the cast of which included Liam Neeson and Billy Connolly. Years later, he said of Neeson, 'He has a really noble presence in the flesh, almost kingly. I know my own limitations though – there's no way I'm leading man material. These guys are brave, standing in the middle of the stage

in front of the entire audience. I like being sat behind my piano. It props me up in case I fall over!'[13]

His unique, instantly recognisable voice – once memorably described as being like 'gravel stirred in melted chocolate'[14] – was well-suited for dramatic delivery. Another brilliantly talented musician and composer who died far too young, Martyn Bennett, recognised this when he asked Michael to be the voice on the track 'Liberation' on his final album *Grit* (2003). Although Martyn maintained that it was all an accident, as Michael happened to be on Mull at the time when he was making the recording, nevertheless he knew what he was being given to work with: Michael read an English translation of a Gaelic psalm and, by the time Martyn had finished mixing the track, was somewhat surprised to find that he sounded like a minister. 'I think that's what he was after, to tell the truth,' Michael concluded, adding that he was thinking he might become a minister.[15]

In October 2008 he took on the role of Niel Gow (1727-1807) in old age, in *Burns and Gow*, a radio drama written by Bryan Beattie and produced by Rab Noakes's company, Neon, for Radio Scotland. Robert Burns was played by Jimmy Chisholm and Pete Clark played the tunes. In the play, Gow's wife Margaret has just died, and Gow has taken up his fiddle to compose his famous 'Lament for the Death of His Second Wife'. As he reflects on his own life, he remembers the occasion twenty years earlier when Burns, now also dead, came to visit. The play pitches the puppy-like enthusiasm of Burns against the more sedate worldliness of Gow as they discuss class, revolution, work, money, poetry and music. It was set in Niel Gow's home at Inver by Dunkeld, familiar territory to Michael as the scene of family caravan holidays as well as his unhappy, long-distance dealings with Björn Ulvaeus. He had also written his song 'Niel Gow's Apprentice' for Dougie MacLean, and the song co-written with Rod Paterson, 'The Bawbee Birlin', is to another Gow tune, 'Farewell to Whisky'. The connections were historical but they were also personal.

Those connections are memorialised today in the form of a bench installed by an ancient oak tree beside the Tay where Gow is reputed to have composed many of his tunes. The bench was carved by Nigel Ross, and Michael's lines, 'I'll sit beneath the fiddle tree / with the ghost of Niel Gow next to me' were inscribed on its wavy edges by Andy McFetters. The original bench was destroyed when a branch from the oak fell on it during a storm in 2011, but was replaced in 2013. [16]

*

Michael's collection of nine short stories, *Karma Mechanics*, was published as a digital book by his old friend Mick McCluskey's Intro2 Publishing imprint in 2004. Experimental in form, with a heavy emphasis on dialogue – 'Saint Catherine's Day' and 'Stevenson Street' are effectively scripts, although especially in the latter he plays with the format for comic effect – they never reached a wide readership, but there are some powerful scenes amidst a lot of very dark humour. What follows is one of the stories, 'Joe the Horse', which was

perhaps inspired by some of his experiences of London in the 1970s. It is a wonderful example of the dictum 'less is more'. Raymond Carver would have approved.

'Go and eat where the humans eat,' she said. I was lost, in the forest, immersed in it. That's a wonderful thing though – it's the best job in the world.

(Following page) Michael's drawing 'The One Armed Fishwife's Heroine' was the cover illustration for his short story collection *Karma Mechanics*.

The One Armed Fisherf's Heroine A/P   Michael Mana '96

Joe the Horse

One of my workmates had just shown me how to take a tenner from an unopened wage packet. He used a pencil in the corner with the money showing and said that if you were quick enough you could get away with it. I think he was using me for a test pilot or at least trying to. I wasn't for it and instantly remembered that hellish feeling of standing outside the Headmaster's door, waiting. This occupied my thoughts all the way from Oval Station to Clapham Common.

Once back in the flat I ran a bath as it was a Friday evening. I had two days off and I wasn't skint. I could go out for a pint later and meanwhile I could lie in the bath with the Runyon Omnibus. As I smoked in the soapy water I read about the open air which is, as you know, full of policemen, then realised that the water was getting cold. I had a decadent habit on a Friday of leaving the heater on so that I could have two baths.

A certain amount of water was drained away and then I added the hot stuff into a generous smearing of Industrial Bubble Bath.

I built a huge mound of bubbles and dug a tunnel into them so that I could strike a match and watch the effect which was that I felt not in a dingy Clapham bathroom.

I returned to the Omnibus and was reading about Harry the Horse and Little Isadore betting on a sure thing in the fifth at Schenectady when I realised that the water was getting cold again and that there was no audible sign of my flatmate Joe.

Deciding to go for a third bath I wondered if Joe had maybe nipped in to the bookies to bet on a sure thing in the fifth at Worcester. A hot horse, that being a horse that cannot possibly lose a race unless it falls down dead and while Joe's hot horses often lose without falling down dead, this doesn't stop Joe from coming up with others.

I ran the third bath and carried on reading until I heard his key in the lock of the front door and then the clump clump of boots on a dingy London staircase, that clump which made everybody sound like Christie the murderer. He didn't even knock on the door, straight in and over to the toilet.

'Well Joe!' I said.

'Aye!' said Joe.

I noticed that he pished straight into the water with no attempt to quieten it on the sides so I thought he'd definitely been to the bookies and was not apparently rejoicing in the Friday feel.

'I thought we might go for a pint later Joe, what do you think?'

'I'm not in the mood.'

'Oh come on Joe it's Friday.'

'Nah!'

I could see him in some horrible betting shop in Victoria, they're always horrible like Social Security offices. I could see him tearing up the receipt and behind him I could see a man spraying the shop from a tank on his back which bore the legend MISERY.

'We could get a couple of women, a wee dance or that.'

'Nah!'

He put the lid down and had a seat.

'It's a Friday Joe, beer, lassies, music.'

'Nah!'

'The Bolton girls!' I made sure he saw my seriously raised eyebrows.

Moan.

'They're very good dancers.'

'Nah!'

'Come on Joe, it's Friday. I'll get your beer if you're skint.'

'I'm not skint.'

'Have you been to the bookies?'

'Aye.'

'How much did you lose?'

'I didn't lose.'

'Well what?'

'I won three hundred quid!'

'What, and lost it again?'

'No!'

He took a thick wad of notes from his inside pocket, squinting at it through the fag smoke.

'…cksake Joe. Heathrow. The Tay Bridge Bar!'

'Nah!'

This was becoming infuriating.

'Well Joe, I'll spend my miserable wages myself. Imagine working all week for a pish scene like this on a Friday.'

'I'm just no in the mood.'

'Right!'

Silence.

Eventually he took a deep smoke and spoke through the fumes.

'I put twenty quid on a known tail biter.'

'I don't know what that means Joe.'

'It means it comes in second every time, so it's worth an each way shot.'

'An unsure thing. And?'

'I put it on the nose and it came up.'

'Therefore you're depressed, I understand.'

'You don't understand.'

'You're right there Joe.'

SILENCE.

'I had my fucking wages in my pocket.'

Notes

1   Interview with Andy Pelc, 13th April 2017.

2   Interview with Frank McConnell,
       11th January 2017.

3   This was not so different from his embracing
       new musical technology. Long before this he
       had installed an electronic notator in his home
       studio, so that as he played the keyboard the
       notes appeared on a stave. If Mozart had had
       one, he joked, the whole of musical history
       would be different.

4   Interview with Andy Pelc, 13th April 2017.

5   Ibid.

6   Francis Boag and Andy Hall,
       The Mearns Distilled (2009).

7   Email from Nicky Marra, 12th May 2017.
       Rhea Martin died in June, 2014.

8   Interview with Andy Pelc, 13th April 2017.

9   See below, p.193.

10   Chitra Ramaswamy, 'Guilty secrets from the
       nation's gravelly voice', *Scotsman*, 21st May 2006.

11   *The Scotsman*, 30th March 2011.

12   Email, 21st May 2017.

13   *Courier & Advertiser*, 11th October 2008.

14   Sheena Wellington mentioned this when she
       gave the laureation address on the occasion of
       Michael being awarded an honorary doctorate
       by the University of Dundee in 2007.

15   BBC Artworks documentary, *Grit*,
       first broadcast 7th December 2003.

16   See below, p.272.

Kitchen conversation

No.6

Michael: Still here.

James: It would seem so. Sorry, was that a question?

M: More an observation. St. Ill Here, the patron saint of stubborn health complaints. Although I might be confusing him with St. Ubborn.

J: I was going to ask you about an event you did at Stirling Castle but now I think you'll just take the piss.

M: Try me.

J: You played there in 2003 ahead of Van Morrison. Up on the esplanade. That must have been a big deal. And I was wondering how that felt?

M: I didn't have time to think about it. I was on at 7.30 and then I had another gig in Edinburgh at 9.15. So you can imagine I wasn't in a very contemplative mood, I just had to do my set and leave. I supported Van Morrison again, in Perth, a couple of years later. I've always loved his music, from *Astral Weeks* on. He's a great example of what you can do with a guitar and three chords. Sometimes simplicity is what is called for. My problem was I tried to be too clever.

J: It hasn't stopped people covering your songs. There's a long list – Barbara Dickson, Rab Noakes, Annie Grace, Leo Sayer, Fairport Convention, Hue and Cry, Billy Connolly, Wendy Wetherby, Frankie Miller, Kiki Dee – allegedly, although I can't track that one down – June Tabor, Sylvia Rae Tracey, Tom Mitchell, Loudon Wainwright, Alan Gorrie, Colcannon.

M: Colcannon?

J: That's a recent one. Colorado-based traditional Irish band.

M: Yes, I know. But I didn't know they had done one of mine. Which one?

J: 'Botanic Endgame'. It's great. Very Irish. Did you ever tour in Ireland?

M: I would have liked to. Peg and I went there on holiday a lot. I played in Cork and I would happily have done an Irish tour but it never came about.

J: That was important, wasn't it, the family links back to Ireland?

M: Maybe that was how I tuned into it initially, through that inheritance, but there was more than that to my affection for Ireland. We used to go over when I was wee. Ireland was a very different place from Scotland then. There was none of that reserve, that caution that we are weighed down with here. People just spoke what they thought and nobody accused them of being stupid. You see it in the literature – James Joyce, Samuel Beckett, Flann O'Brien. There's an appreciation of the absurd, a welcoming of it, that just upsets a lot of Scottish people. It meets this hard wall of common sense here and there's no way through.

J: Do you think that's a cultural thing, a Calvinist hangover maybe?

M: Well, you should know. That is not a pleasant concept – ministers coming out of the walls at you. But that stuff seeps. I've met plenty of Catholic Calvinists, some atheist ones too. In Ireland people don't even think the absurd *is* absurd.

J: When I first read Flann O' Brien, in my teens, I thought he must be a signed-up member of the Surrealist movement. I didn't realise he wasn't really trying to be surreal.

M: Do you know he died on April Fool's Day, 1966? I was there. Not actually *there*, that really would have been strange, but we were on a visit to relatives in Dublin.

J: Dundee isn't entirely free of absurdity.

M: This is true. Well, there were a lot of Irish folk who settled in Dundee. Maybe that stuff seeps too. St. Uff, the patron saint of integration. That kind of movement enriches the communal mental soup. Hmm. Tinned mental soup. Probably a good cure for Calvinist hangovers. A can of mind and a tin of think so. Don't mind me, I am just indulging in ladle speculation.

Collaborator

The Taakeraperter haes a van
valves and tubes and a watterin can,
whiles he drehvs in the poorin ren
doon to the Pitterthegither again,
the Pitterthegither haes a shed
tools that bide whar they've ayeways
  behd,
they bunce thur haeds and mak thur
  plans
for a commonwealth o' Elvis fans

'A Secret Commonwealth o' Elvis fans'

For all that Michael disliked sharing his core work of writing songs or music with anybody else, those who collaborated with him in other ways found it a hugely positive experience: he was hardworking and a perfectionist, but also considerate, respectful of the ideas of others, and often the one person in the room who could spot what was going wrong or identify whatever was required to make something right. People came away from working with Michael feeling that they had learned much without being taught anything. He opened up possibilities that they hadn't realised *were* possibilities. There are countless examples of these – almost always successful – collaborations. This chapter describes just a handful of them.

In May 1989 Rab Noakes was appointed Head of Entertainment at BBC Radio Scotland in Glasgow, a job which gave him responsibility for every musical show and genre on the station except jazz and classical. He started work in July, and almost immediately also landed the job of musical director for a new television series, *Your Cheatin' Heart*, commissioned from playwright John Byrne in the wake of his highly acclaimed, BAFTA-winning 1987 series *Tutti Frutti*.

Rab Noakes:

> As the production unfolded, we real-ised that we weren't going to use records as the soundtrack, all the songs for the show were going to be specially recorded with the actors as the singers. It was going to be a massive job, and hugely time-consuming, so I asked if I could have someone to work with me on it, and the series producers said yes. Michael was who I had in mind, and as it turned out he had a lull in his own projects so he agreed. So that's how we wound up doing *Your Cheatin' Heart* together. We had some marvellous times, but it was tough for Michael as well. He said that being in the BBC building felt like being in a post office. Producers are always on about budgets and it was no different on this occasion, but we were deliver-ing thirty-eight backing tracks and twenty-six pieces of finished music for the price of one Tears for Fears backing track... Anyway, Michael handled most of the on-location stuff, I handled the admin, and we shared the recording sessions between us. [1]

Michael spent the best part of a year working on *Your Cheatin' Heart* as musi-cal co-director, and said it almost killed him. He shared an office with John Byrne – 'which is all right if you're going to share with anybody' – but his allergic reaction to institutions kicked in, causing stress and weariness alleviated by moments of real magic. Rab Noakes remembers coming late to the studio one day and finding Michael and Guy Mitchell, the American 1950s pop star who played Jim Bob O'May in the series, pumped up with excitement because Michael had just coached Guy to harmonise with himself on 'It Keeps Right On A-Hurtin'. Mitchell was from an era where recording yourself singing harmony parts was not done, and he was delighted with the result – as indeed was Michael for having facilitated it.

*

Collaboration sometimes grew from what at first sight looked like confrontation. On another occasion, unrelated to *Your Cheatin' Heart*, Michael showed Rab a disturbing letter he had received from an anonymous Fifer who objected to his song 'I Don't Like Methil'. Michael wasn't sure how to respond to this individual, who signed off as 'Outraged' and whom he seemed to have greatly upset. Rab however recognised the handwriting as that of his old Great Fife Road Show compadre John Watt, composer of, among other immortal songs, 'The Kelty Clippie' and 'Fife's Got Everything'. 'He's winding you up,' was Rab's considered opinion, and indeed not long afterwards John penned his riposte, 'I Don't Like Dundee'. As Michael pointed out, he had really been defending his home city from metropolitan sniping: Methil was a soft target, selected in part because it received the same treatment. Thereafter the two corresponded and met in a spirit of friendly rivalry and sometimes shared a platform, performing the two songs back-to-back to great appreciation.

*

Another form of collaboration was as a producer of other musicians' work. Michael had an ear for quality and a quiet yet determined way of bringing out the best in individual and collective performances. For the distinguished piper and bagpipe maker, Hamish Moore, Michael's role as producer was intimately bound up with his wider personality:

> Dick Lee and I recorded *Farewell to Decorum* in 1993. Here is what Michael wrote on the sleeve notes:
>
> > A good producer always heats the pot first, then into the jungle with Hamish and Dick, Specky Knobbage and a thousand switches, hundreds of k-bytes and old hieroglyphics, battling monsters and mounted polis to rescue the pipes from the warlords and hurl the blues at the sun and moon.
> >
> > These sessions were precious. Sometimes I left my shoes at the door. The players all excelled in skill and spirit and the music was an adventure. This is as it should be, and long may these men hurl.
>
> This sums it up really. It was an extraordinary experience.
>
> Michael and I stayed in Rod Paterson's flat in the High Street during the two (separate) weeks of recording sessions.

Michael was happy being called either 'Michael' or 'Mick' but *not* 'Mike'!

We woke every morning and then went to a particular wee cafe in the High Street for breakfast; always the same cafe, always the same fry-up. Michael always stopped at the same newspaper seller and bought a *Scotsman* and a *Glasgow Herald*. He would scan through one as we ate our breakfast and the other as we drank our coffee. Then a taxi for Granton to Pete Haig's studio. Pete was delightfully renamed 'Specky Knobbage' in the sleeve notes because he wore glasses and his desk had a thousand knobs.

We laughed a lot.

Mick took his baffies to the studio and dug himself into a comfy studio couch for each day's recording.

The work was long and hard and he, with humour and good nature, made sure we got it right.

As producer he kept his ears (and eyes) on us, the arrangements, the tuning and the content, but also made a few invaluable contributions himself, the most notable being the singing of the last verse of Hamish Henderson's 'Freedom Come All Ye'. His interpretation was magnificent and he did it in one take. When he made his way back up from the basement recording room to the control centre, we all congratulated him on the take. Mick stunned us by casually saying, 'Aye, it was simple, lads, I dropped my draars tae sing it.'

Michael's take is a vital part of the last track on the album, '12.12.92 –

A March for Democracy' which is a collage of sounds of the great march of that day demanding a Parliament for Scotland. We needed a dog barking on the track and with a glint in his eye Mick decided we should sample Brian Wilson's dog from *Pet Sounds*; and we did, and laughed!

At the end of each working day we immediately found a pleasing and easy routine, arriving for three pints in Bert's Bar in Stockbridge, a bus up town, a fish supper in the Grassmarket, and back to the flat.

Once back in the flat I would be thinking about bed after a wee cup of tea while Mick got to work, sitting on the floor he would roll a large cigarette, put the TV on with the sound off, and start singing, humming, writing.

One morning when we met for breakfast he handed me an envelope with some of his night time scribblings on it. This I still have as a treasured possession and on it was the embryonic version of 'Schenectady Calling Peerie Willie Johnson'.

These times shared with Michael were precious for me and in amongst all the memories of the studio, the fish suppers, witnessing the making of what was to become one of his best songs, the laughing and the baffies, the most wonderful experiences were just walking down the street with him; taking a dander with him, as he did with St. Mungo, and listening to his extraordinary observations on absolutely everything he saw. He was unique. [2]

*

Frank McConnell's recollections of working with Michael have pleasing echoes of Hamish's. Very rarely, when rehearsing or touring together, did Frank and Michael expose their personal emotions, but this was not because they did not enjoy sharing one another's company. On the contrary, for Frank those days of being in a van with Michael, listening to and learning from him, were some of the most enjoyable of his life.

How did this man, for whom school was such a bad experience, know so much? One of the few things he seemed to have absolutely no knowledge of was cooking and nutrition. He was a man of habit when it came to food. He always ate his breakfast proportionately: the various elements of the cooked breakfast would be reduced at the same pace so that before the plate was finally cleared it had proportional amounts of tomato, egg, bacon, black pudding and sausage. I think that's an analogy for his songwriting craft – editing and narrowing the various parts down until what was left was the finished item.

'Less is more' applied to Michael in many ways including his fashion sense. He had a particular pair of sandals which he wore on tour all one summer so that by the end his feet bore a tan and white pattern corresponding to that of the sandals. Twenty years later on the second tour of *A Wee Home From Home* he was wearing the same sandals, and the same blue jacket as well. [3]

186

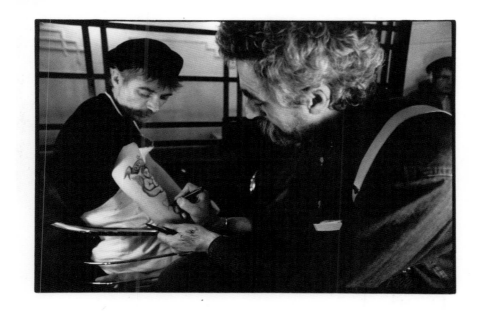

(Left) Michael with Guy Mitchell and (below) being decorated by John Byrne during the making of Your Cheatin' Heart.

187

(Preceding pages) Michael
recording 'Liberation' with
Martyn Bennett for
Martyn's album *Grit*.

(Above) Michael with
long-term collaborator
Frank McConnell.

Eilidh Mackenzie first met Michael in 1992 at Balnain House in Inverness, when she was working for the National Gaelic Arts Project. Her colleague Blair Douglas, a good friend of Michael, had suggested inviting him to a weekend event for aspiring Gaelic songwriters, as an encourager and facilitator. Eilidh recalled him 'getting a little frustrated at our timidness and then perhaps even a little excited as he built up a song (with linguistic help from Kenna Campbell, I think) in a language he did not understand – he seemed flushed with a desperate effort.'[4]

The following year, Eilidh and her husband Ken Barker moved to Dundee, settling initially in Broughty Ferry. Eilidh joined a writing group at the University, where she became friendly with another member of the group, an elderly woman also from the Ferry who, having accepted a lift home, insisted that Eilidh come in for a cup of tea. The conversation quickly moved to music. The woman had a cassette tape recorder and was keen to play Eilidh 'the best local music'. It was Michael's *Gaels Blue*. 'Never before or since has listening to an album affected me as much as that. She gave it to me for a borrow and that was that. This was the man I had briefly met in Balnain House. And of course once I had heard him live I began to understand the real craftsmanship of his work.'

In 1996, when Eilidh and two of her sisters, Gillie and Fiona (who together with her form the group Mackenzie), were looking for someone to produce their album *Camhanach* for the Macmeanmna label, she suggested Michael as a possible producer, and to her delight he agreed. During the recording process over the next year the Mackenzie sisters spent a fair bit of time with him, as well as with his brother, Chris, and another Dundee music stalwart, bass player Ged Grimes (of Danny Wilson, Deacon Blue, Simple Minds). 'My most vivid memory of this process was Michael's need to get inside the texts and understand the songs. He wasn't content with an approximate translation – he went off at tangents about the meaning and the sound. Sometimes he seemed really distant and other times the intensity was quite profound. The atmosphere while recording was lovely. It felt like we were all living in a very supported place. And his own mother was very ill during this time; it must have been a particularly difficult time for Michael and for Chris.' (Margaret Comerford Marra, née Reilly, died on 25th April 1997.)

Over the next couple of years Mackenzie promoted their album at a few gigs including a home trip to Lewis. Michael, Chris and Ged went with them as their band and then, in 2000, Eilidh joined Alice Marra and Maggie Fenwick on backing vocals for 'All To Please Macushla' on *Posted Sober*.

In 2009 Eilidh asked Michael to narrate on her album of Gaelic songs written round the Ann Patchett novel *Bel Canto*, and to sing and play piano on the song 'You Misunderstand Me':

> He was extremely encouraging to everyone involved and again intent on getting his interpretation of the song

and the character to the point where he was satisfied. There was a wee lane outside the studio in Glasgow and I remember fresh-air break times out there and his intensity when he asked about the song's meaning and then as I began to tell him he asked me to not tell him after all as he preferred to imagine his character and play it that way. So Michael worked in his own wee world, in a way – but I imagine it was a very detailed, particular world.

'If I had to sum Michael up,' Eilidh concluded, 'it would be with these words – edgy, intense, kind, encouraging, master of minutiae.'[5]

*

In 1994, the Dundee Rep Women's Singing Group was established by Anna Newell. It is far better known as Loadsaweeminsingin, a name which came out of an exchange between Anna and Michael when he met her as she was putting up a poster advertising the group. She explained that she needed a title for the project and that it involved loads of women singing: Michael said he thought *that* should be the title. Formed from a powerful and passionate band of women from all over the city, the group was directed by Anna for ten years before she handed the reins on to Sarah Harrop. In January 2015 the group came under the new direction of Alice Marra. Despite evolution over more than twenty years it still has members from its first incarnation. Loadsaweeminsingin, from its very name to its great energy and deep commitment

to local communities, was exactly the kind of outfit Michael enjoyed working with. Anna Newell's memory was of a 'diminutive, deeply unassuming man from Lochee' who was top of the wish-list when they were awarded a grant to commission new works from songwriters. The song he wrote for them was 'Muggie Sha''. One of the other commissioned writers was Sheena Wellington. 'He was nervous before they sang it,' she recalled. 'We were all nervous, but he was almost wringing his hands worrying about whether he'd got it right, if he should have changed this bit or that line. I said, "Michael, do they like it?" "They *say* they like it," he said. But that song is a classic. And it's a remarkable song because not only is it funny but it also shows Michael's knowledge of human nature, and his empathy for these women who were the cast-oots of society.'[6]

This is how Michael introduced it during a solo gig at The Shed in Hovingham, North Yorkshire in 2010:

> I have a pal in Dundee, a fellow called Jock, and Jock drinks in a place called the Polepark Bar, but no Dundonian calls it that. We call it Bissells. And Jock was in there one night having a pint, and the man who runs the pub came up the stair from the cellar, and he had in his hand a sheaf of papers, fifteen sheets of paper, I've got photocopies of them at home. The best way to describe these sheets is that they were 'Unwanted' posters. There was fifteen people involved, fourteen women and one man, and each sheet had two photographs, one from the front, and one

192

from the side, and down the side of each sheet a very detailed description, including all injuries and disfigurements, and at the bottom of the sheet was the autograph of the Chief Constable of Dundee. And these fourteen magnificent women and one magnificent man were barred from every single pub in Dundee. That's a lot of pubs. And, like yourselves, I was overwhelmed with admiration. That's a lot of pubs to be barred from. I wanted to celebrate, particularly, these women, these fourteen fabulous women. And my first idea was to make great big screen prints of them, you know like Andy Warhol type of prints, and fill the gallery. But Jock pointed out that one of the women had the same surname as himself, and although she wasn't his grandmother she very easily could have been. I understood. Now there's a wonderful choir in Dundee, a women's choir, fifty-strong, they're called Loadsaweeminsingin, they're a great choir, if you ever get the chance to hear them, go along, they're great. And occasionally I write for them. I was trying to make something for them but I couldn't find a way in, and then I attended a wake for my uncle Willie, and at the wake my auntie Agnes was telling a story, and she said, 'There was three of us there, there was me, Kathleen and Muggie Sha'.' So I said, 'Who was that other woman?' And my auntie Kathleen said, 'Dinnae tell him, Agnes, he'll write a sang and he'll call it "Muggie Sha"'.' I said, 'Thank you very much,

Auntie Kathleen.' And that night I thought, it's a very singable name. If Muggie Sha' was born in Hovingham her name would be Margaret Shaw. You wouldn't rush to get your pen to write a song, would you? But Muggie Sha', I thought, that's pretty good, so I made a composite character out of these fourteen women and I called her Muggie Sha'. Now this song is in the full-strength language of Dundee, so I will hopefully meet you at the end.

This was a collaboration not only with the choir, but also with his aunties and with the long-dead heroes of those police mugshots.[7]

Anna Newell later described a more substantial interaction between Michael and Loadsaweeminsingin, in 2004:

When we at the Rep cooked up the idea of a Gilbert and Sullivan-style operetta for forty women in Dundee, there was only one man for the job. We embarked on the most amazing adventure which resulted in a gorgeous, ridiculous, deeply moving and extraordinarily political piece of nonsense music theatre, *If the Moon Can Be Believed*, with this amazing, gorgeous, ridiculous, deeply moving and extraordinarily political man. I have rarely worked with anyone so extraordinarily talented or so humble....

Before the first night, he made individual cards for each of the nearly thirty-strong cast with personal messages of gratitude and support. I'll bet all of the women still have those cards, as I do. We all loved him so very deeply and still miss him so very much. [8]

Michael wanted a challenge beyond the confines of the three-minute song or a theatre producer's requirements. He had long admired the scope of musicals and opera, from *Guys and Dolls* through Gilbert and Sullivan to Puccini. 'I'm pitting myself against those standards,' he told journalist Kenny Farquharson. 'I want it to be solid.' The storyline came from Irish writer Michael Duke, a former associate director at Dundee Rep, but it was a fantasy tailor-made for Michael Marra, as it plugged directly into his aversion to officialdom and his suspicion of authority and rules:

'It's about a group of truants – plunkers as we call them in Dundee – who, as they get older, just keep it up. They hide in the forest and keep it going into adulthood. And they start their own society.

'People come and join them. Some of them go out to work in the normal world, pretending to be members of society but only to get funds to keep their own society going. There are complications because the police come looking for one of them, but basically their society prevails because of how they conduct it.'

The working title [*Nan Garland*] was eventually superseded by *If the Moon Can Be Believed*: 'I've never met a woman called Nan that I didn't like. And it's also a name that women are not given these days, and I like that.' [9]

The forest commune goes by the name of Absentia, and Michael clearly had fun elaborating on its philosophy with the free spirit of Loadsaweeminsingin in mind:

In Absentia we work away among the
    everyday
But we are heavily disguised
There in secret we protect the interest
    of our sisters

In Absentia we merge and interact
    with fellow humans
Who behave like they're machines
So we join the chorus of complaint and
    petty nonsense

In some respects, the commune reflects Michael's own ideas:

Our educational programme is
    perceived to be the best
Learning all we need to know,
    we disregard the rest

He was enthusiastic about exploring the idea of an independent commonwealth of women. It chimed with his respect for the role of women in Dundee's history – 'Dundee women have always been two or three steps ahead of Simone de Beauvoir,' he used to joke – and also with his wider appreciation of the female sex. Whenever he sang Robert Burns's 'Green Grow the Rashes' he introduced it by praising Burns's courage for asserting, in the final verse and the final decade of the 18th century, that God was a woman. [10]

In 2009, Michael was able link his interest in the history of radical women and human rights to working with another choral event when he was commissioned to compose a piece for 'Choired for Sound – the Big Sing', part of Dundee's Fest 'n' Furious music festival. His composition, 'The Wrights of Man', told the story of Fanny Wright (1795-1852), the Dundee-born free-thinker, early feminist and socialist, and her sister Camilla. The Wrights emigrated to the United States and set up an egalitarian community which gave sanctuary to former slaves, some of whom Fanny bought in order to emancipate them. This daring experiment took place in the 1820s and 1830s and was a direct challenge to prevailing conditions in pre-abolition America. Michael's piece was the finale of the main Fest'n'Furious concert on 3rd October 2009, and involved more than 150 singers from several choirs.

*

In 2005, at Celtic Connections, his powerful yet subtle speaking voice was again in demand. He was the narrator of Robert W. Service's poem 'The Cremation of Sam McGee' in Edmonton-born cellist Christine Hanson's six-part suite of the same name, scored for eight instruments. The concert was enthusiastically received and in September that year the composition was recorded over four days in Ardgour on the western shore of Loch Linnhe. The band included Kevin Murray (guitar and mandolin) and Aidan O'Rourke (fiddle), both of whom had of course been in a studio with Michael on previous occasions. Michael's notes for the CD were typically generous:

Christine emerged triumphant from a very long fistfight sporting a Pinteresque keeker applied in instalments during her formative years.

She then decided to build a cathedral and could have used film, paint or the printed word, but she chose music and went off with Sam McGee to fight amongst the Northern Lights. She rose up twinkling from that scrap and her work is sublime. These delights are the first of many from a great artist.

*

One of the longest and most fruitful collaborations in Michael's career was with Saint Andrew. Andy Pelc studied at Duncan of Jordanstone College of Art, graduating in the late 1970s. As a student in Dundee he had seen Skeets Boliver playing at Laings but didn't know any of the band members until he met Stewart Ivins around 1979. Andy was housesitting for somebody in Garland Place and Stewart came around one afternoon, bringing his pals Eddie Boyle and Michael with him.

The flat was a really bohemian-type place – expensive, unusual visually, a Biba world of peacock feathers and stuff – and I'd been making bread that morning, so I answered the door wearing a pinny, which Michael continued to remind me of for years after that. I am pretty sure he did not know what to make of me at first, but he told me later he thought I was seriously gay. He was quite quiet. I knew who he was. He was being cool, so I was cool as well. I thought, I'll play him at the same game. I shoved on *Blue* by Joni Mitchell, he perked up at that, he was quite impressed, and he did have a piece of my bread.

There was some kind of anniversary party for Groucho's Record Store and Breeks Brodie got Stewart Ivins to organise a kind of Bolivers reunion for it. Breeks says to me, 'You sing a bit, don't you?' 'Well,' I says, 'I've been known to shout.' Anyway, I had a word with Stewart and I was allowed to go up and do three songs with the reformed Bolivers. Then I started to work more regularly with Stewart, Eddie Marra and Gus Foy. That was really the start of the Woollen Mill. So it was round about that time that I started to meet Mick more often. [11]

Andy developed the persona of Saint Andrew, a Dundonian who, having spent the 1970s touring the USA at the head of a band called the Cosmic Kilties, was made homesick on seeing the Corries playing in Tampa, Florida, and came back to Dundee 'to get himself some mince'n'tatties'. Their act's combination of raw musical energy and bizarre humour led to Saint Andrew and the Woollen Mill being in great demand in and around Dundee in the 1980s: a band which served up a head-on collision between Vegas schmaltz and Celtic kitsch fuelled by a tank of rock'n'roll.

Although Michael did play with the Woollen Mill his relationship with Andy was more one-to-one and focused on song-writing and studio work. This was a rare exception to Michael's general preference for working on songs alone. Andy Pelc:

I remember saying to him once, 'Yes, Michael, we all know you don't *do* the collaborative process,' but in fact the work we produced on *The Word On The Pavey* and *Hubris*, that came about through bouncing ideas off each other. My role wasn't just singing the songs. We worked on the ideas together, and the more we collaborated, the stuff I would suggest lyrically or structurally, they were taken on board by Michael. The glossary of terms that accompanies the *Pavey* CD, for example: Michael would say something, I would bounce off that and inject an additional level of bontality [12] into the process. I considered myself to be an improver *if* the opportunity arose. The basic grooves, the melody, the crafting of a tune, that was Michael. He would give me a groove, a starting-point, and we'd be sitting in the room and I would rant off at different tangents. We would keep wee bits and review them: that works, that disnae, can we make that simpler, and so on. Even going back to the *Stagecoach* show, which for me was just the best game of Cowboys and Indians imaginable, when we were writing the dialogue for that all the cast were contributing. The songs were more Michael's, and in fact there was a big difference between *Stagecoach* 1 and *Stagecoach* 2, a lot of the songs changed to being Michael's original compositions.

There was a part of Mick's brain – a small part, not the whole thing – that

Saint Andrew in full regalia.

related to one small part of my brain, and the rest of our brains probably had nothing in common. We had crazy, off-the-wall, getting-a-bee-in-your-bonnet conversations that we couldn't have had with anybody else. It's one of the things I miss most about not having him around. We could go anywhere in these conversations, which might come to nothing or might turn into an idea for an album. We loved language, we loved talking about stuff, we loved the irony of things, we got angry about a lot of things, but that was where the creativity came from.

Michael was a pretty astute kind of guy, and I always took it as a great compliment when he would go with one of my suggestions. He wouldn't do it just to please me, he would do it because he liked it and could see it working. But I was never under any illusion that when Michael worked with me, I was a kind of vehicle for him to bring out stuff that maybe he couldn't risk his own artistic integrity on. The Saint Andrew thing was a nice wee vehicle. But then again, every single track on these two albums, they're quality numbers, the lyrics are poetry and of course they are underpinned by some fantastic grooves and great tunes, and lovely playing.

So yes, we would bounce stuff off each other to make the material, but when it came to actual performance, live gigs, the Dundee Rep shows and so on, there was never any on-stage banter between us then. Come showtime all Michael wanted to do was stay in the background, do what he had to do, play the piano and so on. It always heartened me greatly when I would come out with something on stage and look over and he would be creased up over the piano. But that kind of thing was never planned, it just happened.

One time Michael was interviewed for radio down at the Printmakers' Workshop in the Seagate, I can't remember the exact circumstances, it might have been a show of his own artwork, but I met him afterwards and he was raging, because just before the interview started, he was miked up and ready to go and the interviewer says, 'Be funny!' We used to use that as a kind of currency after that, 'Now remember – be funny!' As if you can just order that up. And anyway, Michael always prepared very meticulously. He was extremely skilful at delivering a show. He didn't need someone telling him how to do it. [13]

The first Saint Andrew CD, *The Word on the Pavey*, came out in 1999 on Michael's Mink label. Its twelve tracks include gems like 'It's Rare T' Be Alehv', 'Ananingina-neana', 'This World is Phuhl o' a Number o' Things', 'Dinna Ast Me (Eh Dinna Ken)' and 'Woodwork Woodwork'. Far from being a collection of novelty songs, as some might mistakenly think, the album is a rich mixture of excellent musicianship, perfectly pitched vocals, fine tunes, and lyrics in 'the full-strength language of Dundee' with plenty of excursions to other parts of the country and indeed across the Atlantic. Word about *The Word* spread rapidly until only one box of the first pressing of CDs remained unsold. At this point Andy and Michael fell out.

Neither Andy nor anyone else can now remember what they fell out about, except that it wasn't money. It would have been something insignificant, no doubt, since – in Andy's words – the two of them habitually behaved 'like an auld married couple', but it didn't feel like it at the time. According to Andy, Michael got himself drunk, took the box of CDs down the disused railway track at Newtyle, birled about in order to lose his bearings, dug a hole and buried the CDs in it. He was, apparently, determined that they should be permanently lost to posterity. However, this version doesn't quite accord with that of Matthew Marra, as some time later Michael was able to draw a map accurate enough for Matthew to go and retrieve them. Thereafter, if Peggy was selling CDs at gigs she sometimes came across a survivor from this batch and had to give it a good dicht to get the mud off it.

Andy is the first to admit that his relationship with Michael was not one that left much space for anybody else, and that this could make things extremely uncomfortable for a third party. Chris Marra opted out of working on the next Saint Andrew CD for that reason: 'If there were three in the room, Michael and Andy would feel that they were entitled to behave as badly as they possibly could, and you were the referee. And it was total and constant. With *Word on the Pavey* Allan McGlone managed it by having them in the studio at different times. If Michael and Andy were in there together they would just wind each other up. They made *Hubris* in Michael's studio in Newtyle, so that would have been three of us in that wee room. No.'[14]

There are just six tracks on *Hubris*, which came out in December 2009. It has a rawer, rougher feel to it than *The Word on the Pavey*, and is several degrees further up the anarchy scale in terms of subject matter and language. It does contain, in 'Cattle-baistquine', probably the world's finest ever serenade to an Angus farming lass; a splendidly philosophical mantra based on the game of shinty in 'Beh Shinty Live Beh Shinty Deh'; and the truly insane 'Secret Commonwealth o' Elvis Fans' which manages to link Elvis Presley to the Reverend Robert Kirk who was allegedly abducted by fairies in the 1690s. *Hubris* – which was originally to be called *Ratify My Hubris* – is the kind of record that you marvel at while being quite glad you weren't inside the heads of the folk who put it together.

*

In 2008 Michael was invited by Jan Hannah, artist and education worker at HMP Noranside in Angus, to work with long-term prisoners on a songwriting project. Every week for a year Michael visited the prison and encouraged a group of men to express themselves through song. He took their material home to his studio and with the help of the Zipped Baffy house band (Kevin Murray, Chris Marra and Alice Marra) recorded eleven of the songs on a CD called *Numbers*. Iain Anderson featured it as the album of the week on his BBC Radio Scotland show but for legal and bureaucratic reasons the CD could not be produced for sale.

A typically sensitive and generous note from Michael on the CD cover thanked 'all the classmates whose songs are not included as every piece of work affected the entire process. Keep writing.' Three of the men provided vocals for their own songs, Michael sang the others, one of which, 'Eternity Has Just Begun', was his own:

> A good joke in jail is a priceless thing
> Very rarely comes along
> Like a lick of paint on a rusty soul
> Relief from topic number one
> If I try to see the funny side of
>   anything I've done
>
> There may be a smile but the smile is
>   a lie
> Nine out of ten there's a tear in the eye
>
> When you hold a photograph
> The way you once held a gun
> That's when you know that
> Eternity has just begun
>
> The truth in the big house is seldom
>   heard
> Mostly scratched upon the wall
> Same old testament of blood and Jake
> It's plain enough though it's only a
>   scrawl
> If I made a mark here, recording my
>   fall
>
> I'd cry like a baby in the darkest
>   night
> Make that lonesome swim for the light
>
> When you hold a photograph
> The way you once held a gun

> That's when you know that
> Eternity has just begun

*

One of Michael's longest-lasting collaborative relationships was with the poet and playwright Liz Lochhead. 1987 saw the first (Communicado) production of her play *Mary Queen of Scots Got Her Head Chopped Off*. On the last night of what had been a triumphant tour, in the autumn of that year, Liz and her husband Tom held a post-show party in their Glasgow flat. Liz remembers that, as one theatrical family dissolved, she heard of another about to form and a name that would come to mean a lot to her. She and Tom were talking to dancer Frank McConnell, who had played Riccio in the play and had also been the production's movement coach, and to Gerry Mulgrew, the director. Frank and Gerry were planning to have the next day, Sunday, off to get rid of their hangovers and then, on the Monday morning, were going to be joined by one Michael Marra. Mulgrew would be directing and helping the other two to devise a show mainly of dance and music – 'but a story too!' – to be performed by McConnell and Marra.

Liz's husband Tom, who had been a student in Dundee and knew of Skeets Boliver and Michael's music from those days, was greatly impressed that Gerry and Frank had managed to attract such a collaborator. What Liz remembers being impressed by (and half-terrified for them, too) was that in less than forty-eight hours they would be going into that empty rehearsal space with a vague theme but absolutely no script and not even a firm title.

The show, of course, became *A Wee Home From Home*. When Liz saw it, she found it 'moving, menacing, hilarious, charming, nostalgic, tough, complex, light and deep.'[15] She loved both it and the performances, especially Michael's. They met backstage, and their friendship and interest in each other's work grew from there.

In 1992 Liz's father died and left her a small legacy. She decided to risk £2,000 on mounting a shoestring, profit-share production of her Scots version of Molière's *Tartuffe*, which she would direct and play a small part in too, at the Edinburgh Fringe in 1993. It received great reviews, and partly thanks to these it was staged again at the Tron Theatre in Glasgow the following year. This time it had a miniscule budget but one that at least meant that the actors were paid Equity minimum rates. One of Liz's ambitions was to work with Michael as an actor. She offered him three minor but significant parts, which he accepted: as Flipote (Madame Pernelle's maid – 'hilarious', Liz recalls); Monsieur Loyal the bailiff ('menacing'); and the deus ex machina character who reverses everything and provides a happy, albeit ironical, ending to the play, the Prince's Officer ('absolutely magisterial').[16] This production also gave Liz the opportunity to fulfil another of her ambitions: during the play's run, Michael and she put on three late-night revue-type shows, performing songs, poems and monologues together. It was the inception of what became *In Flagrant Delicht*.

The title was Michael's suggestion and, though it lasted the lifetime of the show, it initially caused some difficulties for those not familiar with the phrase *in flagrante delicto*: audiences and reviewers alike often referred to it as *In Fragrant Delicht*. An interaction between them consisting of songs, stories, poems and monologues, the show started with childhood memories and moved on to address art, love, grief, comfort – and was by turns funny, poignant and moving. The basic material remained the same but each would add new material as appropriate and each acted as a foil for the other's humour and observation. Liz, who herself admits that she is not the world's greatest singer, found Michael endlessly patient as he coached her to join him on 'Baps and Paste': she got through it by deciding that the woman whose words she sang 'didn't have a musical note in her either.'

Off and on, for a dozen years and more, Liz and Michael charmed audiences throughout Scotland and as far afield as Australia and Washington, D.C. 'We didn't seek out opportunities to perform it but we kept getting requests and then we'd build a run, if we could, to make the preparation work worthwhile.' In 2006 they embarked on a 28-gig tour of *In Flagrant Delicht* which took them through Central Scotland, up to the West Highlands, the Hebrides and Orkney, down to the Borders and north again to Shetland. It was a great adventure but put Michael under considerable pressure as he had to drive them everywhere. It was on this trip that they concluded that they preferred a 'largely inferior hotel' to a 'superior B&B'.

'I couldn't tell you when we last did the show,' Liz said, 'because we never thought of it as being over. Sometimes a year or two might go by without us seeing each other but then the chance to do it again would come up. We never said, this is the last time. If Michael was still alive I think we would still be doing it.'

They worked on other projects together, such as Theatre Babel's production of *Beauty and the Beast* at the Tron in December 2001. Liz wrote the script and Michael the music. He performed all the songs and narrated the tale from behind the piano. 'Anybody who ever worked with him always wanted to do it again. It was an experience that generally involved a lot of laughing. It was never a problem collaborating with him, although it could be a strange form of collaboration for him, separately and independently writing music and lyrics which nevertheless had to fit with the rest of the show, but Michael was able to work like that. And whether the project was big or small, amateur or professional, well-paid, poorly paid or unpaid, you always got the same 100% from him.'[17]

I attended a wake for my uncle Willie, and at the wake my auntie Agnes was telling a story, and she said, 'There was three of us there, there was me, Kathleen and Muggie Sha'.' So I said, 'Who was that other woman?' And my auntie Kathleen said, 'Dinnae tell him, Agnes, he'll write a sang and he'll call it "Muggie Sha"'.' I said, 'Thank you very much, Auntie Kathleen.' And that night I thought, it's a very singable name.

(Left) Michael and Liz Lochhead in their show *In Flagrant Delicht.*

Early days of The Hazey Janes (left to right, Andrew Mitchell, Matthew Marra, Alice Marra, Liam Brennan).

(Left and below) Touring *Houseroom* with The Hazey Janes. Alice Marra: 'Even when he was so ill, he was still being hilarious and we were all laughing all the time.'

The last collaboration undertaken by Michael – with his own children – was perhaps the sweetest of all. Towards the end of 2011 Gordon Maclean of An Tobar in Mull suggested that The Hazey Janes record some songs with Michael. Although it wasn't known outside the family, Michael was not well by then and for Alice it was as if Gordon had instinctively homed in on the need to act quickly. A selection of Michael's songs was made; The Hazeys learned and rehearsed their parts in Dundee before the end of 2011; they and Michael went to Tobermory in January 2012 for four intensive days in the studio; they toured the new CD, *Houseroom*, in March; Michael died in October. The timescale was brutal, but the experience was joyous.

The Hazey Janes formed in the late 1990s, with Alice Marra on guitar, keyboard and vocals, Matthew Marra on bass guitar, Andrew Mitchell on guitar, keyboard and vocals, and Liam Brennan on drums and vocals. When a journalist asked Michael, early in the band's career, if their indie-pop folk-meets-Americana sound was influenced by his own music, he was quick to deny it. Nothing to do with him, he insisted. He'd known all four band members for years, and regarded Andrew and Liam as 'his bairns' as well. He'd neither encouraged nor discouraged their venturing into the music business, but he knew how tough that world could be and felt fearful for and protective of them all.

For Alice and Matthew, the collaborative process went back to childhood, even if they didn't realise it at the time. Alice:

He wasn't there very much. I have a lot of my old news jotters from P1 and P2, and the pictures I drew in them are always of me waving at a train. He was always going to Glasgow or Edinburgh or somewhere else. And when he was at home he was in his studio hard at work. So there are not a lot of memories until I got a bit older and started to get into music. Well, first of all it was the rubbish music – he couldn't bear that I was listening to the likes of Kylie Minogue – but once I got beyond that and was starting to sing, this would be when I was in High School, he clocked very quickly that I could sing in harmony, so he would ask me to come through and sing on demos. We'd do these double or triple-track recordings with me singing on top of myself, I could do that really easily, so he was always trying to get me into the studio, maybe if he was writing songs for a theatre show and needed to show the actors the sound he was looking for. There are still a lot of demos of me singing songs that he'd just written that would then go on to be in a show. And I would do it, but I was a young stroppy teenager so it was like, 'Oh, do I have to?' I feel guilty about that now, not giving him more time, but I was a teenager I was more interested in hanging out with my mates.

His room was quite intimidating too. I used to be scared of the Elvis Costello poster that was on the wall. We were told that he was busy and we mustn't disturb him so it was like,

'What is going on in there?' It was dark and full of smoke. So you would go to bed and you'd hear the piano coming up through the floorboards most of the night, but it wasn't annoying, it was a kind of comforting thing to hear that. If Andy Pelc was there it was different, it was just the laughter coming from downstairs, and you'd maybe go halfway down the landing, peeking down to see what they were up to. It was intriguing. [18]

Matthew too was a little afraid of Michael's room, 'the weird stuff on the walls', but other memories were slightly different from those of his sister:

He would work until about three, most nights. He worked in shifts. He would get up and read the paper right through, every word, then he would go ben the hoose and do a bit of work, have a sleep in the afternoon, get up and do a bit more. We'd all meet at mealtimes. If it was me and him at home in the afternoon it would be, 'Right, let's mak a breenge, get the fire on, tidy up a bit for Peg coming home.'

Until we did *Houseroom* with him, it felt like we'd never worked together musically, but in fact when I think about it we were collaborating the whole time for years before that, just making up daft songs in the house, getting the wee keyboard out, there was a lot of that. He was always singing wee kind of themes for friends or family members, and some of these would eventually turn up in songs as melodies or little phrases. And he would make songs as presents for people's birthdays, things like that. When I was about sixteen, Peg bought him and me a sampler for Christmas, between us, so there would be times when I'd leave something on it for him and then he would find it, do something with it and vice versa. I remember for one of my birthdays he sampled Peg saying 'Happy birthday, Matthew' and played around with that, he loved that kind of thing. And for years Alice sang on demos that he put together in the house. So at those levels there was always a bit of collaboration between us. [19]

Alice did sing backing vocals on 'Constable le Clock' and 'All to Please Macushla' on *Posted Sober*, and (as 'Zug Luciano' – 'Zug' being a nickname invented for her by Matthew) on the Saint Andrew CDs. There had been live performances together too, with The Hazey Janes backing Michael at Christmas gigs in the Westport Bar and Fat Sam's in Dundee, or joining him for a benefit gig for Dundee FC when the club was in financial trouble, and one or two other charity gigs. The *Houseroom* CD, however, was the first and last time they recorded with him. Matthew again:

We knew what we were going to do. Michael had given us all a CD with about fifteen demos on it. We picked six of the songs, rehearsed them in Dundee, so when we got to Mull we knew what we had to do. It was all quite straightforward.

Matthew Marra in the hallway
of the family home in Newtyle.

The annoying thing is if we'd had another day it could have been twelve tracks. We were there for three or four days and he was quite ill by then, although we didn't realise just how ill. A lot of it was down to a raised eyebrow rather than having to speak if something wasn't sounding right. That raised eyebrow could say lots. Even just a movement of the head, you could see what he was thinking. But mostly it went very smoothly. We knew what we were doing, and Gordon was absolutely brilliant on the engineering side of things, he knew exactly how to make it work. [20]

Gordon Maclean is not so sure that a full-length album would have been possible. It was clear that Michael was having to gather his energy between takes. Also, Michael liked the EP format: a project based on five or six songs wasn't too intimidating. Even when he was well, Gordon reckons, it was important not to scare him off. As on *Quintet*, all his solo parts were done in single takes. Michael loved being in the studio with The Hazey Janes, listening to them doing their harmonies, which were recorded ensemble, not individually. He was very impressed by their professionalism. On 'Underwood Lane', some whistling was required. It fell to Liam to be the whistler. When he demurred, Michael's unwavering voice came over Liam's headphones: "It's got to be you, son.' And it was.

All six tracks on *Houseroom* are of the highest quality. The song 'Houseroom' had been a possibility for *Posted Sober* but had not been selected. Now, given Michael's

illness, it seemed to have acquired even more power in its insistence on how comparatively fortunate the singer of the song was:

If you ever catch me moaning
Show me where to go
If it's how tough my life is
Singing on the radio

Don't give me houseroom
Don't be polite
While some voice is silenced
For a loaf of bread in the dead of night

'Ceci N'est Pas Une Pipe' is an attack on artistic conformity and timidity, dedicated to Henri Matisse and asserting his greatness with its repeated demand, 'I've come to see Matisse'. 'Mrs Gorrie' is a wonderful teenage-crush song honouring a real neighbour from Clement Park days. Its reggae beat was based on a two-bar loop Michael sampled from a track by the 1960s Jamaican band The Ethiopians:

She moves like a flamingo
Hair gold, eyes blue
You can feel her senses tingle
From the tips of her heels
To the heights of her bouffant

When I grow to be a man
I'll find a woman like her if I can
If I fail then that's ok
I'll keep on looking anyway

'Flight of the Heron', a tribute to the footballer Gil Heron, is discussed later in this book. [21] 'Underwood Lane', named after the street in Paisley where Gerry Rafferty was born, is dedicated to John Byrne, with whom Michael had worked on *Your Cheatin' Heart*. Around 2005 Byrne had written the book for a musical structured around Rafferty's back catalogue, but that idea had not come to fruition, and in October 2006 Byrne approached Michael to write new songs for the story he had created. 'Underwood Lane' was Michael's first response, but the project did not proceed – or, at least, Michael had no further involvement in it.

The last track, 'Heaven's Hound', is dedicated to Michael and Hilda Craig. Michael Craig is a long-term fan who for more than a decade maintained an on-line blog called 'Marra Musings', recording news of all kinds about almost anything related to Michael's work. Michael (Marra) used to say that Michael (Craig) knew more about him than he did himself. In other circumstances that could have been perceived as persecution, but the two men had met and kept up a regular friendly correspondence. 'Heaven's Hound' is, quite simply, a beautiful coda to the *Houseroom* EP and, it is tempting to suggest, to all of Michael's recorded music. It has distinct echoes of 'The Fold', the last track on *Silence*, as well as of 'Frida Kahlo's Visit to the Taybridge Bar'. A couple are struggling on a 'long and rocky road' and the wife is close to collapse, but entry to Heaven is deferred by the power of love and the love of life:

> O I had a dream I had made Heaven's Gate
> There was no sign of you
> So they told me to wait

> On that Heavenly shore
> In the light we'll arrive
> We have always our love here
> To keep us alive
> So help me for we have a long way to go
> Before we bathe in the light
> Of that Heavenly shore

Houseroom is a superb set of songs which perhaps has not had the recognition or exposure it deserves. Alice felt that it was swallowed up by everything else that happened after her father died. Nonetheless, the memories of making and touring the CD are overwhelmingly good ones:

> When I think of him when we were younger I just remember him laughing. He was always being really funny in that clever daft way, there wasn't much serious conversation, it was just a lot of fun. He was very entertaining. Even right up to that last tour we did with him when he was so ill, he was still being hilarious and we were all laughing all the time. [22]

Matthew agrees. 'There's a great photo from the tour that followed, of Michael, Liam and me all pishing ourselves laughing, which just kind of sums up how it was.'

Gordon Maclean's suggestion that they should seize the moment was clearly good advice.

Mrs Gorrie, a neighbour of
the Marras in Clement Park,
celebrated by Michael in the
song that bears her name.

Notes

1 Interview with Rab Noakes, 21st July 2016.

2 Email, 21st April 2017.

3 Interview with Frank McConnell, 11th January 2017. Another breakfast story comes from Mary Marra: 'I remember them staying with me in Dumbarton, and in the morning I said to him, what would you like for your breakfast, and he looked horrified at me and turned to Peggy: "Peggy, what would I like for my breakfast?"'.

4 Email, 27th May 2017.

5 Ibid.

6 Interview with Sheena Wellington, 13th May 2017.

7 The complete folio of some forty pages, dating from 1905, was sold at auction by Curr & Dewar, Dundee auctioneers, in April 2014 for £1,500.

8 *Resolis Remembers Michael Marra* (Resolis Community Arts pamphlet, 2014).

9 *Sunday Times*, 11th January 2004.

10 A late addition to the libretto of *If the Moon Can Be Believed*, with its lyrics slightly adjusted to fit the context, was a much earlier song of Michael's, 'Soldier Boy'. This song is the opening track on Alice Marra's 2017 album of her father's songs, *Chain Up the Swings*.

11 Interview with Andy Pelc, 13th April 2017.

12 Andy Pelc: '*Bontality* refers to a mixture of bonce and mental – we use the words *bontal* and *bontality* regularly.'.

13 Interview with Andy Pelc, 13th April 2017.

14 Interview with Chris Marra, 10th March 2017.

15 Interview with Liz Lochhead, 26th May 2017.

16 Ibid.

17 Ibid.

18 Interview with Alice Marra, 9th May 2017.

19 Interview with Matthew Marra, 26th April 2017.

20 Ibid.

21 See below, p.219.

22 Interview with Alice Marra, 9th May 2017.

Kitchen conversation

No.7

J: This won't take long. There is something I want to say. I'll be brief.

M: As the man requested of me when I asked if I could play Rommel's piano.

J: That's it, really. Brevity. Saying more by saying less. I don't know if you'll remember this, but I was doing a book event once, just along the road at Alyth, and you came to it. There was quite a good turnout, and you slipped in and stood at the back and you left early.

M: I didn't want to put you off.

J: Well, you didn't because I never saw you. It wasn't until a couple of days later that you told me you'd been there. You thought it had gone well.

M: I was relieved. I was worried for you.

J: I understand that now. Anyway, I was grateful that you'd come to listen. And I was grateful, too, that you read a couple of my novels. Especially the really big one, because I knew your preference was for conciseness, and that was not a concise book.

M: No, but I did read it, all six hundred and seventy pages of it.

J: Which was a huge time commitment. I knew you were a careful reader, a considering reader. It meant a lot to me that you paid that kind of attention to detail.

M: Presumably the detail was there for a reason. Therefore attention should be paid.

J: Not everybody reads like that or thinks like that. Well, anyway, what I want to say is, I had this book of short stories coming out in 2012, and short stories were more your kind of thing, so I wanted you to have them as a gift. You know, the way sometimes Marianne or I would open our front door in the morning and you'd have left a wee gift on the step, a CD compilation you had put together or something special you had made. Once you left her all the bits and pieces to build a miniature boat – whittled sticks, a paper sail, an anchor and so on. It was all in an old Ferrero Rocher box, and you'd named it 'My Little Boatyard'. Well, I was going to put this book of stories through your letterbox and run away, which is kind of what I imagine you used to do. It was to be a surprise. The dedication said, 'For Michael Marra, who *really* knows how to make less more'. But the book didn't come back from the printers in time. It missed you by about two weeks. So you never got it and I just wanted to explain that. It was to be a way of saying thank you for everything. And I'm sorry I didn't get to say it.

Thank you for everything.

Football

And there on the field what appeared to be
A working model of the one big thing
They could dance and sing
A working model of the one big thing

'Reynard in Paradise'

'Reynard in Paradise'
by Vincent Rattray.

'I can't exaggerate,' Michael's brother Nicky said of their childhood, 'how important football was for us.' The beautiful game was something that would remain beautiful for Michael throughout his life. He could see through the ugly things that accreted to it – the obscene amounts of money, the occasional outbreaks of violence on or off the park, the sectarianism of the Old Firm, the commercial exploitation of the game through merchandising and selling television rights – but none of these could take away his pleasure in football at its simplest, the moments of grace and magic, the way it can be, at its best, an international language of shared humanity.

For him, additionally, as an artist, it provided endless material for songs and for reflecting on wider matters. No surprises here, but there was usually something subversive about the way he chose to illuminate life through writing about the game he loved. 'Men can be graceful / This much I know' he wrote in 'Reynard in Paradise', but this was from the perspective of a fox. Elsewhere he once wrote, 'If [English] had gender for things, like a proper language, all the best things would be feminine, even football itself although it's played by men it would be feminine, like music and education…'[1]

Michael himself was a good player as a teenager, Nicky recalled:

> He was what they would call a tasty winger, but he did not like physical contact. So he would play on the wing and when we got older, into our twenties, we played in a team called the Thomson Street Academicals. One time he'd been on holiday with Peg in Barcelona, we were in the traditional white tops, white shorts, white socks, and he had these bands of ebony between the white blocks of cloth, totally tanned from this trip, and he was standing canoodling with Peg on the line. You'd put a ball out to the wing and have to shout to him, because he was otherwise engaged. This was moving up a gear into amateur, Sunday morning football, and Michael didn't like that because it was hard, physical, and he developed bad knees. I'm not sure if that was for real or an injury of convenience. When they moved to Newtyle he loved playing two-touch at the side of the house there. That was mind games. Ask Matthew. If you went in the lead he would start giving you all this talk, highly competitive, and if you relented he was in, merciless.[2]

Despite this gamesmanship, there was an absence of malice in Michael's wider appreciation of football. He was a Dundee fan from the age of ten when they won the Scottish League in 1962. In the European Cup campaign that followed, Dundee started off by beating FC Cologne 8-1 at home. It was the first game Michael had seen under floodlights and he had never experienced excitement like it. As the years went by, however, supporting Dundee was more about resilience than ecstasy. A sense of humour was essential. He was also, along with Peggy, Alice and Matthew, a keen follower of Celtic, which was considerably more rewarding in terms of trophies and titles. He resisted the tribalism of the game and found incomprehensible its appropriation by bigots and fanatics in other parts of the country. For Michael, football was always bigger than any one team. He did, however, struggle to empathise with Rangers F.C., a club he generally referred to as 'the Forces of Darkness', or just 'the Forces' for short. But he still managed to inject humour into the Old Firm rivalry in his song 'King Kong's Visit to Glasgow', in which the fans at Celtic Park urge Kong's angel to take him elsewhere:

> so he bumps into the floodlights
> and the crowd began to sing
> why don't you take him to Ibrox
> there we think he might blend in

*

When World Cup or European Championship finals were in progress, Michael and the rest of the family found it hard to step away from the television screen. In fact a summer without one of these tournaments was regarded as a kind of wasteland as far as entertainment was concerned.

Part of the pleasure of watching the games was making wry observations on, for example, the prevailing fashion in players' hairstyles, as well as decrying the nonsense spouted by over-excited commentators. Of the 2002 World Cup he commented:

> I liked the Turkish laddie with the Samurai hairstyle, you see how dignified that elaborate barnet was, handsome is as handsome dis. The moment came and there he was, beautiful goal. I've only missed three or four matches and have really enjoyed most of it, apart from the guys havering and the jingoism, it has been good and my sleeping habits are different. I needed a brisk lie doon after South Korea v. Spain. Great stuff. [3]

*

The two football-related songs on *On Stolen Stationery*, 'The Wise Old Men of Mount Florida' and 'Hamish', have been mentioned in an earlier chapter, but it's worth adding that when Prince Rainier and Princess Grace flew to Scotland to watch the second leg of Monaco's UEFA Cup tie against Dundee United, they stayed with friends at Meigle, just a couple of miles up the road from Michael and Peggy's home. If only they'd known, they could have popped in for a cup of tea. The match took place at Tannadice on 30th September 1981. Monaco were 5-2 down from the first leg but won in Dundee 2-1. Hamish MacAlpine, United's goalkeeper and the principal subject of Michael's song in spite of Grace Kelly's cameo appearance, later said that the United players preferred to go for a pint after the game rather than meet one of the world's most famous and glamorous women. It was just under a year later that Princess Grace died in a car crash in Monaco.

High romance and the down-to-earth touched again when Michael was performing in Turin in January, 2000. He prepared for this trip by asking Frankie Robatti, a neighbour in Newtyle, to translate the introductions to his songs into Italian. Michael learned them by heart and delivered them like a native speaker to a very appreciative audience. Between songs he told them of the time he had met the great AC Milan and Italy player Gianni Rivera in the Nethergate in Dundee, in May 1963 when Michael was eleven. They shook hands. AC Milan were at Dens Park for the second leg of the European Cup semi-final. Their players looked like film stars, while the Dundee players were all peely-wally. As Michael was speaking a man in the front row stood up, turned round and began to count back through the years on his fingers. When he signalled his satisfaction that Michael's claim was correct, the entire audience roared its approval.

That trip was not without its drama elsewhere. When he arrived at Turin airport, Michael accidentally bumped his guitar case against a sniffer dog which began to bark furiously. Suspected of being in possession of 'sostanze stupefacenti', Michael and his bags were taken aside and he was subjected to a strip-search, which – of course – proved 'negativo'. Half an hour later he was free to proceed.

*

There is nothing down-to-earth about the link between Michael and Gil Heron, the subject of his song 'The Flight of the Heron'. Gil Heron was the first black professional footballer to play in Scotland. He was also the father of the musician, poet and political activist Gil Scott-Heron. Jamaican-born Heron, a former boxer and all-round athlete, was playing centre-forward for the Detroit Corinthians when he was spotted by Celtic scouts and brought to Glasgow for the 1951-52 season. He was known as the Black Arrow and moved at what was said to be 'camera-shutter speed'. Off the park, he must have made an astonishing impact in grey, post-war Glasgow, walking around town in sharp suits and coloured shoes. A team-mate remembered that he used to hang out in the music department of Lewis's department store, listening to the latest American imports. But the physical nature of the Scottish game was not to his liking and Celtic released him after one season. He went on to play for Third Lanark and then Kidderminster Harriers in England before going back to Detroit.

All the elements of this story appealed to Michael and are captured in the song he wrote and dedicated to Gil Heron. In 2008 the journalist and political commentator Gerry Hassan went to New York to visit Gil Scott-Heron, whom he had once seen perform at the Dundee Jazz Festival. Michael asked him to take a demo of the song as a gift. At this time Gil Heron was still alive, although he and his son were estranged. When Gerry arrived at Scott-Heron's flat, just off Broadway in Harlem, he was not sure what to expect, but Scott-Heron, a little greyer, a little thinner than when Gerry had last seen him, welcomed him in with an 'infectious, glorious smile'. What happened next was extraordinary:

He led me down a narrow, long hall, and after we passed one door, he indicated we turn second right into his bedroom. This was his main place of work. A disorganised, dishevelled room, but a place where Gil sought out some peace and sanctuary.

I wondered where to sit, and Gil motioned that the bed was fine, so as I perched on the side of his bed, taking in the state of the room, he went off to get some drinks, and the house cat, 'Paris', came in and checked me out.

I am meeting Gil to give him the recording of Michael Marra's 'The Flight of the Heron', a tribute to his father's days at Celtic, along with a handwritten note from Michael about writing the song.

I sense that this is a special moment of anticipation. Gil puts the track on his home entertainment system and opens Michael's letter. When the opening words begin, 'When Duke was in the Lebanon' in Michael's evocative, soulful Scots voice, I realise that I am at the scene of something profound, and that I am part of it.

As the song reaches its second verse, 'From Jamaica to the Kingston Bridge', I know that Michael's music has touched Gil's heart. There is as the song closes a moment of silence, and both of us are close to tears. [4]

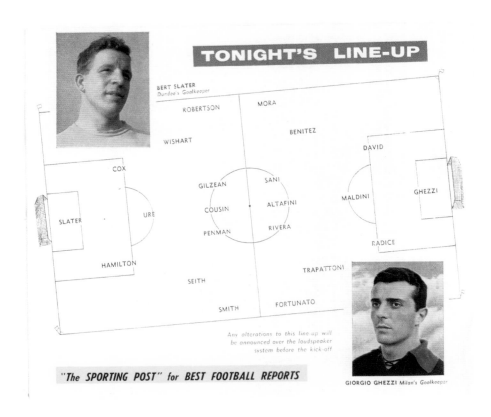

The team line-up for the
Dundee v. AC Milan
European Cup semi-final,
May 1963.

AC Milan's Gianni Rivera,
with whom 11-year-old
Michael shook hands in
the Nethergate, Dundee.

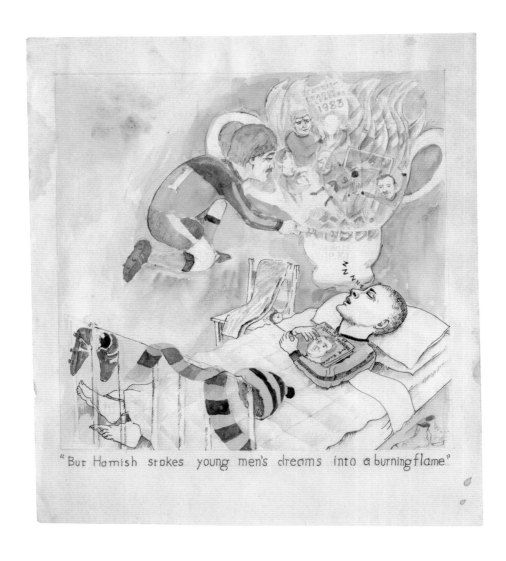

"But Hamish stokes young men's dreams into a burning flame"

The artist John Johnstone
responded to Michael's
song 'Hamish' with
these illustrations.

The figure wearing glasses is
Michael's oldest brother Eddie.

The three-line chorus really sums up Michael's feelings about the power of football to demolish barriers:

> Higher, raise the bar higher
> He made his way across the sea
> So that all men could brothers be

Scott-Heron told Gerry that he would like to record the song himself but there is no indication that he ever did. Gerry found him 'diffident, fragile, even humble' and was struck by the similarities with Michael, even though their roots and journeys had been so different.

Gil Heron died in December 2008 aged eighty-six, and his son Gil Scott-Heron died in 2011, aged sixty-two.

*

In 2004 the naturalist and writer Jim Crumley published a novel called *The Goalie*, based on the life of his grandfather, Bob Crumley, who had played in the Dundee team which won the Scottish Cup in 1910, served in the First World War and subsequently become alienated from his family. About much more than football, the story was adapted into a radio drama-documentary. Jim was anxious that, for one vitally important part of the programme, the right voice be identified. In the book the appearance of skylarks at significant moments symbolise hope, and Jim also quoted the lyrics of Hoagy Carmichael's 'Skylark'. It was concluded that it had to be Michael who sang the song for the radio show. The chapel of Dundee University had good acoustics and a good piano, so that was where the recording was done. Jim recalled:

Skylark – the word – is the first two syllables of Hoagy Carmichael's song. When I heard it that very first time sung in Michael's unique delivery and slung over the top of what he called his 'industrial' piano-playing, I knew I would never hear it any other way from that moment on. [5]

Not for the first or last time, Michael got under somebody's skin and into their heart, and not just because of his voice but because he understood the way the song related to the story.

*

Perhaps his most sublime song about football is 'Reynard in Paradise'. Dedicated to Bernard MacLaverty, one of his favourite authors and a master of the short story (these facts are not unrelated), it manages to connect the city to the countryside, football to freedom, the beauty of a fox to the beauty of men, and it even carries an echo of Burns's 'Song: Composed in August' ('Westlin Winds') with its condemnation of blood sports. This is how Michael would introduce it at gigs:

This is a song about football, it's a song about the urban fox, but I think more than anything it's a song about human beings. I was listening to the radio one Saturday afternoon, and it was a football match taking place in Glasgow between Aberdeen and Celtic. And during the course of the commentary the commentator said, 'An amazing thing has just happened, a beautiful and healthy fox has just run on the park.' Did anybody see it, on television? I saw it later, it was fabulous. He was running alongside Jackie MacNamara. Absolutely gorgeous. And so was the fox. Anyway, I began to wonder why such a wise creature would put himself in such a precarious position, because any game of football you get at Celtic Park there's sixty thousand people all howling and screaming. It just didn't seem to be the right place for a fox to appear, but there he was. So I began to wonder where he'd come from. I thought maybe he'd come from a wealthy part of Lanarkshire. [Laughter] I didn't know that was a comical thought. Then I thought, well, maybe a member of his family had been killed by the hunt, and he had moved into sophisticated Glasgow, tired of the rural way of life. Something like that. But anyway, no matter what reason, I wrote this song, and during the course of the song, the fox revises his opinion of mankind, having watched Aberdeen play Celtic.

Thus a true story became a fable in Michael's hands. 'Men can be graceful / This much I know', the fox says, but he speaks in Michael's voice.

Notes

1   Undated letter to Nicky Marra.
2   Interview with Nicky and Mary Marra, 13th January 2017.
3   Thanks to Michael Craig for this swatch of Marra World Cup wisdom.
4   Gerry Hassan, 'A Scottish Story of Spirit and Grace', *Sunday Times*, 7th December 2008.
5   *The Courier*, 30th October 2012.

Kitchen conversation

(with Peggy Marra)

No.8

James: Let's go back to just after you and Michael got married. That was November 1972. You were living in Dundee and you were teaching at Auchterhouse Primary School. Michael was playing in Hen's Teeth, but by 1973 Hen's Teeth was coming to an end, with Dougie MacLean pursuing his own career and Michael doing a lot of solo gigs too. What else was he doing to earn money?

Peggy: We were living in Wellgrove Street and he was working on a building site at Inchture, going out there every day on the bus. But that changed in the summer. There was a really nice guy we knew in town, and he was on the bus that Michael took to his work one day, and he was going away travelling. Michael came home and told me the story, and we decided to go travelling too when the school term was over. He gave up his job and we got a ferry to Norway, then hitchhiked through much of Western Europe, just going where the lifts took us. We were camping, mostly. We ended up in Berlin. We didn't know we were going to end up there, but we were in a lorry that took us to West Berlin. We hadn't quite understood that you had to go through East Germany to get to Berlin, but the driver was very friendly, he looked after us. One thing I remember was he kept telling us about Kartoffelsalat, potato salad. That word stuck with us, it would come up regularly for years after that. 'Let's just have some Kartoffelsalat.'

J: Did either of you have any German?

P: Not really. We just had 'Kartoffelsalat'.

J: I had a similar experience travelling in the Czech Republic and Slovakia and Hungary in the 1990s. In a lot of places we found that German was the *lingua franca*. My then partner said she knew some German but it turned out the only phrase she did know was 'Das ist ein Spiegelei', which means 'This is a fried egg'. It's amazing how far a phrase like that can get you when it's all you have.

P: Kartoffelsalat.

J: Exactly. I'm guessing that you might have been the organising force on that European adventure, but what about when Michael was spending so much time in London, when he had the contract with Polydor? This would be 1979, 1980, and by then you were living in Newtyle. How did he get up and down to London. By train?

P: No, he usually flew. We'd moved to Newtyle in 1975. I used to drive him to Edinburgh Airport very early in the morning, then drive back and go into school at Auchterhouse. I joined him in London when I was on maternity leave before Alice was born, and then Alice and I went down sometimes while he was recording *The Midas Touch*. Polydor put Michael up in a hotel when the recording was going on, but at other times he'd stay with a friend of ours, John Cook. And, later, when he was doing theatre work in Edinburgh or Glasgow, he would stay in friends' flats rather than drive back and forth to Newtyle.

J: For many years his agent was John Barrow of Stoneyport Associates in Edinburgh, so presumably a lot of bookings for gigs and so on would come from him. But you must have been handling a lot of the logistics.

P: Yes, I was. I dealt with John over the years, first of all by phone and then by email, but I never actually met him. In fact it wasn't until 2010, when Michael won a *Herald* Angel award for his Fringe show, that I did meet him. It was very short notice – just the day before – and we didn't have time to arrange for other family members to be there, but I asked my friend Dorothy, who stays in Edinburgh, to come along. So we went to the Festival Theatre for the presentation, and John was waiting for us – I knew what he looked like from photographs, but he didn't know me – and Michael says, 'John, you've never met Peg, have you?' pointing at Dorothy. Dorothy played along and we kept that up for quite a while that morning before we told John who was really who. That was typical Michael.

J: So many folk I've spoken to have said, 'If it hadn't been for Peg…' Sheena Wellington, for example, was full of praise for you. 'We all owe Peggy a huge debt,' she said, 'because without her care we wouldn't have got half of what we got from Michael.' And Michael knew that. Sheena said he would say, 'Come on, Sheena, you know I'm no allowed anything sharp. Talk to Peg.' I suppose what I'm getting at is, all right, John Barrow was his agent, but effectively you were his management.

P: Well, Michael would say that, but I didn't particularly like – being accused of that! People would say, 'I want to book you for such and such,' and he would say, 'Ask Peg. Don't ask me, ask Peg.' So, yes, I took care of it all, but I would hate to have been given a title.

J: But you did do it. Because he wouldn't, or couldn't?

P: He could have. Of course he *could* have. But he was not interested. Too boring! And then when it got to the stage where he didn't know about a gig until two days before it, how could he have done it? How could he have kept his own diary and remained calm, seeing all this work ahead of him?

J: One might think the stress and pre-gig nerves would have got easier over time, but it didn't?

P: It definitely got more difficult.

J: The first time I was ever in contact with you was back in 1996. I was co-compiling a dictionary of Scottish quotations. I didn't know either of you, of course, but I wrote to him asking if we could quote some extracts from his song lyrics. It was you who replied. I've got the letter up in the attic somewhere. You said that was fine, but you corrected some of the lyrics, which we'd probably just copied down from listening to the songs. In retrospect, it looks like Michael said to you, 'You deal with this.'

P: Yes, but sometimes it might seem like I was replying on his behalf, but he was telling me what to say. It would depend what it was. Eventually it got to a stage where it just became his default for everything: 'Ask Peg.'

J: But on the other hand when he was working in a studio or on a show he would deal with that side of things himself, so it was as if more routine matters just bored him.

P: That's what I said. 'It's boring, it's for Peg. She likes boring.'

J: Did you resent that?

P: No, I had always done it. It increased, of course. I would be up at six in the morning, doing emails, then I was off to work so I couldn't deal with anything else until I came home again, so it could be quite awkward.

J: Presumably quite a lot of your weekends were spent catching up on stuff as well.

P: That's right.

J: So he relied on you a lot for some of the practical things. What did you? –

P: *Every* practical thing.

J: Everything?

P: Well he could, of course he *could*, put petrol in the car, but if he was going for a gig the car would be there, ready, with the petrol in it.

J: Did you pack his suitcase if he was going away for several days?

P: Probably. I mean, yes, his bag with all the practical things, the clothes and that, but he had his own bag and that would be full of a whole lot of completely different stuff.

J: Did he care what you packed?

P: Well, on the one hand he was so uninterested himself in his appearance, but on the other hand he was very observant of how other people looked. He would pass judgment on footballers' hairstyles on TV, that kind of thing, but it wasn't just footballers, it was everybody. You had to watch your hairstyle. If I was going anywhere, maybe to meet someone for a coffee, it would be, 'And the costume?' He wanted to know before I went out.

J: And in spite of apparently not being that interested in his appearance, he was very particular about some aspects of it. His beret, for example. He wore the beret – Frank McConnell told me he got quite distraught when they were touring and he lost it – and that made him instantly recognisable as Michael Marra.

P: People would hear that he'd lost his beret and send replacements.

J: There was another time, Rod Mackenzie, father of the Mackenzie sisters told me, when he was playing at the old An Lanntair in Stornoway Town Hall and he'd come across without his own ironing-board to put his keyboard on and Rod drove back up to his house at Gress to collect their ironing-board for him to use. So he must have

been conscious of his image, of going to do a gig with the beret, the ironing-board and so on?

P: Yes, because he became somebody else. He had a green shirt, which I've still got, that he wore. As soon as that shirt went on, that was it. He wouldn't do a gig without it, although I remember there was once when he had to, he'd forgotten to take it or something, and he had to do the gig in a white shirt. Not happy.

J: So it was like getting into character?

P: Definitely. He didn't ever want to do a gig without the beret or the green shirt. Unless it was something where he had to wear a costume or a suit for some other reason, but then that was him in another character.

J: Is that also why he learned the introductions to the songs, which are often almost word for word the same on different occasions? Because that was him playing a part? And maybe, too, because he didn't want to have to ad-lib?

P: Yes, although sometimes he did, and sometimes the intros were much longer, the full thing, and other times they were fairly short, that would just be determined by how he felt it was going at the time.

J: So my question from a few minutes ago was going to be, what did *you* rely on *him* for?

P: Nothing practical! All the laughs.

Nothing sensible. Everything that wasn't sensible or practical.

J: That's important, though.

P: Absolutely. I always remember my mum saying, not long after we'd met – I can't remember what I was telling her, it couldn't have been that we were getting married – but she realised it was serious and she said, 'Well, I knew that because you've always got a smile on your face.' I would turn round and he'd be sitting there with this really ridiculous face that he was making, just daft stuff. The daft stuff, that's what I relied on him for.

J: Andy Pelc told me a story about when he and Michael used to write a column called 'Showbiz Tam' in the *Dundee Standard*, the local Labour Party newspaper, in the 1980s. It was a spoof on the *Daily Record*'s 'Showbiz Sam'. On one occasion they put in a reader's letter which said, 'Hi Tam, I'm hoping you can help me. I'm a huge fan of local singer-songwriter Michael Marra. I've got all of his records. I know he is on tour soon and I wonder if you know if he is playing in the local area because it would be great to see him. Yours, Peggy Marra, Newtyle.'

P: He used to send me postcards if he was away touring. A card would arrive the day after he'd got home and would say something like, 'Hi Peg. I am upstairs in bed. Love Michael.'

J: The thing that Alice and Matthew say they remember most is loads and loads of laughing.

P: Absolute hysterics sometimes, all of us. We just laughed. All The Hazeys – Andrew and Liam too – would say that.

J: Michael used to come out with things that were both extremely funny and very astute, very perceptive. Something I find I do a lot now, if there's some dilemma I'm facing, I ask myself, 'What would Michael think? What would his take on this be?' And I wonder if Michael bounced stuff off you like that, if he said, 'What would Peg think?' and if he'd come home and ask you, 'How do you think I should deal with this?'

P: Yes, he would. And isn't that funny, what you've just said, because Matthew is so much his father's son. We have a thing now: 'What would Matthew do? What would Matthew say? We'd better ask Matthew.' He's taken on that role.

There are so many things that have happened that are continuations or completions. Like Sheena Wellington taking Michael out in his pram in Clement Park, and now all these years later Sheena's been working with Alice on the Singer Machine Choir project at the Dundee Design Festival. More than sixty years on, and the connection is still there. Things come full circle.

J: There's continuity, but there's change too. I'd love to know what he thought of the politics of the last few years, the independence referendum and Brexit and so on. I think I understood where he was coming from in terms of his political principles, but he never seemed loud or even explicit about, say, independence. Maybe that's because he was wary of being associated with a particular political party.

P: He was very much for independence. It caused me a bit of angst after he wasn't here because there were all these things happening, especially with the referendum. I remember Eilidh Mackenzie getting in touch, she was performing at some event to do with independence and she wanted to sing one of his songs. I said, 'Yes, and Eilidh, could you please say at that concert that Michael would have been there, he would have been going for independence?' And Eilidh said she hadn't been sure. And because of the Marra family background, the whole history of the family and the Labour Party, I think people got the wrong impression, but Michael would have been up there. I don't know if she said it, but the fact that she asked made me want to set the record straight.

J: You said to me once that you haven't been able to listen to Michael's music since he died. Is that still the case?

P: I'm not keen. Matthew came into the car the other day with a CD and said, 'Can you listen to this in the car?' I didn't realise what he was meaning when he said it, I thought he meant 'Is the CD player working?' so I said, 'Yes, I can.' He said, 'I think it's quite good.' So he put it in, and it was *A Wee Home From Home*. And then he realised what he'd done, we both realised, and he took it out again. I can be driving and listening to the radio, the Bryan Burnett

show or something, and he'll say he's going to play one of Michael's songs – last week it was 'All Will Be Well' – and I have to put it off. But sometimes it catches me by surprise, and I get a fright.

You know, he only ever phoned me twice in all the years I've worked at Airlie Primary. Once was when he got the *Herald* Angel award in 2010. The other time was in 2012 to tell me that Alice and Matthew and the band were going on tour in Europe with Wilco. He was so excited about that, he needed to tell me straightaway. And he was delighted for them, he so wanted to go with them. He was really ill, but he still wanted to go. We sat every night and watched the photos going up on Facebook, because they kept a diary, and we could see these huge venues they were playing in Italy and Spain. It was so important to him, it was the last thing that was so important to him. They got back at five o'clock from that tour on the day he died. And you know why? Celtic. Celtic were playing, and the roadie wanted to get back for the match so he booted it up the road, otherwise they wouldn't have been in time. That's true. And they were there in the hospital, telling him, 'Celtic have scored against Barcelona.'

J: And you were all there.

P: Well, yes. They just made it. It was very significant, that whole Wilco thing, he was so chuffed for them. All The Hazeys had come out to the house to say cheerio to him before they left. That would have been in September, we were all out in the garden. And Colin Reid was there too, Alice's partner.

J: Colin's in the band Cuddly Shark, is that right?

P: Yes. He hadn't met Michael before that day. In fact that was the only time they did meet. We didn't know then how much a part of the family Colin would become, and what a support for Alice he would be through everything. They got married last year and Michael would have totally approved.

Well, it was a beautiful day, we were all in the garden and Michael was sitting there saying, 'I wish, I wish I could go with them.' And then all these fabulous photos were coming in from the tour. He would say to me, 'Where are they today?' It was huge, it was brilliant. And they did get home in time.

Causes and Effects

There's love in this world for everyone
Every rascal and son of a gun
It's for the many, not for the few
Be sure it's out there looking for you
In every town in every state
In every house and every gate
With every precious smile you make
And every act of kindness

'Farlow'

Michael always read the papers and listened to the news with great intent. He absorbed vast amounts of information about the world and the state it was in, and filtered what he learned through his own principles and political instincts, the foundations of which lay in his upbringing in Lochee. He often kept his views to himself, but he certainly did not shy away from expressing them when necessary. Eilidh Mackenzie wrote of him, 'Rather than being opinionated, he held many opinions and gently led you to look at things from other, sometimes initially obscure, perspectives,'[1] which seems a fair assessment. Often, he preferred to show his support for something he believed in through performance rather than talk. Charities and political causes alike benefited from his willingness to turn up and play.

Tayside for Justice in Palestine was a group on whose behalf Michael made several appearances. His brother Nicky was involved in the Dundee-Nablus Twinning Association so there were family links too, but Michael would not involve himself in anything that he himself couldn't commit to. He played at the TJP group's 'Stovies and Olives' fundraising concert at the Queen's Hotel in 2004, and again in 2008 after the Israeli invasion of Gaza when his presence combined with heightened public awareness to ensure a packed-out event. Only ill health prevented him continuing to give his services to this particular cause. Other notable charity concerts included the 'Who's That With Chris?' fundraiser for Roxburghe House, the hospice which had cared for Eddie Marra (the poster was one of Eddie's paintings, showing Chris alongside Tina Turner); and the 'Euphonia' concert for the Samaritans at the Bonar Hall, remembered by many not only for a superb set by Michael but also for Saint Andrew's role as compere and overseer of the raffle.

He gave his time and expertise to other one-off charitable projects. One example was a CD, *Ordinary Angel*, released by Macmeanmna to raise funds for the Scottish Liver Fund. This was an album conceived and planned by Sheila and Stephen McCabe from Skye. Sheila died of cancer in May 2005 at the age of forty-one. *Ordinary Angel* was a compilation of her favourite Scottish musicians and singers, including Rod Paterson, Donnie Munro, Mackenzie and Peatbog Faeries. Michael contributed two tracks, 'The Homeless Do Not Seem to Drink in Here' and 'Chain Up the Swings'.

*

In the spring of 2006 Michael went to Washington, D.C. as one of a group of Scottish artists which included Liz Lochhead, to perform during 'Tartan Week'.[2] On entering the USA he had his fingerprints taken. This annoyed him. He felt he was being treated as a potential criminal even though he had done nothing wrong. His sense of injustice chimed with something that had been bothering him for a while, the case of Shirley McKie. This is the story as told by Shirley's father, Iain McKie:

When my police officer daughter Shirley was first accused, in February 1997, of leaving her fingerprint at a murder scene in Kilmarnock, and then charged with perjury, the furthest thing from our minds was that the whole affair would rumble on for the next fourteen years and indelibly mark Shirley's life for ever .

Over those years many extraordinary things happened to us. Some were traumatic and frightening. Some were life-affirming and uplifting.

In May 2003, my wife Mairi and I attended the 'Burns An' A' That' festival concert at Culzean Castle, Ayrshire. The highlight of the evening was the appearance of world-famous American singer Patti Smith who with Michael Marra performed Robert Burns's 'Sweet Afton'.

We were captivated by Michael's singing but the evening passed and was quickly forgotten amidst the turmoil of our campaign.

The years after the Culzean concert were taken up with trying to force the Scottish Executive (as the Scottish Government was then known) and

Crown Office to admit that the fingerprint officers at the Scottish Criminal Record Office (SCRO) purposely misidentified Shirley's fingerprint to protect a murder conviction and their own reputations, which were under relentless attack. Little did we know that Michael Marra, like thousands of others, was following the progress of the case and was angered by the stubborn 'head in the sand' approach of the Scottish Executive.

There was a sudden resolution in February 2006 when Shirley was awarded an out-of-court settlement of £750,000 by an Executive which denied any wrongdoing.

In justifying this settlement, the then First Minister, Jack McConnell, addressed the Scottish Parliament and called the SCRO misidentification an 'honest mistake'. It was our firm belief, and that of hundreds of fingerprint experts across the world, that it might be a mistake but it certainly wasn't honest.

Unknown to us in April of that year Michael Marra, who was participating in a 'Tartan Week' event in Washington, D.C., had his fingerprints security-checked on entering the United States. As he stated later, this action brought Shirley's ordeal to mind and, feeling angry that he hadn't spoken up before, he quickly penned, 'I Am Shirley McKie', a powerful and damning indictment of the Executive's behaviour and misuse of power. His message was that honesty can only be encouraged by example and that any

one of us could be a Shirley McKie.

We first heard from Michael a few weeks later when he wrote to us enclosing a copy of 'I Am Shirley McKie' and seeking our blessing for the song he had written.

Anybody who has experienced trauma in their lives, and what appears to be a permanent uphill struggle against the powerful, will perhaps understand how hearing his words of encouragement, hope and support were almost too much to bear after years of facing the implacable and uncaring face of bureaucracy and government.

Mairi and I were moved to tears as his words brought home the pain of the past years and seemed to summarise what Shirley's fight had been about.

In May of that year, Mairi and I attended Mauchline's 'Holy Fair' as Michael was appearing and we had arranged to meet.

Originally conceived as a celebration of Scottish Presbyterianism, over the centuries the Holy Fair had become central to Ayrshire's celebrations of the life and works of Robert Burns. Given Burns's at times visceral condemnation of those he saw as hypocrites in the Kirk this evolution seemed to appeal to the Scottish psyche.

Our conversation in a narrow alleyway, a few feet away from a packed main square, was in some ways surreal. Instead of being faced by a confident, outgoing 'personality', here was a man, modest almost to the point of shyness, who insisted on playing down any part he had played and intent only on emphasising Shirley's bravery in the face of bureaucratic stubbornness. After a few minutes he left, mounted the stage and changed into the polished, charismatic performer the crowd had been waiting to see: a man apparently content to let his words and music speak for him.

We viewed Michael's performance from the grounds of the Mauchline Parish Church which border onto the square.

After a few songs Michael launched into 'I Am Shirley McKie'. As he started singing we sighted Cathy Jamieson, the then Justice Secretary and local MSP, enter the square and make her way through the crowds towards the stage. More than anyone Jamieson had represented the total failure of an abject government bureaucracy to face up to its responsibilities towards Shirley and represent the public interest instead of its own incestuous ones.

The irony was not lost on us when she suddenly turned and quickly left the square.

Did Michael know she was there, did Jamieson hear Shirley's name ringing out, did she fear facing the condemnation being so eloquently expressed on stage? We will never know but the satisfaction we felt as she hurriedly retreated was irresistible, and the whole action being played out before us seemed powerful and symbolic and only served to reinforce Michael's words:

Don't call this the home of the brave
Don't call it the home of the free
Don't call it the home of the handsome
Or any noble name that might come
    back to haunt you

We lecture children if they're telling
    lies
They will not prosper and they will not
    thrive
That's the message we teach our youth
It will not work if you don't tell the
    truth

And even the First Minister must
    sometimes stand naked

Over the years Mairi and I continued to enjoy Michael's words and music. We were planning to attend one of his concerts when his programme of forthcoming events was cancelled and then his untimely death announced in October 2012.

We knew that Scotland had lost one of its finest ambassadors for truth and justice. A man to whom we would be eternally grateful. A man of peace, unafraid to stand up against hypocrisy and the misuse of power, and with the unique talent to move others through his humble use of words and music.

A wonderful man. [3]

*

Michael was a republican, a socialist, an environmentalist – but he resisted labels being stuck on him or anyone else. That was the problem with labels – they tended to stick. He always had a very keen sense of being a second-class citizen because of his Irish ancestry and Roman Catholic upbringing, since the British constitution, unwritten though it is said to be, is actually founded upon privileging particular (Protestant) Christian churches and faiths over all others: legal and political power, with the monarchy at its heart, has been intimately and explicitly tied to the supremacy of Anglicanism in England and Wales, and Presbyterianism in Scotland, since the 17th century. Whatever historical reasons there may have been for this – and Michael had a clear understanding of why and how things had happened in the past – to him it was way beyond the time when this situation was still defensible or acceptable. Yet nothing was done about it. Any suggestion of a written constitution that would assert and protect the rights of all citizens equally was dismissed by the very people whose own interests and authority would be undermined by it. As with the injustice of the Shirley McKie case, this angered Michael. It led him to have a deep mistrust of the political system and of all political parties. As he grew older he found himself more and more alienated from the one party – Labour – which for so long had represented working people but which increasingly seemed to him to be more interested in representing itself.

In January 1992 British Steel had announced that the Ravenscraig steelworks at Motherwell, the great icon of heavy industry in the West of Scotland, would close later in the year with the loss of thousands of jobs both at the plant and in connected businesses. The Labour Party had been in opposition for thirteen years and seemed to Michael to be ineffectual in preventing such devastation of working-class communities: Ravenscraig was final proof of that. He had already allied himself, under the name Artists for Independence, with a group of other writers and musicians who believed that only through self-government could the Scottish people truly gain control of their own political destiny and thus exert influence over social and economic policies that directly affected their daily lives. In the run-up to the General Election of April 1992, Michael made public appearances with others from the group, who included Pat Kane, Ricky Ross, Lorraine McIntosh, William McIlvanney, Edwin Morgan and Liz Lochhead. Labour led by Neil Kinnock was widely expected to defeat the incumbent Conservative Government under John Major, but in fact this did not happen, the Ravenscraig closure went ahead and Scotland was subjected to another five years of Tory rule.

I never heard Michael hold a brief for any political party. He was suspicious of the motivations of professional politicians whether they claimed to be of the Left or the Right, for or against Scottish independence or anything else. He was much happier being involved, however loosely, with something like Artists for Independence – a grouping of friends whose work he already knew and respected, an alliance or movement with a common objective or, as he sometimes put it, a camp. You can pitch your tent in a camp but you can also strike it and move on if the campsite becomes overcrowded or detrimental to the environment. There was something about having the freedom to pack up and go somewhere else that appealed to Michael, even if in other respects he was very much a home bird, happiest in his own place among his own family.

*

Being out in the fresh air, a temporary gypsy, was important to Michael throughout his life. Childhood summers were spent outside in Dundee, and then there were caravan holidays at Inver and further afield. All this tied into the concept of 'backwoodsmanship', a term shared with Andy Pelc, as the latter explains:

> The whole being outdoors thing started off with Peter McGlone, the sax player in the Bolivers. Peter and I were very keen anglers. Michael's father was a very keen angler. I don't think Michael ever did much fishing with his father but he'd been around it. He had a pair of wellies, he had a Barbour coat, he went camping up at Aviemore in a tent, so he wasn't unaware of the outdoors thing, but our term of 'backwoodsmanship' basically meant being out on the banks of the River Ericht, usually in the summer months, staying overnight and building a fire. So Michael would come with Peter and me, and he would take on the role of 'the expert', showing us how to whittle, how to build a fire, even though he'd only really known it from watching cowboy films. Peter and I would fish away, Michael was into whittling, big-style. He would attach feathers and things to his sticks, on strings, make them kind of symbolic, and throw them up into the trees above our base camp, and over the weekend or even over a whole season or years these things would be dangling down. One time the local farmer came by and was chatting away, he spotted these things and we feigned ignorance, the farmer's opinion was that it was maybe tinkers or travellers that had put them up there. Michael loved that, the fact that he had created that sense of mystery or puzzlement. He loved being out in nature, it took him away from his world of a smoke-filled room and a piano in much the same way it took me away from my wee flat down a badly lit street in the west end of Dundee. We liked driving, because when you're driving you can put on music, you can take yourselves off to strange places for cups of tea.
>
> The Marras had the caravan up at Inver too, Kevin Murray and I went up there one weekend. There was a major falling-out over sausages. Three men living in a caravan and fighting about sausages. I stormed out with my fishing-rod, went over the river Tay, came back three hours later with a three-pound sea trout, and all was well![4]

Another aspect of his engagement with the outdoors and with nature was Michael's fascination with an osprey nest a few miles from his home. Every year the adult pair would arrive in the spring and repair their own home on top of an electricity pylon –

> That big bunchy structure of sticks and
>   moss not
> ramshackle in the least but
> firm, safe as houses in the high winds,
> not perched but planted

– as Liz Lochhead describes it in her poem in memory of Michael, 'The Optimistic Sound'. As often as he could, Michael would go to a nearby vantage point and through his binoculars watch the ospreys catch fish and take turns to sit on the eggs, waiting for them to hatch and the chicks to appear, eventually to take their first tentative flights. As skylarks did for Jim Crumley, so for Michael the ospreys came to symbolise all the beauty, hope, resilience and renewal of the natural world. They were very special for him, especially in his last summer. Most days, Andy Pelc would pick him up and drive him to see the ospreys. 'He loved the ospreys, the idea of the ospreys,' Andy said. 'He loved salmon, what salmon do, what ospreys do, he got off on nature in that spiritual sense.' And then they'd drive somewhere else, sampling the cafes and hotels of Angus and Perthshire for cups of tea. 'We never spoke about his illness. We spoke about everything else.'[5] That was how Michael wanted it.

*

In the summer months, if the weather was dry, you would often get no answer to a knock at the front door of the Marras' house in Church Street, Newtyle. You had to walk round the back, and there you might find Michael, working on his boat. Or playing with it – the line between work and play was a fine one. The boat was not really a boat. You could not sail away in it, but you could imagine it. Michael could, anyway. It was an assemblage of branches and tree-limbs and other bits of wood that he had gathered or that friends would deliver, almost like offerings. They brought sticks from the New Forest, sticks from the Pacific Ocean. Alice Marra remembers the boat as a place of sanctuary for him:

> I don't know why it started, but it was very important to him, especially in the last few years of his life. He would deconstruct and rebuild it, he had mirrors and other things worked into it, it was a kind of sculpture really, one that he could keep adding to, working on. People would bring things to him to add to it, driftwood from the beach and things like that.
>
> The boat reminded me of those drawings he would do with felt-tip pens, with really straight lines and the spaces that he would colour in. The placing of the sticks in rows and patterns, the making of the boat shape, was maybe similar to that.[6]

He was always pleased to show you the boat, but he didn't really show you anything. It was there for you to look at, admire, guess at. It was a structure for something that would never actually sail, and it wasn't his job to tell you what it would or should look like. It was a space for his imagination, and by extension – if you allowed yourself the time and liberty – for yours.

Michael and his boat
in the back garden at
Church Street, Newtyle.

She suddenly goes,
'Oh, Mr Marra, you've
got your torture button
switched to ON.'

And I says to her,
'What do you mean,
my torture button?'
She says, 'Your torture
button on the back of
your head. Everybody
has one.'

Not long before Michael died, Gordon Maclean was over from Tobermory and he went to see him in Newtyle. They sat out in the back garden beside the boat, talking of this and that – not about his illness. The breeze was blowing through the struts and spars of the boat, making it ripple and float. 'It was a precious time,' Gordon said. 'I'll never forget it.'

Then Gordon went on:

> Both as an artist and a human being Michael was a one-off. One of the things that made him stand out was that he was so clearly not a 'product': nobody had moulded and shaped him. He always resisted such pressure, or reacted against it. Good music, he believed, like all good art came from everywhere and anywhere. There was not a drop of prejudice or racism in him.[7]

The same term was used by Liz Lochhead in assessing Michael's importance not just to her but to so many others with whom he interacted:

> He was a one-off. He turned everything upside down and made you see it differently. His way of looking at things was so exciting and illuminating – even if he revealed it just by an off-the-cuff remark or a wee joke. He changed me in ways that nobody could change him. Once you had known Michael, you wanted to conduct your own life as much as possible as he conducted his, with that quiet

confidence in his own brand of integrity. An awful lot of people who knew Michael became better people because of knowing him. [8]

And Rab Noakes also emphasised how unusual he was:

> It can't be underestimated how unique Michael was. You can sing Michael's songs – I put 'Guernsey Kitchen Porter' onto my latest album and 'Niel Gow's Apprentice' on an album I did in the early 90s, so you can find a way into the songs – but you're not going to catch the same things that Michael Marra did. He's inimitable in that sense. And he has no successor either. [9]

Who knows, though, down what paths younger musicians and songwriters may venture after listening to Michael? One of the important things that happened in 2017 was the digital release of most of his back catalogue, together with the live album *High Sobriety* (from a concert at the Bonar Hall in Dundee in 2000) and *Dubiety*, the album that should have followed *The Midas Touch* but was shelved by Polydor. It had become notoriously difficult to find Michael's recordings: now they were available again, to be heard not just by those who already knew them but by new generations of listeners.

2017 also saw the release of Alice Marra's album *Chain Up the Swings*, which features Alice singing twelve of her father's songs backed by a fully-charged line-up of the Gaels Blue Orchestra (with both original members and new, younger musicians involved):

> Gordon Maclean was at the party on the final night of The Hazey Janes' 2013 tour with Deacon Blue, and he said to me, 'By the way, Alice, you need to make an album of your dad's songs.' It was his idea about The Hazey Janes working with Liz [Lochhead] as well. Basically, if Gordon has an idea it's always a good one. So I said, 'Okay, I will do that.' I thought I'd be making it with him, but going back and forth to Mull was going to be too complicated, so I spoke to Allan McGlone and Derek Thomson. I also thought it was going to be piano and vocal and not much else, a bit jazzy-folky, but Allan had a lot of other ideas and it became very much a collaboration between me, Allan, Derek and Chris [Marra]. Beyond having a preference for doing some of the songs from the theatre shows I had no idea which songs I wanted to do. We had about thirty songs in the beginning, demo'd them all, and then by a process of elimination got down to the twelve that are on the album. The difficulty was working out how to sing the songs and how to arrange them. I thought maybe the ones that were in the wrong key for me, well, just forget them, but some of them turned out to be the right songs to do. Then I thought I had to sing them differently from how Michael sang them, but actually that wasn't the case either.

And I worried about doing a song like 'Goodnight to Lovely You', a song I really like, because he might have thought it wasn't good enough, that it's a good tune but the lyrics aren't strong enough. But the songs are there to be sung. [10]

Folk are still singing the songs of Robert Burns two hundred years after his death precisely because they are still here to be sung – sometimes well, sometimes badly, sometimes 'traditionally' (a loaded term) and sometimes given new interpretations. Michael's versions of Burns's songs were not to everybody's taste, but they were – at the very least – one songwriter's acknowledgment and honouring of another. And although there were many covers of his songs during his lifetime, perhaps *Chain Up the Swings*, five years after Michael's death, marked the moment when his songs were 'released' to everybody to sing, the moment when his name really did make it into brackets.

One day you'll find Joni Mitchell and everything will be okay.

(Facing page) Lyrics of 'Hermless': 'My contender for National Anthem of Scotland', Michael noted, before scoring out 'contender'.

Hermless *

Wi' my hand on my hert
And my hert in my mooth
Wi' erms that could reach ower the sea
My feet micht be big but the insects are safe
They'll never get stood on by me

Chorus.

Hermless hermless, there's never nae better
I ging tae the library. I tak oot a book   fae me
And then I go hame for my tea

I save a' the coupons that come wi' the soup
And when I have saved fifty three
I send awa' fifty, pit three in the drar
And something gets posted tae me.
Chorus.

There's ane or twa lads I could cry my chums
They're canny and meek as can be
There's Tam wi' his pigeons
And Wull wi' his mice
And Robert Mc'Lennan and me

Chorus

Hermless hermless

* my ~~candidate~~ for National Anthem of Scotland.

247

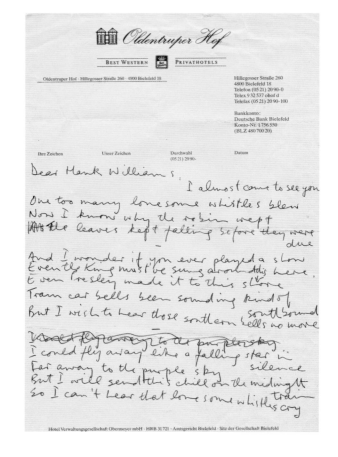

On borrowed stationery, the
lyrics of 'Dear Hank Williams',
written by Michael for his
brother Eddie.

If we are to talk of successors and influence, where better to start than with his children, Alice and Matthew? What was it like growing up having Michael Marra as their father. Matthew:

> You don't have anything else to compare it with, so I just assumed that other people's dads were like my dad. When he was working, that was separate, so we didn't really see that side of him when we were wee, but everything else was just normal family life. Just the usual things – playing football in the garden and so on. He was always pretty ruthless when we were playing two-touch. Maybe in my teenage years I wouldn't really want to go out there and play, but then I got through that and right to the end we'd go out to the front garden and kick the ball around. [11]

But in some ways Michael *was* different. Alice:

> For somebody who didn't go to school that much and left school early, he knew an amazing amount. When you're little you think that your dad knows everything – everybody thinks that about their dad – but I remember having conversations with friends when somebody would say, my dad knows everything, and I would be thinking, no, but my dad really *does* know everything. Anything you asked him, he had an answer. We did a lot of quizzes, that was always a big thing in

the evenings, the four of us with a quiz book, and he would get every single question right.
>
> People imagine we must have grown up in a house which was constantly full of music, but it wasn't like that. When he finished working, he didn't want more music. When he came out of his room he wanted to watch TV. But I do remember one time when I had Kylie on really loud, he said, one day you'll find Joni Mitchell and everything will be okay. And I did! [12]

And there was one occasion when Michael said something to Alice which revealed a little of his own consciousness of being different: 'We were driving in the car one time and he said, "Zug, what would you do if I was a normal old boy?"' To which she had no ready answer; no answer at all, in fact.

I suggested to Andy Pelc that every person who knew Michael got their own version of him. This wasn't a deliberate act of dissemblance or control on his part, it was that different people drew different responses from him. Andy agreed: 'I think that's right. What makes me proudest of having known Michael was I got a version of Michael that nobody else got.' He then told the following story:

> He turned up at my flat one day, unannounced. I opened the door and he walked straight in, his head was down as it sometimes was, he sat down and didn't say anything. 'You all right? You want a cup of coffee?'

Yes. So I made him a coffee. He says, 'I've been having this fantasy, this recurring dream. The broon nurse [district nurse] comes around to see us, and she's going through my hair with a Derbac nit comb, and she suddenly goes, "Oh, Mr Marra, you've got your torture button switched to ON." And I says to her, "What do you mean, my torture button?" She says, "Your torture button on the back of your head. Everybody has one." "Oh, I never knew that everybody –" She says, "Aye. Are you wanting me to turn it to OFF?" I says, "Aye." So she turns it to OFF and you know what, everything's just fucking great again.' [13]

There is something poignant about this story, showing as it does that there could be dark zones in the passages of Michael's brain. But the telling point is the one that demonstrates Michael's capacity for empathy: *everybody* has a torture button. Eilidh Mackenzie has a similarly moving anecdote:

> On one occasion, probably after a *Bel Canto* recording session, I was travelling back to Inverness by train from Glasgow and shared the journey as far as Perth with Michael before he got off to catch the connection to Dundee. We had what is possibly my favourite shared Marra conversation. He told me of a wee lad with dyslexia who had taken his written schoolwork home to show his mum and on seeing the red pen corrections of his teacher had announced to his mother that

there were now red spiders marching across the page. The retelling of this story seemed to fill Michael with absolute joy.

Shortly after Michael's death I introduced his song 'Hermless' to children in schools in Inverness and Ross-shire through the Youth Music Initiative scheme. One wee lad, originally from Poland, who was in the early stages of English acquisition, cried and smiled every single week and managed to tell me he thought it was the most beautiful song he had ever heard. I came to expect his smiling tears every week of the six and he never disappointed. [14]

*

Michael's unique take on life and his ability to bring the best out of others came up again and again in interviews or correspondence with those he worked with. One of his longest-standing friends was the singer Rod Paterson:

> I first met him, briefly, in Woodlands Folk Club, Broughty Ferry, around 1971. I did one or two floor spots, but he made regular contributions, amongst which was a twelve-bar blues which started, 'Last time into Bell Street, didn't have any excuse...' [Bell Street is the address of Dundee's central police station.] The line 'Willie Fitzgerald, don't you put the hose on me' referred to the US National Guards' hosing of anti-Vietnam student rioters in Chicago some years earlier, but transferred the hose into

the hands of Dundee's uninspiring Lord Provost to howls of laughter. I thought then, 'This boy's trouble.'

I next met him, in Edinburgh, during the Festival in the 1980s. He was gigging nights with Saint Andrew at the Cafe Royal, and promoting his album *Gaels Blue* in an afternoon slot at the music venue, the A1 Club, to two men and a dog.

The songs hit me like a thunderbolt: it seemed to me that we were both aiming for the same goal. He was giving pop music a Scottish lyrical twist, while I was trying to give traditional Scottish song a 20th-century musical treatment.

Around this time we were both involved in STV'S *Moonlight and Love Songs*, filmed in Dougie MacLean's studio. I had introduced Michael to Dick Lee's sax/clarinet playing, and together they recorded some Burns songs. When Dick asked Michael for artistic direction on 'Ae Fond Kiss', he stroked his chin and replied. 'Think o' a deid bairn floatin' just under the water.' Dick did and they nailed it in one take.

Kindness is a quality I haven't heard mentioned among the many tributes since his death, nor courage, but my memories of him usually involve one or other, or both. [15]

*

Someone who knew Michael his entire life was Sheena Wellington, who grew up as he did in Lochee. 'There are going to be thousands of PhDs done on the work of Michael Marra,' is Sheena's belief. 'It's a rich field. I mean, who would have Princess Grace of Monaco and the advert for Taylor's Coal in the same song? Who would do that apart from Michael? You listen to his songs and think, this is unbelievable. It's great but it's unbelievable!' She continued:

> When he left the school it wasn't because he wasn't clever, he was just too big for the space. He had that bump of curiosity that led him to explore. He had a very perceptive eye. He could see things that we all see but don't notice. Michael noticed things. And yet talking to the man offstage, you wouldn't know there was something special about him. A lot of artists, when they come off the stage, they're still the personalities that they were when they were performing, and there's nothing necessarily wrong with that. But if you met him in the bar afterwards and didnae know that he was Michael Marra, you would not have found oot that he was Michael Marra. [16]

*

That reluctance to be the centre of attention, coupled with his suspicion of some of the corporate side of the music world, undoubtedly had an impact on Michael's career and on his output. Ricky Ross, lead singer with Deacon Blue [17], expressed admiration for Michael but some frustration as well:

> I saw Michael playing with Skeets Boliver when I was sixteen or

seventeen. He was the 'local rock star', the one who went off to London and made a record. Looking back from nearly forty years on, it's unfortunate that the bad time he had in London left him with such a diffident attitude towards the music industry, especially since in other areas of life he showed such generosity of spirit and gave so many people the benefit of the doubt. I think his antipathy to the industry probably meant some of his work remained less properly 'finished' than it could have been. It was also frustrating that his recorded music was often difficult for people to find. His songs should have been better known in his lifetime than they were.

Having said that, I respect his reasons for being wary. He was an artist and that meant he could be spiky and sensitive. He was full of contradictions, as we all are. If he hadn't been he couldn't have made the songs that he did from the stories he found all around him.

This year is fifty years on from *Sergeant Pepper*. Will Michael Marra's music still be played and listened to fifty years from now? Maybe not the records per se, but the individual songs, yes, I think so. He wrote so many songs that speak to people's hearts. They are about us. They speak of a Scotland that we who live here understand. He poked fun at our sensibilities not by recycling clichés but in a much more nuanced way. He enabled us to look at ourselves much as the writer Sean O'Casey enabled the

Irish to look and laugh at themselves.

I remember two things he said to me that I feel came from his own experience. One was when I was moaning about something I was involved in that wasn't going too well. 'Ricky,' he said, 'you're allowed three tantrums on any one project.' The other was when I was having my own difficulties with some aspect of the industry. 'Listen,' he told me, 'no one can ever stop you making music.' These are lessons I took from him that have resonated ever since. [18]

*

Ray Laidlaw, drummer and mainstay of the band Lindisfarne, recounts how he came across Michael's music:

I first became aware of him in the 1980s when Lindisfarne performed at a number of festivals where Michael was also on the bill. A mutual friend of ours was Rab Noakes, who had also mentioned Michael in glowing terms but for some reason I got the idea that he was a singer of traditional Scottish songs.

In 2000, another Scottish friend of mine, Duncan McCrone, asked me to contribute some drums to an album he was planning. One of the songs we recorded was Michael's 'The Lonesome Death of Francis Clarke'. I was captivated by this song and realised that there was a lot more to Michael Marra than I realised.

I have been lucky in my musical career and have spent many years playing songs by Alan Hull and Rod

Clements, both formidable songwriters. The very high standard of their work raised the bar for me and if a song doesn't have that special something I quickly lose interest. Outside of my Lindisfarne pals my personal favourite writers were Leonard Cohen, Bob Dylan, Mark Knopfler, Randy Newman, Warren Zevon and a few more. As I began to search out Michael's back catalogue I discovered that here was someone whose songs could easily be measured up against the music of my long-time heroes. Michael had a fantastic gift for melody and language. He created wonderful aural scenarios that impressed, intrigued and amused me in equal measures. That happens very rarely.

Learning that Michael was playing a gig not far from his home in the North-East of England, Ray went along and was 'knocked sideways by his musicality, his innovative performance style and then, after the show, was charmed by his gentle and modest persona.' Ray organised a gig for Michael in his home town of Tynemouth and introduced him to an entirely new audience: 'My neighbours still talk about that very special gig. Michael was a true original. It's a shame that more people in the mainstream of music weren't aware of his talents when he was alive but I don't think he would have coped well with fame and adulation. I fancy he was fond of the simple life.' [19]

*

Alan Gorrie of the Average White Band also heard about Michael and Chris Marra in the 1980s, from his old friend, drummer Donny Coutts. Donny identified the Marras as the 'new' Dundee talent to watch. However he did not become familiar with the Marra songbook until *Gaels Blue* 'took his fancy', followed by *Posted Sober* which remains 'one of my top ten favourite records of all time, by anyone':

When Donald Shaw invited us to play Celtic Connections, and asked me who I would pick to add a local Scottish side to our concert, I immediately nominated Michael as I really wanted an excuse to work with him, and knew there would be a soulful compatibility in our collaboration.

He had an immediate effect on the rest of our band when he walked into rehearsals for the first time, sat down at the piano, and we began 'Flight of the Heron'. When we moved on to 'All Will Be Well', it was game over. Brent, our lead vocalist had to video it on his phone, he was so moved by Mick's honesty and presence.

The concert itself was very special, though we didn't really get a chance to hang out together as we were so busy with our own programme and another guest performer too. Nor did we know that Mick was ill – I had been up to Newtyle to go over our plans the week prior, and he was full of bonhomie (and we blethered more than we worked) – and it wasn't until I asked Peg later about the possibility of our reprising the partnership for a Celtic Connections event at the Ryder

(Top) Michael Marra,
Doctor of Laws (University
of Dundee, 2007).

(Above) Receiving his *Herald*
Angel from Simon Callow
in 2010.

Cup in Chicago that she told me of his condition.

Anyway, suffice to say it is one of the standout moments of my career – right up there with Marvin Gaye joining us onstage, and other wondrous bits of serendipity and good fortune. Hence my being inspired to write a piece for his memorial concert, which turned out to be 'The Future'. At least we were able to put forth a full-blown recording of that and 'Letter From Perth', with Chris and some of Mick's Dundee cohort, into the pot for the Optimistic Sound charity, the forerunner and bow-wave for El Sistema in Dundee. Hopefully a fitting tribute to him, his music, and his poetry. [20]

Michael also considered sharing a stage with the Average White Band one of the highlights of his musical life, but had a slightly different take on the rehearsal experience. He told me that to begin with he thought these very cool musicians weren't paying much attention to the skinny old white guy in the beret, but then somebody mentioned not only that his song was for Gil Scott-Heron's father but that he'd corresponded with Gil Scott-Heron. Suddenly his kudos went through the roof!

*

Trying to have the last word on Michael Marra is like trying to ban the dawn chorus or stop a river flowing. There are too many competing voices, too strong a current. In writing this book, I could have spent months asking people to sum him up, and

for every definitive assessment that would seem to have nailed it, another would have popped up that saw him from a completely different angle. Yet there is consensus on one thing: he is irreplaceable.

His voice managed to be both true to its local origins and universal in its humanity. The likeness to Robert Burns is incontestable. On the occasion of his receiving the honorary degree of Doctor of Laws from the University of Dundee in 2007, the laureation address was given by Sheena Wellington, who said:

> Mention Michael Marra to anyone who has worked with him and you find both huge respect for his music and deep affection for this gentle gifted man. He has given numerous concerts for charities and in his own quiet understated way he has been a constant supporter of the fight for justice and the right of people to live free from fear and want.
>
> Michael Marra sits awkwardly as his home city's bard, a troubadour voice for the working-class heart of an increasingly cosmopolitan town and in the true Dundee tradition he is both proud and self-deprecating, wry and tender, outward-looking and homely.

Michael was also honoured by Glasgow Caledonian University with the degree of Doctor of Letters in 2011. The citation for his Bank of Scotland *Herald* Angel award in 2010 described him as a 'national treasure' and praised his 'complete mastery of his material and his relationship with his audience'.

When Gary West gave his inaugural lecture as Professor of Scottish Ethnology at the University of Edinburgh on St Andrew's Day, 2016, he acknowledged Michael's place in a broad movement that continues to make connections between different aspects – oral, folk, pop, literary and classical – of Scottish and international culture:

> I think back on some huge cultural moments that have happened even just in the last few months: Greg Lawson's reworking of Martyn Bennett's *Grit* at the Edinburgh International Festival; *Pilgrimer*, James Robertson's re-imagining of Joni Mitchell's album *Hejira* in beautifully crafted Scots; and the powerful presence of the late Michael Marra to be heard in both of these wonderfully inspiring moments of art…
>
> There is a strong cultural movement afoot… challenging, politically charged, intellectually curious, with an edge of the radical, a vivid awareness of what has gone before, and a sharpening vision of what yet might be. And it is highly creative…
>
> If Hamish Henderson's vision was to forge a folk-centred cultural future that was Gramsci in action, this movement of today might yet be Henderson in action. Or Martyn Bennett in action. Or Michael Marra in action. And it is marvellous in our eyes![21]

But since there has to be a last word – in this chapter, anyway – let it be that of another songwriter, Karine Polwart, somebody with whom Michael had performed and whom he greatly admired (her album *Traces*, released two months before he died, was the last CD he bought). It would, I think, have pleased Michael to have read this appraisal from another worker at the same seam.

Michael had a songwriter's voice like no other. And I'm not talking about the gorgeous gravelly sound he made when he opened his mouth but about his eye and his ear for people and place and particularity. I heard his songs first when I was living in Dundee, just off the Magdalen Green, the year after I finished university. He appeared through my bedsit door on a mix tape put together by a lovely, skinny man from Birkhill called Dougie, who would, as a result of his good taste in music, amongst other things, become my first big love. Michael was nestled in there with John Martyn, Leonard Cohen, Dick Gaughan and James Taylor. It tickled me no end when I heard him later on a radio show talking about how perfect a song 'Sweet Baby James' is, because I'm sure it was on this first tape from Dougie alongside 'General Grant's Visit to Dundee' and 'Happed in Mist'.

I fell in love with 'Happed in Mist' because Chris Guthrie from *Sunset Song* was a teenage heroine to me. And then the thing that struck me was the reek of place. Dundee, Angus, Newburgh. And later still there's Mount Florida, Ullapool, Invergowrie Bay.

I walked to Newburgh one day with

Dougie as a result of 'Racing from Newburgh'. We got waylaid en route at Balmerino and stomped into town just in time to see the last bus leaving for Dundee. It was an epic thirty-six mile, Michael Marra-inspired pilgrimage! We didn't get home until two in the morning…

There's this misconception that some songwriters have, that to make a thing sing to someone else, to make it universal, you have to rob it of all its local colour and nuance and rhythm. For me, the opposite is true. The specificity is what allows us to make the connection, to imagine real bodies in space.

There's such humanity to Michael's songs, even when he's writing for laughs. He's expert at satire but doesn't sneer. 'Baps and Paste' is one of the funniest songs I've ever heard but I never for a minute think Michael's being cruel. He's just got it. And that's maybe part of why he is so loved in his own city.

I have a few personal favourites, of course. 'The Lonesome Death of Francis Clarke' breaks my heart. It's riddled with quirky local references – Blind Mattie, the Mackay Twins, the Blackness Foundry. And, like so many of his songs, there's a wink in the title to the songs of his own heroes, especially a recurring nod to Dylan. Most of all though, there's solid empathy for the maverick outsider, the one who's a wee bit broken by life but absolutely in love with it too. In this case, it's the tale of an ancestral black-sheep uncle.

But Michael renders him luminous in this lyric, singing to his love bathed in the moonlight. And the final line of the bridge – 'there must be a twinkling seam of Love' – well, it's like some kind of manifesto for life, a philosophical underpinning. In fact, there's a redemptive quality of light in so many of his songs. It's there in 'Frida Kahlo's Visit to the Taybridge Bar' too. She's another beautiful, wounded, eccentric soul, freed from all pain in that bar and flooding us with her 'scarlet light'.

There are songs that amount almost to hymns for the stuff that brings people together. 'Hamish' is a gorgeous example of that. Who would think to write a song about the Dundee United goalie? And who would even care about such a song if they weren't into football? But at the Celtic Connections celebration of Michael in 2013, it was Rod Paterson who finished me off, singing 'Hamish stokes young men's dreams into a burning flame'. That song says something huge about hope, and grace, and a kind of everyday heroism.

There's tremendous positivity in a lot of the songs. I can imagine Michael in the alternate version of his life, the one he walked away from, conjuring 'Like Another Rolling Stone', with some corporate Brill Building executive at his back saying, 'Hey, this could be a great song, but what the hell is a fife? And can you just ditch the fiddle and the tent and…' But those idiosyncrasies are perfect.

There's a beautiful quote attributed

to Woody Guthrie that says, 'I hate a song that makes you think you are not any good. I hate a song that makes you think that you are just born to lose. Bound to lose. No good to nobody. No good for nothing.' I reckon Michael held that in his heart as a writer too, because it's his humility and his humour and his humanity above all else that distinguish him. [22]

Listen, no one can ever stop you making music.

Notes

1 'Michael Marra; A Gentleman Genius; Our National Bard', in *The List*, 25th October 2012.

2 This engagement was followed immediately by a booking at the Arts Centre in Washington in what was historically part of County Durham: he thus did back-to-back gigs in Washington, D.C. and Washington, C.D.

3 Email, 21st May 2017.

4 Interview with Andy Pelc, 13th April 2017.

5 Ibid.

6 Interview with Alice Marra, 9th May 2017.

7 Interview with Gordon Maclean, 17th May 2017.

8 Interview with Liz Lochhead, 26th May 2017.

9 Interview with Rab Noakes, 21st July 2016.

10 Interview with Alice Marra, 9th May 2017.

11 Interview with Matthew Marra, 26th April 2017.

12 Interview with Alice Marra, 9th May 2017.

13 Interview with Andy Pelc, 13th April 2017.

14 Email, 27th May 2017.

15 Email, 21st May 2017.

16 Interview with Sheena Wellington, 13th May 2017.

17 Michael toured Europe with Deacon Blue in 1991, and – completing a kind of family circle – The Hazey Janes supported Deacon Blue on their 2013 UK tour.

18 Interview with Ricky Ross, 15th May 2017.

19 Email, 25th May 2017.

20 Email, 9th March 2017.

21 'Performing Testimony: towards a creative ethnology for the 21st century', lecture at the University of Edinburgh, 30th November 2016.

22 Email, 29th May 2017.

Michael in the National Theatre of Scotland's inaugural production *Home*.

The Singing Moth

All will be well, you may do as you
  please
No harm will befall you, while I live
  and breathe

'All Will Be Well'

Michael was diagnosed with lung cancer in May, 2012. By that time he was already very ill, and had played what was to be his last gig, a sell-out show at Dundee Rep with The Hazey Janes on 30th March. He underwent treatment during that summer, but died on the night of 23rd October in Ninewells Hospital, Dundee. He was sixty. The family issued a brief statement: 'We are devastated by our sudden loss but are comforted by the kind words of so many people who loved Michael, his music and his spirit. His life's work has told our family story, and the story of his beloved Dundee. Michael's songs are his legacy, given to Scotland by one wee boy from Lochee.'

I was on a train to London when Marianne phoned to tell me the next morning. I sat with my head against the window pane and 'cried like a baby in the darkest night'. Over the months, we'd seen him getting thinner and thinner, becoming more and more exhausted, yet I'd somehow believed that he was going to be well again. The things I was on my way to do in London seemed utterly unimportant. I felt his loss like a heavy, empty hole inside me, and I was not alone. Across Scotland and around the world, thousands of people – many of whom knew him only through his recordings or from having seen him perform – found themselves bereft when they heard or read the news. The journalist and writer Lesley Riddoch was on her way from Skye to Perth when a friend phoned her. That evening she wrote a moving tribute which included the following:

> Dundee has lost its bard. And Scotland has lost one of the few people who ever really understood it – kindness, squalor, hilarity, warts and all… Like Robert Burns, Michael was driven by compassion, humanitarianism and a deep-seated fury at cruelty – whether that was the callous cruelty of war… or the cruelty of men towards women.
>
> All Michael's work was characterised by humanity and – despite the mess humanity has made of the planet – optimism. [1]

There was an outpouring of grief and a plethora of glowing and grateful obituaries which, all his family are agreed, he would have found profoundly embarrassing. Hundreds of people attended his funeral at Dundee Crematorium on 30th October. It was a very moving occasion, with moments of mirth shining through the sadness. Frank McConnell reminded me of one beautifully significant touch. When the coffin was brought in the music played was 'Inchworm' from the film *Hans Christian Andersen* – that song that Michael had loved from childhood. In the film, the cobbler Hans (played by Danny Kaye) passes the schoolhouse where the children are learning their times-tables by rote. He looks in at the door and the schoolmaster, who believes Hans is always distracting his pupils with his fairy tales, peevishly shuts him out. Round the corner his orphan apprentice Peter points out the first inchworm of the season among the marigolds. Danny Kaye sings, 'Inchworm, inchworm, measuring the marigolds, you and your arithmetic, you'll probably go far. Inchworm, inchworm, measuring the marigolds, seems to me you'd stop and see how beautiful they are.' The contrast between the inchworm's progress and the dead hand of education on the children's imagination and engagement with the world could not be greater. The inchworm, of course, will in time turn into a moth. 'Remember,' Frank said, 'when Michael worked at Smith & Hutton's boatyard they nicknamed him "The Singing Moth".' [2]

Notes

1   www.lesleyriddoch.co.uk, 24th October 2012.

2   Interview with Frank McConnell, 11th January 2017.

Kitchen conversation

No.9

Michael: Are you working?

James: I'm just finishing something off.

M: That's good. Although that can be the hardest part. Letting go.

J: You're right. You have to be as sure as you can be that it's ready because, once it's out there, that's it. You can't call it back.

M: What is it you're finishing?

J: A book.

M: Another novel?

J: No, this one's factual. You're in it. It's about you, actually.

M: Hm. I knew something was going on.

J: You don't sound pleased.

M: Did you expect me to be?

J: Not really.

M: I don't suppose I have a say in this? About being in this book?

J: Again, not really. Sorry.

M: You don't surprise me.

J: What might surprise you is the number of appearances you've been making since you left us. Without having any say about it.

M: So things haven't changed much then?

J: I was at the McManus last week. You're in there too. A portrait by Calum Colvin. That photograph of you was a study for it.

M: Calum's a great artist. I can't complain about that.

J: Are you complaining about the book?

M: Well, I think you could be more usefully employed.

J: There is also a display cabinet in the McManus – part of the same exhibition – full of Michael Marra artefacts.

M: That's a step up from a butler's pantry anyway. I think. But the McManus is a museum, which is worrying.

J: It's also an art gallery.

M: What kind of artefacts?

J: Your ironing-board, your keyboard, your beret. Some of your books and CDs.

M: Anything that might surprise me?

J: There's a pair of insoles for your baffies, made out of carpet. You won't have seen those. Johnny Briggs who has the Persian carpet shop in Stonehaven made them for you.

M: I remember him. I did a gig there and he'd spread these marvellous rugs all over the stage. I was impressed by the forethought that had been given to the comfort of my feet.

J: He made the insoles for you but unfortunately, before he could get them to you, you had gone.

M: You're not talking about the night of the gig, I assume? That would have been fast work.

J: No. Later. He gave them to Peggy at your funeral.

M: This is one of those conversations that could be heading for metaphor territory. Where, as you know, I do not like to go. You mentioned other appearances. Such as?

J: There's a portrait of you by Donald Smart hanging in Lochee Library. Your words are on a bench by the River Tay next to Niel Gow's Oak, and there's a waymarker beside the Dighty Burn with a wee rhyme by Jim Crumley about you. One of your fans made a tapestry portrait of you. It's really good.

M: Has anybody opened a shop to sell all this merchandise? Are there Michael Marra dolls?

J: Not yet. But there is a tattoo.

M: A what?

J: There's a man who has a tattoo of you.

M: Now you are taking advantage of my gullibility. Where is it?

J: Kilmarnock.

M: Where *on his body?*

J: His leg. I'm not sure which one. It's a good likeness too, and almost as hairy as the tapestry.

M: Is this the fame I eluded all those years?

J: You could say that. What else? There's a beer called Hermless. Your back catalogue has been re-released digitally. There have been tribute concerts, people have been performing your songs and recording new versions of them.

M: People are singing my songs?

J: Oh yes. That's what they're there for, isn't it? 'People don't need your biography, they need your songs.' You said that.

M: Then why bother with the book?

J: Just to provide a bit of context, Michael. Can you tolerate a bit of context? Give it houseroom, even?

M: Why do I get a sense that one of my songs is about to be used in evidence against me?

J: For me, that one's right up there with the best of them. There are those lines that go,

If you ever hear me grumbling –
Don't give me houseroom
But a scornful look
As some soul makes a midnight sprint
Through a sniper's sights
For a library book

M: The situations are not comparable.

J: Nevertheless.

M: Hm. I'd better let you get on then. One thing, though.

J: What's that?

M: Do I get the last word here?

J: Why not?

M: To the left of us fly the monkeys in the trees,

And to the right of us flows a stream,

To the back of us, old foolish notions,

And ahead of us lie our dreams…

267

(Left) Michael in *Border Warfare*
(Wildcat Theatre, 1989).

(Above) Banner outside
Dundee Rep for the
An Optimistic Sound tribute
concert, 28th September 2013.

Posted Later

There's a light at the end of the tunnel
I can see it keeking through
Big light must shine on someone
May as well be me and you

'Letter from Perth'

Since Michael's death, the months and years have been marked by many tributes and events celebrating him and his work. The following pages record just some of these – from full-scale concerts to beer, buses and a tattoo.

December 2012:
A televised tribute to Michael, including an emotional performance of 'Hermless' by Ricky Ross, forms part of the annual Hands Up for Trad Awards. Later in the month sees Neon Productions' (Rab Noakes's company) television tribute *All Will Be Well* and, on 1st January 2013, the *Michael Marra Family Album* programme presented by Janice Forsyth on Radio Scotland.

2013:
The charity, Optimistic Sound – Michael Marra Music Trust For The Young People Of Dundee, is established by the Marra family with the aim of bringing the Sistema Project to Dundee and setting up a Big Noise Orchestra in the city.

28th January 2013:

All Will Be Well: Tribute concert at Glasgow Royal Concert Hall, Celtic Connections. Rab Noakes hosts an array of performers including Alice Marra, The Hazey Janes, Eddi Reader, Dougie MacLean, Tom Mitchell, the Mackenzie Sisters and Kris Drever, Hue and Cry, Riley Briggs, Rod Paterson, John Spillane and Sylvia Rae.

4th February to 26th April 2013:

A retrospective exhibition of the work of Vincent Rattray, titled *Synchronise Our Eyebrows* (a line from Michael's operetta *If the Moon Can Be Believed*), is held at the Hannah Maclure Centre Gallery in the University of Abertay. When the exhibition was first being planned it had been hoped that Michael would write something about Vince's work. After Michael's death Vince's family and gallery curator Clare Brennan decided to give the paintings, many of which were untitled and had not been seen in public before, titles taken from Michael's lyrics, as a way of marking the friendship between the two men and celebrating both their lives. One comment by Michael is prominently displayed in the exhibition: 'Vince's powers of observation were acute and he reserved a single most eloquent raised eyebrow for the charlatan.'

1st March 2013:

A print of Michael's collage of Frida Kahlo is presented to the Tay Bridge Bar by Peggy, Alice and Matthew. The picture takes up residence in one of Michael's favourite haunts, and the scene of the Mexican painter's return to Earth in one of his best-known songs, following a suggestion from publican Jimmy Marr that a memorial should be created to Michael in the bar. On the occasion Mr Marr presents the family with a cheque for £500 for Optimistic Sound.

23rd March 2013:

After the original bench was destroyed by a branch from Niel Gow's Oak falling on it during a storm in December 2011, a new bench is unveiled by Peter Fullarton of the Forestry Commission at Inver on a path beside the River Tay. The small ceremony, which takes place during a light snowstorm, is attended by Michael's family and celebrated fiddler Pete Clark. The bench is inscribed with words from Michael's song for Dougie MacLean, 'Niel Gow's Apprentice'. The pieces of the first bench are now in Andy Pelc's garden.

April 2013:

Peggy, Alice and Matthew are invited to judge a songwriting competition at Glenfarg Festival where Michael was a regular guest. Proceeds are donated to Optimistic Sound.

5th April 2013:

Launch at Abertay University of Sistema Scotland's campaign to establish a Big Noise Orchestra in Dundee.

14th May 2013:

Evening Telegraph readers vote for Michael's name to appear on one of nine new double-decker Dundee buses. Other names selected include Billy Mackenzie, Jim McLean, Bob Shankly, Brian Cox and Lorraine Kelly. The name on the bus is unveiled at a ceremony in Caird Park in July 2013.

15th August 2013:

Publication of *Whaleback City: the poetry of Dundee and its hinterland* (edited by W.N. Herbert and Andy Jackson, Dundee University Press). The book is dedicated 'To the immortal memory of Michael Marra' and its contents include the lyrics of five of Michael's songs.

28th September 2013:

An Optimistic Sound. Tribute concert at Dundee Rep. Alice Marra hosts the evening. Performers include Dougie MacLean, Eddi Reader, Rab Noakes, the Mackenzie sisters, the Mackay Twins, The Hazey Janes, Karine Polwart, Anderson, McGinty, Webster, Ward and Fisher, Saint Andrew, Sheena Wellington, Frank McConnell (who danced with Clare Brennan), Rod Paterson and Liz Lochhead.

23rd October 2013:

On the first anniversary of his death, a portrait of Michael by Donald Smart is unveiled by Alice and Matthew Marra at Lochee Library. A plaque bearing words from 'Hermless' is also unveiled, and Andy Pelc, accompanied by Kevin Murray and Chris Marra, leads the assembled audience in a rendition of the song.

8th November 2013:

Michael is posthumously given the 'Spirit of Dundee' award at the *Evening Telegraph* Dundee Born and Bred Hero Awards.

29th March 2014:

Resolis Remembers Michael Marra, a Highland tribute concert organised by Resolis Community Arts, takes place at Resolis Memorial Hall. Performers include The Hazey Janes, the Mackenzie Sisters, Rod Paterson, David Gilbert, John Douglas, Riley Briggs, Eddi Reader, Saint Andrew and the Rare Wee Helps, and Frank McConnell. All proceeds go to the Optimistic Sound charity.

June 2014:

A series of six new waymarkers are commissioned by the Dighty Connect environmental group, to replace old mileposts that used to stand alongside the Dighty Burn that runs through Dundee. Each waymarker is a four-sided, flat-topped pyramid about two and a half feet in height, decorated with bright mosaics incorporating a thread of words like a continuous poem. Jim Crumley supplies the words, including, on one of the waymarkers in Trottick, the following: Breengin' alang the straight an' narra, singin' an' growlin' like Michael Marra.

25th September 2014:
A golden ale called Hermless, brewed by the MòR independent brewery at Kellas, is launched in tribute to Michael at the Tay Bridge Bar, with money from the sale of the beer on the night going to Optimistic Sound and thereafter £10 being donated to the from every cask sale. Matthew Marra designs the pump clip, basing it on a keyboard image originally drawn by his father, with Michael's signature overlaid. Peggy pulls the first pint, and Matthew drinks it.

30th November 2014:
Andy Hall's book *Still Light* is launched at the Scottish Parliament. The dedication reads: 'This book is dedicated to the memory of Michael Marra whose art touched the soul of Scotland'.

1st December 2014:
Optimistic Sound EP (CD) released to raise funds for the Optimistic Sound charity. Featuring four of Michael's songs – 'Like Another Rolling Stone', 'When These Shoes Were New', 'Dear Hank Williams' and 'Monkey Hair' performed by The Hazey Janes with Chris Marra, Derek Thomson and a string quartet comprising members of the Royal Scottish National Orchestra.

24th December 2014:
Digital single 'Julius' performed by Drew Larg and the Gaels Blue Orchestra released to raise funds for Optimistic Sound.

28th December 2014:
The Bard is Well: Songs of Michael Marra takes place at Clark's on Lindsay Street, Dundee. This celebration of his music has since become an annual event.

April 2015:
Tim Dalling of the New Rope String Band releases 'Mr Michael Marra', his personal tribute to Michael on his album *Eve's Bonie Squad*.

11th May 2015:
Dean Owens releases his album *Into the Sea* (Drumfire Records) which includes 'Sally's Song (I Dreamed of Michael Marra)'., the final words of which are 'another good man's gone'. Dean Owens explained: 'This song came to me in a dream around the time that Scottish singer-songwriter Michael Marra passed away. In the dream Michael was sitting at the piano singing a song and this was the melody he was singing. There were no words I could remember apart from "it'll all work out" and the name Sally stuck in my head for some reason. Around that time I'd gone for a wander through the old neighbourhood [Leith] where I grew up. There was a housing scheme called The Fort that had been my playground. It had recently been knocked down. Some of the characters from my childhood make an appearance in this song.'

6th November 2015:
Release of 'Letter from Perth'/ 'The Future' AA single by Alan Gorrie and the Big Light Band, to raise funds for Optimistic Sound. 'The Future' is Gorrie's own composition in honour of Michael.

27th May 2016:
Remembering Witch's Blood, a one-night re-imagining, using digital technology, of the 1987 community theatre production, takes place at the West Ward Works, Guthrie Street, Dundee. Michael's voice singing 'Penitence' is heard on a tape-loop and Alice Marra performs 'Humphy Kate's Song'.

27th July 2016:
Mary Ann Kennedy releases her Gaelic version (translated by herself and her mother Kenna Campbell) of Michael's 'Mother Glasgow', featuring Finlay Wells on guitar, on the internet.

11th November 2016:
Michael is inducted into the Scottish Traditional Music Hall of Fame, at a ceremony in Dundee's Marryat Hall.

17th June 2017:
Release of 6-track CD by Liz Lochhead with The Hazey Janes and Steve Kettley, *The Light Comes Back* (Tob Records). The last track is a musical arrangement of Liz's poem 'The Optimistic Sound', written after Michael's funeral and also published in her collection *Fugitive Colours*.

3rd February 2017:
Release of Michael's back catalogue for digital download. Simultaneously released are *Dubiety* (which should have been his second album after *The Midas Touch*) and *High Sobriety*, a double live album of his concert at the Bonar Hall, Dundee in 2000.

3rd February 2017:
Digital and CD release of Alice Marra's *Chain Up the Swings*, on which she covers twelve of Michael's songs, backed by the Gaels Blue Orchestra. The album is launched at Celtic Connections the next day at a concert in St Andrews in the Square, Glasgow.

23rd March 2017:
An article in the *Fife Free Press* rates Michael's concert at the Rothes Halls, Glenrothes in November 2004 at number 54 in the '100 greatest gigs staged in Fife – ever!' Not too impressive, perhaps, although the competition did include The Beatles, the Who and the Kinks, who took the first three slots. It was indeed a great concert, made all the more so by the fact that when Michael opened with 'Mac Rebennack's Visit to Blairgowrie', with the lines

> Then the word goes round
> You get these guys dressed like Elvis
> Come on stage, make a noise
> Who's to say he ain't one of those
>   creatures?
> Who's to say he ain't one of those
>   boys?

there was an Elvis impersonator performing in the auditorium next door.

14th May 2017:

Liz Lochhead appears on *Desert Island Discs*, BBC Radio 4. This is the first time in the programme's history that a song by Michael has been picked by a castaway. Liz does it in style by picking two: 'Green Grow the Rashes' from the live album *Michael Marra with Mr McFall's Chamber*, and 'Mother Glasgow'.

6th July 2017:

Calum Colvin's portrait of Michael is unveiled at the McManus Art Gallery and Museum, Dundee, as part of his exhibition *Museography: Calum Colvin Reflects on the McManus Collections*. As well as the portrait the exhibition includes a case designed by Calum which contains numerous Marra artefacts, loaned by Peggy, including handwritten lyrics, books, beret, record and CD covers and the famous ironing-board.

7th September 2017:

Sistema Scotland's fourth children's orchestra is launched in Dundee. Big Noise Douglas, run in partnership with Optimistic Sound and Dundee City Council, aims to work with around 400 pupils from St Pius and Claypotts Castle primary schools. Alice Marra says that Michael truly believed in the transformational power of music and that it was 'a tribute to his memory that this inspirational programme will today start working to transform the lives of children here in Douglas.'

Etching by Gabriele Gudaityte
inspired by Michael's song
'Frida Kahlo's Visit to the
Taybridge Bar'.

Commemorating Michael:
Hermless ale; Dundee bus.

Commemorating Michael:
Frida Kahlo in the Taybridge Bar.

Commemorating Michael:
tattoo (courtesy of Gavin Wilson).

Commemorating Michael: Woven
portrait (courtesy of Eileen Hughes).

Appendices
Discography

7" Singles

Skeets Boliver
1976
Streethouse Door / I Can't See the Light
(Thunderbird THE 116)

1977
Moonlight in Jeopardy
/ Ain't I Been Good to You (picture sleeve)
(Thunderbird THE 117)

Michael Marra

1980
The Midas Touch / Sleepwalking
(Polydor POSP 108)

1980
The Midas Touch (U.S. release)
/ same on both sides
(Polydor PD 2100)

1980
Hooky's Little Eyes / Foolish Boy
(Polydor POSP 158)

1981
Like a Frenchman (I Said Oui)
/ There's No Such Thing
(Polydor POSP 301)

1983
Hamish – The Goalie
/ The Champions by The Die Hards
(picture sleeve with insert)
(Premier 2 A)

Michael Marra Albums

1980
The Midas Touch (vinyl only)
(Polydor POLS 1016)

Side 1: The Midas Touch, Pity Street, Hooky's Little Eyes, Foolish Boy, Take Me Out Drinking Tonight.

Side 2: Glasgow, Features, Cheese for the Moondog, Benny's Going Home, Taking the Next Train Home.

1984
Dubiety (cassette tape)
(no label)

Side 1: Made in Taiwan, Gaels Blue, Six Feat (Blues for Lowell George), There's No Such Thing, Luna Lumiere, Doc Boone's Number, New German Waltz.

Side 2: Like a Frenchman, Monkey Hair, Julius, When My Eyes Become Accustomed to the Light, The Altar Boys, General Grant's Visit to Dundee.

1985
Gaels Blue (vinyl)
(Mink Records SHS2)

Side 1: Mincing wi' Chairlhi, Racing From Newburgh, The Angus Man's Welcome to Mary Stuart, King George III's Return to Sanity, General Grant's Visit to Dundee.

Side 2: Black Babies, Monkey Hair, The Altar Boys, Gaels Blue (live), Happed in Mist.

1986
They Fairly Mak Ye Work (cassette tape)
(Mink Records KN 2)

Side 1: Jute Mill Song, Jute Bag Moan, Jock Stewart, Brave Men We, Banks o' the Bann, The Lass Wi' the Flax in Her Hair.

Side 2: King of the Wild Frontier, We Drunkards in Our Wisdom See, Sarah's Getting Married, Auld Maid in a Garret, Here Comes the Weak, My Ceiling is an Inch Too High, Calbharaigh.

1991
On Stolen Stationery
(Eclectic ECL CD 9104) (CD)
(Eclectic ECL TC 9104) (cassette tape)

Margaret Reilly's Arrival at Craiglockhart, The Wise Old Men of Mount Florida, Under the Ullapool Moon, Rats, Hamish, Hermless, Niel Gow's Apprentice, Humphy Kate's Song, Like Another Rolling Stone, Here Comes the Weak, The Bawbee Birlin', O Penitence.

1992
Gaels Blue
(Eclectic ECL CD 9206) (CD)
(Eclectic ECL TC 9206) (cassette tape)

Re-issue of original 1985 vinyl only release on Mink Records: Mincing wi' Chairlhi, Racing From Newburgh, The Angus Man's Welcome to Mary Stuart, King George III's Return to Sanity, General Grant's Visit to Dundee, Black Babies, Monkey Hair, The Alter Boys, Gaels Blue (live), Happed in Mist.

1993
Candy Philosophy
(Eclectic ECL 9309) (CD)
(Eclectic ECL TC 9309) (cassette tape)

The Land of Golden Slippers, Don't Look at Me, Johnny Hallyday, True Love, The Violin Lesson, To Beat the Drum, Painters Painting Paint, King Kong's Visit to Glasgow, The Guernsey Kitchen Porter, Australia Instead of the Stars, O Fellow Man, This Evergreen Bough.

1996
Pax Vobiscum (Live in Concert) (CD only)
(Eclectic ECL CD 0616)

Don't Look at Me, Pax Vobiscum, Lieblings in the Absence of Love, The One and Only Anne Marie, Beefhearts and Bones, Chain Up the Swings, Moravian Girls, Here Comes the Weak, Julius, Dear Hank Williams, King Kong's Visit to Glasgow, To Beat the Drum, Painters Painting Paint, The Promised Land.

1998
The Mill Lavvies (CD)
(Mink Records MINK 0002)

Spontaneous Combustion, If Dundee Was Africa, Big Wide World Beyond the Seedlies, Oh Meh Goad (featuring Saint Andrew), Broom Crazy, For To Be Or Not To Be, What to Do, Gin Eh Was a Gaffer For to Be.

2000
Posted Sober (CD)
(Inner City Sounds Records ICS 001)

Albert White Feather, Letter From Perth,
The Butterfly Flaps It's Wings, Botanic Endgame,
Reynard in Paradise, Angela Gunn, Frida Kahlo's
Visit to the Taybridge Bar, Constable le Clock,
All Will Be Well, Pius Porteous, Bob Dylan's
Visit to Embra, The Lonesome Death of Francis
Clarke, All to Please Macushla, Scribbled Down
Drunk (But Posted Sober).

2003
Silence (CD mini album)
(Tob Records TRCD 014)

Silence, The Clock, Gossip, The Bard is Well,
Lily, The Fold.

2007
Quintet (CD mini album)
(Tob Records TRCD 0023)

Schenectady Calling Peerie Willie Johnson,
Peter, Thomas Fraser, If I Was an Englishman
(For Martin Carthy), Mac Rebennack's Visit
to Blairgowrie.

2010
Michael Marra
With Mr McFall's Chamber
(live on tour) (CD)
(Delphian Records DCD 34092)

The Lonesome Death of Francis Clarke,
The Slave's Lament, Hamish (The Goalie),
The Beast, Niel Gow's Apprentice, Happed in
Mist, The Clock, Monkey Hair, Schenectady
Calling Peerie Willie Johnson, Pius Porteous,
Green Grow the Rashes, Farlow, Frida Kahlo's
Visit to the Taybridge Bar.

2012
Houseroom
(CD mini album with The Hazey Janes)
(TOB Records TRCD 0034)

Houseroom, Ceci N'est Pas Une Pipe,
Mrs Gorrie, Flight of the Heron,
Underwood Lane, Heaven's Hound.

2017
Dubiety
(Inner City Sound Records)
(digital release with revised track listing)

Made In Taiwan, I Don't Like Methil, Six Feat
(Blues for Lowell George), Like A Frenchman
(I Said Oui), Gaels Blue (Studio Version),
Luna Lumiere, There's No Such Thing, The
New German Waltz, When My Eyes Become
Accustomed To The Light, Monkey Hair
(Michael's Vocal).

2017
High Sobriety (Live At The Bonar Hall)
(Inner City Sound Records)
(digital release)

Mac Rebennack's Visit To Blairgowrie, I Don't
Like Methil, General Grant's Visit To Dundee,
If Dundee Was Africa, Big Wide World Beyond
The Seedlies, Reynard In Paradise, Peter, Miss
Otis Regrets, Schenectady Calling Peerie Willie
Johnson, Mother Glasgow, Beefhearts And
Bones, Pius Porteous, Frida Kahlo's Visit To
The Taybridge Bar, If I Was An Englishman,
Scribbled Down Drunk (But Posted Sober),
I Love The Alphabet, Green Grow The Rashes,
The Lonesome Death Of Francis Clarke,
Hermless, The Homeless Do Not Seem To
Drink In Here, Baps And Paste, Rockin'
Chair, Two Sleepy People.

Miscellaneous compilations and collaborations

1988
Witch's Blood II (cassette tape)
(Tayside Regional Council)

Dundee Community Festival presents Witch's Blood II – music by Michael Marra

Side 1: Interviews & Comments

Side 2: Music & Drama

1990
Hard Cash
(Special Delivery Records SPD 1027)

Featuring: The Guernsey Kitchen Porter.

1990
Hard Cash
(SPDCD 1027) (CD)
(SPDC 1027) (cassette tape)

Alternative sleeve.

1990
Your Cheatin' Heart T.V. series soundtrack / Various artists

Michael Marra on piano, guitar, backing vocals & percussion. Musical co-director with Rab Noakes.

Your Cheatin' Heart, Jambalaya, Don't Be Cruel, Always on My Mind, Hey Good Lookin', Quicksilver, Running Wild, Deep Water, Tennessee Waltz, You Are My Sunshine, From a Distance, Settin' the Woods on Fire, Your Cheatin' Heart, Half as Much.

1994
Rock & Water
(Eclectic Records ECL CD 9411) (CD)
(Eclectic Records ECL TC 9411) (cassette tape)

Compilation CD featuring True Love (Candy Philosophy), Racing From Newburgh (Gaels Blue) & Like Another Rolling Stone (On Stolen Stationery).

1995
The Tenth Glenuig Music Festival (CD)
(GLEN CD 012)

Featuring live recordings of Lonesome Road, Chain Up the Swings, Mac Rebennack's Visit to Blairgowrie.

2000
Letter From Perth, Scribbled Down Drunk (But Posted Sober) (live)
(CD single with Frida Kahlo)
(CS 002 CDS)

2001
Tobermory Songdreams
(Tob Records TRCD 008)

Local young people collaborated in song writing workshops with Michael over a three week period. Michael plays piano, organ, acoustic guitar and has co-production credits.

Featuring Kirsty MacLeod's Visit to Outer Space, Into the Sun, Eastern Storm, Dream Guy, As the Mayflies Dance, KP, Wonder, I'm Bored, Smiling with You, Many Things, Factor, Get Off the Train.

2005
Ordinary Angel (CD)
(McMeanmna SKYE CD 38)

Featuring: The Voyage (by Johnny Duhan), The Homeless Do Not Seem to Drink in Here, Chain Up the Swings.

2009
The Cremation of Sam McGee
by Christine Hanson
(CD BABY.COM/INDYS CHCDTCOSM01)

Narration by Michael Marra

2009
Numbers
Noranside Songwriting Project

Michael Marra on guitars, piano, keyboards, moothie, stylophone, bass guitar, backing vocals and drums, Chris Marra on acoustic and electric guitars, Kevin Murray on mandolin, guitars, percussion, Alice Marra on vocals. The CD includes ten songs written by long-term prisoners at HMP Noranside and one written by Michael ('Eternity Has Just Begun'). Michael sings lead vocals on eight songs: the other three are sung by the songwriters themselves. Owing to the nature of the project the CD was not made available for sale.

2009
Bel Canto by Eilidh Mackenzie
(Macmeanmna SKYE CD 52)

Michael Marra features as a guest narrator on A Chiad Pog (The First Kiss), vocals and piano on You Misunderstand Me / Little Darling.

2010
The King of Lochee (CD)
(St John's Community Enterprise Project)

Featuring Michael Marra vocals and co-writing credits with Derek Thomson on The Devil Lives in Peel Street, Wullie Fawn & Song of The Fleet. Backing vocals on Lux Dei. Co-writing credit for Clement Park.

2010
Concerto Caledonia (live CD)
(Delphian Records DCD 34093)

Featuring: Marshall-Burns
(Concerto Caledonia with Michael Marra)

Discography compiled by
Breeks c/o Groucho's.

List of Shows, Plays, Films etc

The following is a list of theatrical and other shows in which Michael appeared, or for which he wrote the songs and/or music. This is undoubtedly an incomplete list.

1985

— Musical director and performer in *Bathtime Bubbles* at Edinburgh Festival Fringe and in Dundee (Steps Theatre, and Dudhope Arts Centre).

— Music for *& as in Gilbert & Sullivan* by Howard Burman & N.C. Sorkin, at Edinburgh Festival Fringe.

1986

— Musical director and performer in *They Fairly Mak Ye Work* by Billy Kay at Dundee Rep. Musical director of *Bread Upon the Waters* by Anne Downie (a play about Mary Slessor), Dundee Rep Youth Project.

— Musical director of Community Musical at Craigmillar Festival, Edinburgh.

1986-7

— Musical director of *The Snow Queen* by Stuart Paterson at Dundee Rep.

1987

— Musical director and composer of *Witch's Blood* by John Harvey (Dundee Community Festival).

— Music and songs for Tayport Burgh Centenary show.

— Musical director of *Merlin the Magnificent and the Adventures of Arthur* by Stuart Paterson at Dundee Rep.

1988

— Music, songs and performer in *A Wee Home from Home* by Frank McConnell (Communicado Theatre Company). World premiere at Adam Smith, Kirkcaldy, later at Edinburgh Fringe and on tour.

— Music for *Crying Wolf* by Gerald Mangan (Communicado Theatre Company), Edinburgh Festival Fringe.

— Music and performer in *Fancy Rappin'* (Wildcat Theatre Company, Scottish tour).

— Musical director/composer of *Witch's Blood II* (Dundee Community Festival).

— Songs (in collaboration with John Harvey) and music for *A Bicycle to the Moon* (Communicado Theatre Company, St Bride's Centre, Edinburgh).

1989

— Musical director and performer in *Border Warfare* (Wildcat Theatre).

— Musical director of *Your Cheatin' Heart* by John Byrne (BBC Scotland).

— Music for *Love and Pocket Money* by Frank McConnell (plan B).

1990

— Music for *The Creature from the Mermaid's Purse* by Anne Downie (Communicado Theatre Company, St Bride's Centre, Edinburgh).

1991

— Music for *Man Cub* (Pocket Theatre, Cumbria).

1994

— Music for *Blood Red Berries* by Ron Whyte (Dundee Rep Community Theatre).

1995

— Acts in *Tartuffe* by Molière trs. Liz Lochhead (Tron Theatre, Glasgow).

1996-1998

— Contributes to/performs songs in *The Ken Fine Show* (STV eight-part series on the Scots language).

1997

— Writes monologue for *The Corridor* (Benchtours Theatre Company).

1998

— Musical director and performer in *The Mill Lavvies* by Chris Rattray (Dundee Rep).

— Music and songs for *Eh! That'll be Right* (Dundee Rep Community Theatre promenade production, Caird Hall, Dundee).

2001

— Songwriter and performer in *Beauty and the Beast* by Liz Lochhead (Theatre Babel, Tron Theatre, Glasgow.

2004

— Composer and musical director of *If the Moon Can Be Believed* (Dundee Rep with Loadsaweeminsingin).

2005

— Writes music and performs in *The Ballroom of Romance* by Stuart Paterson from a story by William Trevor, Dundee Rep Community Company & OPEN (Scottish Dance Theatre's Adult Performance Group).

2006

— Acts in *Home* (National Theatre of Scotland) (48 Logie Place, Aberdeen).

2007

— Writes and performs music and songs for *The Demon Barber* (Perth Theatre).

2008

— Acts part of Niel Gow in *Burns and Gow* by Bryan Beattie (a Neon production for BBC Radio Scotland).

— Music for *parallel |parallels*
  (plan B, Dance Base, Edinburgh).

2009-10
— Music, songs and performer in revival
  of *A Wee Home from Home* (plan B,
  directed by Gerry Mulgrew from an
  original idea by Frank McConnell.

2010
— Musical director of *The King of Lochee*
  (St John's Community Enterprise
  Project and Dundee Rep).

2011
— Performs songs and narrates in
  St Catherine's Day by Michael
  Marra (A Play, a Peh and a Pint
  at Dundee Rep in association
  with Oran Mor, Glasgow).

Original film scores

— *Ruffian Hearts*
  (Dir David Kane, 1995)

— *Sheila*
  (Dir Hannah Robinson, 1996)

— *Initiation*
  (Dir Martin McCardie, 1996)

— *The Lucky Suit*
  (Dir Caroline Paterson, 1996)

— *Birth of a Salesman*
  (Dir Claudia Nye, 1996)

— *Caesar*
  (Dir Davy McKay, 1999)

Michael

he deserves a song
at least as wide
as those he gave us
a national anthem

his wee frame
carried gigantic thoughts
glittering with notes
up hills, into bars, into hearts

we were glad he dumped
coal in our bath
the tang of laughter-tears
in our soul

and the delight
he found around
he shared
an invisible teacher

his microscope
revealed the world
and the world
beside the world

he showed us
where beauty is found
an act of kindness
a gift

for us
and our only exchange
the tears
he would not seek

Bryan Beattie

293

All shall be well,
and all shall be well,
and all manner of
thing shall be well.

Julian of Norwich (1342-1416),
Revelations of Divine Love

James Robertson is an antiquarian raconteur and yodeller
not much in demand on the Burns Club circuit. A former
professional basketball point-guard, he occasionally appeared
on television nonentity game shows before developing an
evangelical rash and taking up preaching in the Peerie Wee
Church of St. Agnant (Continuing). Ejected by his flock after
confessing his belief in fairies, he is not expected to return to
the pulpit any time soon. (Image of the author and
his muse by Michael Marra.)

Photograph credits